IN PARIS WITH JANE AUSTEN

IN PARIS
WITH JANE AUSTEN

Three Literary Walks

Vera Quin

Cappella Archive
Limited Editions

Cappella Archive : 2005
Printed : May 2005

© 2005 Vera Quin
Maps © 2004 Veronique Yapp

British Library Cataloguing–in–Publication Data
A catalogue record for this book is
available from the British Library

ISBN 1–902918–22–3

Cappella Archive : Great Malvern : England

*Typeset in a Cappella Archive realization of a Baskerville of 1769
and printed on Five Seasons paper from John Purcell of London.*

Contents

v

Acknowledgement

I am indebted to Veronique Yapp, who has known Paris since childhood, for drawing the maps; to Susan Close, who turned a dishevelled manuscript into legible text; and to John Hunter, Russell Lewis, and Serena Moore, who read the entire manuscript and suggested many improvements.

For Starters

'Think only of the past as its remembrance gives you pleasure,' suggests the twenty-year old Elizabeth Bennet to her fiancé Darcy, himself not yet thirty. As advice, it is the declared purpose of many a sundial – and perhaps more readily followed in later years. Then, with ambition moderated, some burdens lifted and increased leisure, there is time to look back without urgency and retrieve the moment of first encounter with a particular delight: Jane Austen.

For the lucky ones it came in adolescence, the unfolding realisation that over and above the excitement of plot and the enjoyment of characters, there is far-reaching entertainment to be quarried from the way a story is told. Hundreds of books later, with discrimination sharpened and tastes enlarged, it is still the memory of that first illumination that gets labelled in the mind, in conversation, in the rear car window: 'I'd rather be reading Jane Austen.'

Magnetically over the years other pleasures, other insights have accrued. A few are spread out here. They are worth a rummage, as you might if you unexpectedly come upon the clearance sale of a family house. On a whim you wander in, look around. A box catches your eye. You bid, bag it for the proverbial song, bring it home. It is crammed with trinkets, the scrappy memorabilia of somebody's life. They remind you of incidents in your own. Anecdotes crowd in, snatches of music tease the edge of memory, faces come, more or less, into focus, questions hover, change shape, firm up; plans, improbably colourful, sprout and are as rapidly discarded.

But something remains: the day that would have been routine, develops the glow of expanded possibility. 'Yes,' you recollect, 'that was good . . . I wonder . . . would it be fun now if . . . ?' and with luck another plan, a manageable one, will grow until it flowers into pleasure. Paris revisited? Seen from a fresh angle, with enough sideways glances for you to hook memories to, comment, argue, laugh. The start is right here.

The year 1997 was a good one for Jane Austen enthusiasts: a biography by David Nokes, another by Claire Tomalin, the paperback of Park Honan's updated and revised. For long–term aficionados there was a tantalising tit–bit: Tomalin's two sentences mentioning translations into French, supported by two reproductions of the earliest illustrations to the novels. The briefest enquiry showed that, in London, between 1811 and 1818 the novels went through ten editions. Between 1813 and 1828 several translators worked on thirteen French editions, nine of them published in Paris, three in Geneva and one in Vienna.

Vienna. The immediate association is with baroque and Art Noveau buildings steeped in music and the Harry Lime theme an insistent riff. In every sense too far from Jane Austen. Forget it.

		Table One	
		FIRST CONTINENTAL EDITIONS	
1811	London	*Sense and Sensibility*	1st edition
1813	London	*Pride & Prejudice*	1st & 2nd edition
		Sense and Sensibility	2nd edition
	Geneva	*Orgueil et Préjugé*	4 instalments: abridged
1814	London	*Mansfield Park*	1st edition
1815	Geneva	*Mansfield Parc*	4 instalments: abridged
	Paris	*Raison et Sensibilité*	
1816	London	*Emma*	1st edition
		Mansfield Park	2nd edition
	Paris	*Le Parc de Mansfield*	
	Paris	*La Nouvelle Emma*	
1817	London	*Pride & Prejudice*	3rd edition
	Vienna	*La Nouvelle Emma*	
1818	London	*Northanger Abbey*	1st edition
		Persuasion	1st edition
1821	Paris	*La Famille Elliot*	1st edition
1822	Geneva	*Orgueil et Préjugé*	
	Paris	*Orgueil et Prévention*	
1824	Paris	*L'Abbaye de Northanger*	
1828	Paris	*La Famille Elliot*	2nd edition
		Raison et Sensibilité	2nd edition

Geneva recollected was more of a mixed bag. Calvin, the Pro-testant Reformer, too ancient. CERN [*Conseil europen pour la recherche nucléaire*] too modern. Voltaire at Vevey: getting warmer. Byron, the Shelleys and *Frankenstein* (published in the same year as *Northanger Abbey* and *Persuasion*) better still. It sounded worth a detour, though not in winter.

In the short chilly days of early spring one question nagged: ten editions of six novels in only seven years imply an unusual degree of urgency on the author's part. How long did it take to hand–write two copies of each of the six novels, one working copy and another fair one for the publishers? By our standards these are long–ish novels, granted shorter than Peter Carey or Margaret Atwood, but Jane Austen did not have the feel of an empty continent at her back, waiting to be filled with words. They are distinctly longer than Wil-liam Golding or, at the other end of the spectrum, books intended for the young but adopted by adults, like Philip Pullman's or Mark Haddon's. For length they match Rose Tremain (*The Colour* 360 pages), Alice Sebold (*Lovely Bones* 328 pages), or those descendants of the Gothic Novel, Science Fiction: (Brian Aldiss *Heliconia Spring* 361 pages, Isaac Azimov *Nightfall* 352 pages) or the detective story proper (Sayers' *Thrones and Dominions* 367 pages). Just the pen–push-ing took doggedness and a great deal of time. Why did she write?

The sheer compulsion of genius has been suggested. Arguably poverty was the proximate cause. In Jane Austen's day, a woman's only socially acceptable means of coming by 'only a comfortable home', as Charlotte Lucas[1] puts it, and never mind luxury, were: prosperous parents, marriage to a prosperous man, inheritance, governess to a kindly and prosperous family, writing.

In 1805, at the time of her father's death, Jane Austen was thirty and marriage looked extremely unlikely. There had been a happy flirtation with Tom Lefroy in 1796. But the young man's elders quickly put a stop to it: he was quite unable to support a wife for several years and she was portionless. However lightheartedly she skated over the episode in her letters to Cassandra[2], this, her early valuation in the marriage market, must have been depressing. Then in 1802 had come a full–blown, solid proposal of marriage from Harris Bigg–Wither, the younger brother of Catherine and Alathea, two of Jane and Cassandra's close, long–standing friends. The young man was something of a rough diamond: clumsy, tactless, stuttering, heir to a highly desirable estate, with a beautiful, old house in which Jane and Cassandra were staying at the time.

It would be a prudent match, leading to a comfortable, friendly home, the young man might improve, Jane would cease to be a burden to her brothers, she would be able to offer Cassandra a home, she would be well–integrated socially: something she knew would be in doubt on the diminished income after her father's death. She accepted him, thought about it overnight, and in the morning retracted her acceptance. In other words, she chose penury three years later.

For, in January 1805, when the Reverend George Austen died, the only assured income of his widow Mrs Austen, Cassandra and Jane was £210 a year: this included income from the £1000 settled on Cassandra by her fiancé, before his voyage and death in the West Indies. The Austen brothers rallied round and pledged another £250. All told, £450 seemed fine, barely less than Mrs Dashwood, Elinor and Marianne had on reaching Barton Cottage. But Frank and Charles, the sailor brothers, never made any significant prize money; their contributions were sporadic and after 1816 stopped altogether. From 1814, Edward, the wealthiest brother, who had provided Chawton Cottage for the three ladies, was involved in a major lawsuit, which he lost. Henry, the soldier turned banker, ran into financial difficulties in 1815, and the following spring his bank failed, involving Edward in further loss. After that disaster, Henry bounced back into a curacy that paid all of £52 a year. So only the £50 a year from the Reverend James', the eldest brother, remained dependable. And Jane was totally dependent on her brothers.

Neither was there any likelihood of inheritance in the near

future. The proverbial rich uncle, Mr Leigh Perrot, lived on to March 1817; by then Jane herself had only four months left to live. To make matters considerably worse, he left all his estate to his wife, and only upon her death were the Austen siblings to receive £1000 apiece. Jane took it badly.

Did she ever think of going for a governess?[4] There is no hint in the extant letters. Which left writing. Starting in adolescence, she had written burlesques, skits on fashionable novels of the period. These were for entertainment in the family circle, read aloud to laughter and applause. In 1796, soon after the Tom Lefroy episode, she had tried her hand at a proper novel, *First Impressions*, a first shot at *Pride and Prejudice*. Scholars argue whether it was in the letter–form, made fashionable by Richardson some fifty years earlier and taken up with enthusiasm by his French and English imitators. Or was it straight narrative, like *Tom Jones*? Whichever, Jane's father thought sufficiently well of it to suggest it to Thomas Caddell, the London publisher, who rejected it by return of post. Within twelve months she started on another novel which, much later and with some alterations, she turned into *Northanger Abbey*. This was sufficiently good for her to succeed in selling it to a publisher for £10 just a few weeks after turning down Harris Bigg-Wither's proposal of marriage. For a moment, it may have seemed that saying 'no' to the gawky lad was not financially suicidal, even if life was likely to be constrained.

Unremitting inflation, due to the long war against revolutionary and Napoleonic France, steadily tightened the finances of 'our dear trio', as Henry Austen called his mother and sisters after his father's death. Jane knew she had a marketable talent; she may have felt guilty that her refusal of marriage had deprived her mother and sister of comfort; she may have felt bored by her neighbours at Chawton, a small village then as now. 'They were not rich', wrote Jane's favourite niece, Fanny Austen-Knight in 1869, 'and the people around, with whom they chiefly mixed, were not at all high-bred, in short anything more than mediocre . . . ' Writing was perhaps an escape, as much as a hopeful dash for wealth. It amounted to little enough: at her death Jane left £600 in Navy 5% stock, that is £30 a year.

Little as it was, she was delighted to earn it. Besides, by writing she had, echoing Emma contemplating the Knightley brothers and the Donwell estate, given her family nothing 'that could raise a blush'. Novels by women were common, hers were well received in such notice as they obtained; anonymity, commonplace at the time, prevented the wide knowledge of her brothers' inadequate provision for their mother and sisters. She had kept herself sane, her older nieces amused, her beloved Cassandra protective, absorbed, loving: just about enough for a first dividend from writing.

For Starters: Notes

1 *Pride and Prejudice*, vol. 1 ch. 12.

2 Letters to Cassandra: Letters 1 and 2, dated 10 January and 14/15 January 1796, pages 1 and 3 in *Jane Austen's Letters*, ed. Deirdre Le Faye, OUP 1996.

3 The Reverend James, the eldest brother: he was the father of the Rev. J.E. Austen-Leigh, who wrote the *Memoir of Jane Austen*. The second, enlarged edition of this, dating from 1871, is the one that is commonly printed together with *Persuasion*.

4 Governess: Had she read (in numbers between August 1778 and December 1780) in *The Lady's Magazine* any instalments of *The Governess* ('A narrative, written for the amusement and instruction of those young ladies, who have been genteelly brought up, but have little or no fortune')? It is a picaresque novel in which the change of employer does duty for the adventures that befall a conventional hero of such novels. Two employers are set up as particularly risible: one has a house full of animals and the governess is expected to teach the resident monkeys as well as the children of the family. The other is Mrs Classic, who reads all the time, even at meals while 'she devours with great avidity' huge amounts of food. Mrs Classic maintains that 'women are infinitely superior to men even without a learned education; and surely if we were sent to study at our universities, we should make a prodigious figure indeed.'

The Next Step

As the days lengthened and the mercury crawled upward another feature of the list of Jane Austen's publications obtruded. All the early translations into French had run their course by 1828. By then Jane Austen had died (1817) in obscurity. Byron had died in 1824, greatly mourned across the Continent, where he had been a celebrity for his life as much as for his poetry, rather like Pablo Neruda in our day.

Walter Scott, who enjoyed an even greater following in France at both popular level and among the literati, died in 1832, the year that Richard Bentley, the publisher, decided to include Jane Austen's six in his series of Standard Novels. At this stage Austen, Byron, Scott *et al* (including Shakespeare) were seen as contributors to the literature of the British Isles, which was one of a handful of European literatures with competing claims to the crown: in so far as such supremacy can sensibly be granted to any. However the French advanced equally plausible claims to superiority.

Only ten years later, in 1842, Charles Dickens was on his first triumphant tour of North America, acclaimed as the dazzling new writer of novels in English. The English language had slipped out of its European nursery to become the global adult, carrying all earlier English writers to unimagined numbers of readers.

Of course there was a downside: the old grievance about copyright was greatly sharpened. As early as 1826 Scott had complained to Fennimore Cooper, an admirer, about pirating in the infant United States. This became ever more blatant till Charles Dickens, whose American sales numbered millions without a dime to himself, mentioned international copyright at a public dinner given in his honour in Boston. The reaction was predictably indignant.

It took many years of effort (by Anthony Trollope for one[1]) to bring the USA fully into the Universal Copyright Convention, and somewhat fewer for the European nation states to achieve agreement – on paper if not always in fact – on translation rights. Needless to say, neither Jane Austen nor her family made any money out of the translations and the American editions.

Be all that as it may, the question remained – how did the first translations of Jane Austen fit into the French–dominated European literary scene? The answer had to be in Paris. Another look at the list of her first Parisian publishers and a check of the map confirmed that the original publishers and printers had been within agreeable walking distance of each other.

Table Two

	TITLE	LIBRAIRE	ADDRESS	PRINTER	ADDRESS
1815	*Raison et Sensibilité*	Bertrand	R Hautefeuille	d'Hautel	R de la Harpe
1816	*Le Parc de Mansfield*	Dentu	R Bonaparte	Dentu	R Bonaparte
	La Nouvelle Emma	Bertrand	R Hautefeuille	Lebegu	R Hôtel Colbert
		Cogez	R Suger		
1821	*La Famille Elliot*	Bertrand	R Hautefeuille	Cordier	R St G. l'Auxerrois
1822	*Orgueil et Prévention*	Maradan	R Visconti	David	R du Pot de Fer
	Orgueil et Préjugé	Paschoud	R de Seine	Paschoud	Geneva
1824	*L'Abbaye de Northanger*	Pigoreau	Pl du Louvre	Hadamard	Metz
1828	*Raison et Sensibilité*	Bertrand	R Hautefeuille	Huzard	R de l'Eperon
	La Famille Elliott	Bertrand	R Hautefeuille	Huzard	R de l'Eperon

The bait was irresistible, for Jane Austen enthusiasts are tireless walkers. Mapped, well–documented routes take them through the streets of Bath and London, along lanes and paths round Steventon, Chawton, Alton, driving and walking through Kent, strolling in Lyme Regis or climbing the hills inland, sauntering in Southampton and Portsmouth, hiking over Box Hill. Then why not Paris? Granted, Jane Austen never went to Paris, did not even know of the booksellers and printers pirating her work. But modern Jane Austen fans do, and as often as not with one of her books for the week–end. What better product of the Age of Enlightenment for the City of Light?

Of course, fans read and re–read the novels for pleasure, for that easy slip from smile to enjoyment, to delight, from joyful recognition to amused eye–brow raising, from sympathetic head–shaking to decided nods, to the sudden pounce 'Never noticed that before', whether it's a background detail or a phrase pattern repeated at emotionally charged moments. Readers return to Jane Austen much as an extended piece of music returns to its dominant key, going through the seamless texts with fine-tooth comb, to analyse opening paragraphs, wonder about finances of commissions in the army and militia, question references to watches, clocks, elapsed time, reconsider paragraphs that mention landscape (rare), catch metaphors (rarer still), re-evaluate characters (is Wickham a paedophile as well as a fortune hunter?) and how they develop, discuss screen versions, become acquainted with ways of introducing sixth-formers to the novels. Scholars stretch our ideas – we have been led to look at Jane Austen as one woman novelist among many, as a feminist, as a protagonist in the war of ideas, as a clergyman's daughter, as the sister of naval officers; and to ask how did she respond to the politics of her day, to the scandalous laxity of the Prince Regent's household, to leisure pursuits, to the picturesque, to novels by named writers; what else did she read, what did she eat, what kind of clothes did she wear; how did she get on with her family, her friends, her publishers, her neighbours; where did she live and where did she visit, how did she get from one to the other, and for that matter, how do her characters travel, and with what results (momentous in every novel)? All this, and much more, has been mulled over, simmered, blended by the learned, and lapped up by the fans, individually in their homes, in little groups over cups of coffee, in bigger groups in the myriad Jane Austen circles across the English-speaking world, at splendid jamborees. 'There's a glow about us Austenites,' said one lady at the millennial conference in Boston. How right she was!

As addictions go, it is harmless, just boring for the non-involved. That too can be avoided, for who could conceivably be bored on a trip to Paris, even one that has, theoretically, a distant echo of a serious purpose – to get some idea of what the French made of Jane Austen, that prodigy at the birth of England's Great Tradition? And, correspondingly, how does she look to the English-speaking common reader, high on Paris, energised by holiday mood and fortified by French food and wine?

So the plan is to wander along the streets inhabited by Jane Austen's publishers and printers of the early nineteenth century, try to view them in their context, have a good look around, enjoy the views, remember other writers, composers, actors, painters, rally memories, and every now and again touch base, that is revert to Jane Austen. Your French can be non-existent, your command of history as sketchy as you choose. (The Time Line at the end of this book will help.) But you are expected to have a nodding acquaince with the arts in general, to be an avid reader and above all to have a vast capacity for enjoying yourself, even on a bookish walk, through unfamiliar streets of a foreign language capital.

> And she was never one to miss
> The plausible happiness of a new experience.[2]

Could that have applied to Jane Austen herself? Her letters reveal needle-sharp focus on what is going on around her, brisk opinions, many smiles, a zest for books and outings to picture galleries and the theatre. Foreign parts are seldom mentioned and France, the enemy for most of her life, barely mentionable: 'Edward Lefroy is come back from France, thinking of the French as one could wish, disappointed in everything. He did not go beyond Paris.'[3] She certainly knew nothing of her books being serialised in Geneva and 'freely translated' in Paris. But we have been brought up knowing France as a friendly power and favourite holiday destination. So, there's nothing for it – a jaunt to Paris is a must. As you assemble a few things to throw into a bag, you wonder – a Guidebook?

Take this one. It will steer you along the relevant streets at a fair clip (fine for a crisp January morning, or with reluctant teenagers in tow). If you want more information, look at the notes at the end of each walk. Some refer you to paintings or films connected with the particular location, others are anecdotes that fill out the background. If, as you wander along, questions, often more generalised ones, niggle, try one of the related sections. They go more deeply into the background.

And if you want still more, there are notes again, referring you to other parts of Paris to visit, more anecdotes, more books, opera, films. If you are unlucky, you may chance upon the same item of information twice, though the risk is low, since no one reads a holiday book from cover to cover. The repetition is not from school-marm-ish intent to fix the item in your mind, but in the hope that you will not miss out on something particularly arresting or entertaining – good stories are for sharing. So, having picked out your choice of best bits, the rest can serve as a scribbling pad, as long as you write crossing the lines, like Jane Fairfax in her letters to her aunt, Miss Bates.[4] If you never travel without a book, and your pockets take only one, here are gobbets to fill the minutes before the train arrives or the coffee is cool enough to drink.

All set for Paris? You know a handy hotel? Restaurants off the tourist routes? Shops that must be checked out? Exhibitions and theatres to visit? (*Pariscope* can be picked up at the Eurostar terminal.) You are booking the passage . . .

Hold it. Look again at Table One. There were three editions of Jane Austen in Geneva, the first of *Pride and Prejudice* in July 1813, that is six months after its publication in London. At the time, the greatest war the western world had ever known was ravaging the Continent and Geneva was in enemy-occupied territory. What had happened in London and Geneva and the 450 miles or so in between to make the first Genevan edition possible? The explanation is here and the Eurostar journey long enough to read it. No way will it diminish the fun of Paris – just catch the train.

The Next Step —Notes

1 Anthony Trollope. See the excellent biography by Victoria Glendinning, Hutchinson, 1992
2 Stephen Spender: *Ruins and Visions*, Faber and Faber, 1942.
3 *Jane Austen's Letters* edited by Deirdre Le Faye, OUP 1996, letter 145.
4 *Emma* vol. 2, ch. 1.

To Geneva

In 1813, French bookseller John Deboffe was based at 10 Nassau Street, the present Gerrard Place, W1, off Shaftesbury Avenue. The house still stands, a modest eighteenth century building with an added top floor. Until 2004 at street level it was a bookshop, but when last seen, stood empty. Next to it is a very narrow in-fill, inserted into the gap shown on the 1813 maps as a tiny garden. The in-fill abuts another eighteenth century building that occupies the corner into Gerrard Street. The ground-floor is a restaurant, as it was at that time, with a window following the curve of the corner. On its Gerrard Place façade is the inscription:

NASSAU STREET
IN
WHEETENS BUILDING
1734

On 6 March 1813 Deboffe, with pint and pie to hand, put a copy of *Pride and Prejudice* into the monthly package sent to Marc-Auguste Pictet in Geneva, then reluctantly a part of France. The latter was one of the editors of the *Bibliothèque britannique*, a two-part monthly journal, intended to keep continental Europe abreast of scientific, literary and agricultural developments in Britain. The literary sections for July, August, September and October 1813 published substantial extracts from the novel, with linking passages to keep the reader tracking the plot. This version was sufficiently well received to encourage the same treatment for *Mansfield Park* in April, May, June and July 1815.

In France, 1792 was the year that started with a moderate, reformist government and ended with the trial of the king and the guillotine. The wary, even if only modestly-monied, cleared out early. One of them was Joseph de Boffe, a bookseller, who came to London and set up shop at 7 Gerrard Street, Soho.[1] He imported French-language books for the increasing number of French émigrés and with the printer John Baylis took to publishing. He had the perspicacity to back Chateaubriand[2] – then an *émigré* in London with barely a publication to his name.

De Boffe encouraged him to work in his *Essai historique, politique et moral sur les Révolutions* and with Baylis, lent him money (Chateaubriand did not obtain the weekly shilling from the British government during the first few years of his eight–year exile), found him a teaching job in Suffolk; Baylis even housed him in Greville Street, Hatton Garden. They supported him much as, these days, an exceptionally friendly literary agent might a wonderfully promising beginner.

When the *Essai* came out in 1797 it was a *succès d'estime*, more talked about in Paris than in London, but it set Chateaubriand on his literary career. As talent spotter, de Boffe was clearly gifted. For bread and butter he acquired the distribution rights for two French scientific journals – *Annales de Chimie* and *Journal de Physique*. Inevitably, he became well–versed in dealing with customs officials in this country, forwarding agents here and abroad, and mail services throughout northern Europe. These were well developed. For instance, on Tuesdays and Fridays mail went, via Dover, from London to Paris; Mondays and Thursdays a French vessel sailed into Dover with mail in the opposite direction. Additionally, the important Dover to Ostend run[3] worked well until 1793, when a packet–boat was captured by the French.

By 1795, when the Low Countries were under French control, Flushing became the embarkation point for the Ostend run; the packet–boats out of Harwich moved up the coast to Yarmouth, with Cuxhaven – for Hamburg – as their destination. Privateers were a danger,[4] as well as the French navy, providing extra impetus for the construction of less vulnerable packet–boats. The new design was three–masted, 170 tons, carried four 4–pounder guns. There were six passenger cabins, though at 4' 4" by 6' 6", with no ports, they were intended only as sleeping quarters. A 20ft cutter, a smaller jolly–boat and small arms for a crew[5] of 28 completed the hardware. So, even with scope for smuggling reduced, it was relatively easy for mail and travellers to get in and out of England, war with France notwithstanding.[6]

This was essential for the two Genevan Pictet brothers in their patriotic new enterprise. In 1795 the brothers started a monthly translating journal, *Bibliothèque britannique*, to preserve the Genevan virtues of moderation and independence from the prevailing political correctness of revolutionary thinking. The journal came in two sections, *sciences* and *littérature*. The latter, edited by the younger brother, Charles Pictet, in due course published extracts from both *Pride and Prejudice* and *Mansfield Park*. Material for the journal was derived from English publications on science, technology (which included agriculture) and literature, with the declared aim of keeping Francophone readers in touch with English intellectual developments.

It followed that material for the journal was produced in England and had to be transported to Geneva before the editors could select, translate, print, distribute and sell. While the Genevan end of this operation was well under control, collecting material in London was loosely directed from Geneva; transport from London to Geneva was the troublesome part.

Over the years, collecting material caused repeated irritation and worry to Marc–Auguste Pictet, the senior editor, who specialised in science. At first he relied largely on François d'Ivernois, one member of the Swiss diaspora in London. D'Ivernois had two advantages for this early stage of the journal's life – he did not require payment and had numerous, excellent contacts in London. Byron found him boring at the 'Alfred', a club 'a little too sober and literary . . . but one met . . . many pleasant or known people; and it was, upon the whole, a decent resource on a rainy day, in a dearth of parties, or in an empty season.'[7]

Clearly d'Ivernois was in a position to find out what the latest admired work of literature was, and have it sent on. However, as the most prominent Swiss émigré in London, he lacked the time to keep the Pictet brothers regularly supplied with the amount of material needed for a serious literary enterprise. So another émigré, an abbé, was contracted at 12 guineas *p.a.*, to help, in the first instance by placing orders for reviews.[8] The banker was Lucadon, but who paid him? Indeed, who, over the years from 1795 to 1815, paid for the thirteen reviews most frequently quoted,[9] or the thirty-three 'other titles', or the books on historical subjects, theology, travel writing, the novels of Maria Edgeworth, Jane Austen (*Pride and Prejudice* alone cost 14s.10d.) and Scott amongst others, the improving works, many on education by Edgeworth and Hannah More, the raft of miscellaneous publications? The Pictets certainly had credit in London, but who, over twenty years, kept it topped up?

A long shot is the youngest Pictet brother, Mark, who had served in the Royal American Rifles, transformed into the King's Royal Rifles/the Green-jackets, after the War of Independence. Had he made good in Canada or England? Another, more likely possibility, is the British government. Once the *Bibliothèque britannique* was recognised as a cultural fifth column in French-dominated Europe, it would have looked, even to a cheese-paring government, like a cost-effective cause. Besides, Marc-Auguste Pictet, the senior editor, was an agent – unpaid – for Britain. The government did help out, at least with transport, after 1806.

On the face of it, the most likely source of money was the Swiss diaspora in London, well established before the Revolution. For instance, Alexandre Aubert, F.R.S., the astronomer and mathematician, was the very wealthy governor of the London Assurance Co. While the *Dictionary of National Biography* is sniffy about his contributions to *Philosophical Transactions*, he clearly did a very great deal for life insurance at the period when, historically, its development became urgent.

Two more Swiss F.F.R.S. were J. De Salis and H.J. De Salis, of the same extended family that helped the Rev. Martin Planta set up his model school in Haldenheim. Martin's nephew, Joseph Planta, another F.R.S. and London contact of Marc-Auguste Pictet, was the Royal Society's foreign secretary. One of his proposers for the

honour of becoming F.R.S. was Daines Barrington, the cor-
respondent to whom Gilbert White addressed the letters that make
up *The Natural History of Selbourne*. Evidently the Swiss were well
dug in, part of a valuable network, even if not all personally
wealthy.

Assuming that money was forthcoming – and there seems to be
no evidence that it was ever seriously lacking at the London end –
the problems of selecting materials and their dispatch still had to be
solved. In that respect the 12 guinea abbé turned out a broken-reed.
It took two journeys to England, the first in 1797 by the *Bibliothèque
britannique*'s business partner, F. Maurice, and the second in 1798 by
Marc–Auguste Pictet, the senior editor, to set up the connection with
Joseph de Boffe *'libraire français, qui est le seul que d'Ivernois m'a
indiqué . . . il loge à Gerrard Street'* [a French bookseller, the only one
mentioned as competent by d'Ivernois . . . he is set up in Gerrard
Street].

De Boffe ended up with a threefold task – its first, and most curious component, was to find subscribers to the *Bibliothèque
britannique* in England. Why private subscribers here should wish to
pay money for a journal of translations, in order to read, in French,
articles on science and technology originally printed in English, is
one of those questions time has not clarified. The task eventually
boiled down to copies of the *Bibliothèque britannique* being sent to de
Boffe, for him to pass on, free of charge, to Joseph Planta. The latter was to lodge them in the library of the R.S., as part of its store of
scientific journals. This worked irregularly until 1809 and served to
keep the British scientific community abreast of what the
Bibliothèque britannique was doing to publicise British science on the
continent.

Next, de Boffe had to select materials for dispatch. This was easy
as far as journals went. For book selection, additional advice came
from a succession of Swiss residents in London, all more or less
known to Marc–Auguste Pictet. So far, so good. But whenever one
of the editors travelled to Britain (and Marc–Auguste spent three

months here in 1801), he collected a swathe of likely material and carried it home to Geneva, as part of his luggage.

De Boffe's biggest headache was transferring packages from a British port to a continental one, without loss *en route*. Various dodges were tried – sending books in wrappers, open at each end, the way journals travelled; using neutral shipping on the Dover to Calais crossing; using British packet-boats on the Yarmouth–Harwich to Cuxhaven run. Later, Emden in Lower Saxony (East Friesland) was suggested; agents in Amsterdam and Rotterdam were used. There were fifteen months' respite and reasonable mail service during the Peace of Amiens starting in March 1802. When hostilities were resumed in May 1803, de Boffe tried the route to Husum, a port just south of the border with Denmark. Later still, a package might go via Gothenburg in Sweden. The trouble with these more northern routes was that their greater length made carriage charges excessive.

It was time to pull strings. Fortunately for Marc–Auguste Pictet, the senior editor, he had been appointed in 1802 to an official post in Geneva – he was made *tribun*, a representative of 'the people'. With this leverage, he applied to his immediate predecessor in the post, Benjamin Constant, known from the latter's long involvement with Madame de Staël. What Marc–Auguste wanted was consistently favourable treatment for his *ballots* (packages) from London. It didn't work out. So Marc–Auguste tried again, this time going to the top – in 1802 he saw Talleyrand, the French foreign secretary, and got the brush off. Which left de Boffe in London, coping as best he could under a hail of scoldings from Geneva, his efforts supplemented by the kind offices of Swiss travellers. The crunch came in November 1806 – the Continental System closed all continental ports to British shipping, and vice-versa. Marc–Auguste went back to Talleyrand and this time was favourably heard. Talleyrand undertook to ease the *ballots'* safe passage on the last leg of their journey to Geneva on condition that the *Bibliothèque britannique*'s source supplies from London were addressed personally to him in

Paris; packages were to reach France 'through the usual channels', that is, cartel ships.

These were intended strictly for the exchange of prisoners. Both the French and British governments hired, controlled and supervised vessels that carried no guns, armaments or merchandise. However, passengers were allowed, as long as they carried no mail; from England they paid 5 guineas one way and were not allowed to carry gold coin.[10] The exchange of prisoners was supposed to deal in equal numbers from both sides, each group to include 5% of officers. Needless to say, the arguments that in our day beset the EU–sanctioned would–be export of beef, or non–opening of the French utilities market, figured just as acrimoniously two hundred years ago over the exchange of prisoners. Britain predominantly returned prisoners who were old, or very young or sick. Officers on both sides were given parole and often broke it.

Cartel ships plied between Weymouth and Morlaix.[11] As long as de Boffe delivered his monthly *ballot* at the Transport Office,[12] it should reach Geneva without undue delay, thanks to Talleyrand's nod and wink to the Ministère de Police. However there was also censorship of printed matter by the Directeur général de la librairie. This was so effective that no materials reached Geneva between September 1810 and October 1811, that month seeing the publication of *Sense and Sensibility* in London. In the following year, supplies were again very scant and irregular, so *Sense and Sensibility* never made it on to the pages of *Bibliothèque britannique*, which even had to stop publishing for a few months.

There is, theoretically, one very tenuous connection between *Sense and Sensibility* and the editor of the *Bibliothèque britannique*. While Jane Austen was in London in the spring of 1811, correcting the proofs of *Sense and Sensibility*, she was staying with her brother Henry and his wife Eliza. Henry was Eliza's second husband; her first one, in Paris before the Revolution, had been Jean–François Capot de Feuillide, from Gascony, reputed an excellent officer in the French army; taken for an aristocrat, he had been guillotined in

February 1794. On re-marriage to Henry, Eliza kept up her French connections – she had French servants, was in touch with French émigrés. Henry, as a banker, may well have come across his Swiss counterparts. As a couple they socialised in far more sophisticated (more international?) circles than any other Austens of their generation. They sound like the sort of couple who knew of everybody, even if they hadn't actually met them, and were abreast of all the gossip. And in April 1811 they took Jane when they visited the Comte d'Antraigues, an émigré – also from Gascony, like Eliza's first husband – and his wife, a former opera singer. Jane was intrigued by them, while discreetly laughing at Eliza's efforts to organise a musical soirée in her house in Sloane Street.[13]

Eliza must at least have known of d'Antraigues from her time in Paris before the Revolution. He was of the more recent, provincial nobility (that is, his title had been created after 1400, which debarred him from a court appointment) and in 1787 he joined the aristocrats' party which aimed at stripping the monarch of his absolute powers. Specifically *la liberté individuelle, la liberté politique et la liberté de la presse, nous obtiendrons ces trois points pour la nation où nous périrons.*[14] Stirring words, but then d'Antraigues was a friend of Rousseau and d'Alembert, beacons of the Enlightenment, arguing for constitutional reform.

Spring 1789 and the king, Louis XVI, for the first time since 1614, summoned the Estates General, that is the national parliament (provincial ones had met regularly for some years). D'Antraigues attended as a very prominent member of the aristocrats' party. Its faults, apart from the usual internal disagreements, were total opposition to equality in any form, numerical insufficiency and inadequate political nous. It was rapidly out-voted and out-manoeuvred, leading d'Antraigues to suggest *dissoudre cette Assemblée rebelle à coup de canons* [dissolve this rebel Assembly with canon balls – a thought kept in mind some eighty years later, when Haussmann was endowing Paris with its straight, wide boulevards]. At the start of 1790 d'Antraigues left France, defending himself and other aristocrats, not just members of the party, for doing the same:

> La patrie borné à un territoire ne dit rien au Coeur des hommes;
> aimer sa patrie quand elle perd ses lois, ses usages, ses habitudes, c'est
> une idolatrie absurde, c'est celle des Egyptiens qui adoraient des
> brutes.

> [Homeland is a meaningless word. Homeland defined by area has no
> emotional hold over people. To love one's homeland when it has lost
> its laws, traditions, habits, that is absurd idol-worship, like that of
> ancient Egyptians worshipping primitive images.]

So he wrote a combative pamphlet[15] and later slipped out of high-
profile activity into ostensible diplomacy, with the spy's usual
migratory loyalty to anyone who would pay him. In November
1793 (that is, after Eliza, Henry Austen's future wife, had got back to
England), he arrived in Venice, officially in Spanish employ, but
remained in touch with Wickham, the British diplomat and spymaster, trying to organise a *coup d'état* in Paris in the autumn of
1796. Eventually Napoleon caught up with him, and spared his life
in exchange for extensive de-briefing (aka treachery) and all his records, which contributed significantly to Napoleon's police being
much more effective than previous ones. There is even a suggestion
that the murder of d'Antraigues in 1812 was at the instigation of
Napoleon's imperial police, whom he had double-crossed once too
often.

Be that as it may, during 1801-2 he had certainly worked with
Russian, Prussian, Swedish and Corsican agents, to keep the Tsar of
Russia, Paul I, in alliance with Britain, against France. One effect of
this was to keep the Baltic Sea open to British shipping, a fact that
both Jane and Henry would have remembered in 1811, when their
brother Francis was serving with the North Sea Fleet, on the edge of
the Baltic. In London, d'Antraigues was known to William Wickham, the British diplomat and spymaster, long based in Switzerland,
and subsequently at the Aliens Office in London. Wickham's name
and function would in turn, have been known to 'people in the
know', like Henry and Eliza. As they were driving to the

d'Antraigues, 'and the Horses actually gibbed on this side of Hyde Park Gate,'[16] did they put Jane in the picture and mention Wickham? The speculation arises because at about that time Jane Austen would also have started the final re-jigging of *First Impressions* into *Pride and Prejudice*, in which the notably double-faced character is named Wickham.

D'Antraigues had settled in London in 1807, the year Joseph de Boffe died[17]. The latter's business was taken over by his son,[18] who continued the connection with *Bibliothèque britannique*, packages, scoldings and all. The system for sending *ballots* to Geneva seized up in September of that year. Fortunately it was re-started in December, through the good offices of the new French foreign secretary, de Champigny. The following year, young de Boffe moved his business into a smaller house round the corner, in what is now Gerrard Place, but was then Nassau Street. Another dispatch crisis in 1810 (see above) had him re-affirming the regularity of his monthly delivery of packages at the Transport Office[19]. In May 1812 John Deboffe (sic) and B.C. Crocker between them paid the parish paving rate of £1 19s. 0d. (just under £2) on the Nassau Street building. While young Deboffe had an associate[20] to help pay rates, no packages were reaching Geneva. Marc-Auguste Pictet got in touch with the Commissaire de Police in Morlaix, to ask if any ballots for the *Bibliothèque britannique* had arrived on a cartel ship, and beg for them to be forwarded to Geneva. For six months supplies for the journal were reasonably regular. During that window of opportunity *Pride and Prejudice* sneaked in, and was serialised in July, August, September and October. Supplies were again disrupted during the first quarter of 1814, while repeated French defeats led to Napoleon's exile to Elba. With peace, mails normalised for the best part of a year, and *Mansfield Park* got through before the adventure of Napoleon's 100 days – his attempt at a comeback – again disorganised all services.

With the second Peace of Paris, Europe heaved a great sigh of relief. For the Pictet brothers there was the immediate benefit of

ease of access to material for their journal, as well as the wider benefit of Geneva joining the Swiss Confederation of twenty-two contiguous cantons, and the country's perpetual neutrality guaranteed
by international treaty. Charles Pictet, the editor of the literary section of *Bibliothèque britannique*, had been the prime mover in
negotiating that happy outcome. A pity Jane Austen never knew of
him. Her first foreign editor was a man to be proud of.

To Geneva — Notes

1 7 Gerrard Street: The original house no longer stands. Currently the street is flanked by Chinese gateways and the street name, like all the others in China Town, rendered also in Chinese characters.

2 Chateaubriand – He turned into the most eloquent and poetic of the early French Romantic writers. By far the most enjoyable of his works is *Mémoires d'Outre-Tombe*, highly accessible autobiographical writing of great variety and freshness. He was, exile notwithstanding, sufficiently in the swim to describe at first hand, events, places and people that figure in the history books, and indeed in the films, about the period. His family and many friends provide him with anecdotes galore. His mother had been at the boarding school started by King Louis XIV's second wife, for daughters of impoverished nobles; consequently Chateaubriand relays some of the court gossip from that earlier period. Enormously long as the *Mémoires* are, the text is divided into short sections, so the book is ideal for dipping into. The Pléiade edition (which tactfully places 'Digression Philosophique' into an appendix) consists of two small volumes, making it an excellent bedside book.

3 Dover to Ostend run: Important because it connected with the continent-wide Turn and Taxis mail service. Ostend was part of the Austrian Nether-lands and Austria at war with France since April 1792.

4 Privateers a danger: The packet-boats sometimes carried bullion, less likely to be thrown overboard in the event of capture than the mail in weighted sacks.

5 Crew of 28: Service on packet-boats exempted sailors from impressment on to men-of-war.

6 War with France – This became much more difficult after 1806, when the Continental System closed all continental ports to British shipping, and vice versa.

7 An empty season: *Letters and Journals of Lord Byron, with Notices of his Life*, Thomas Moore, vol 1 page 666. Murray 1830.

8 Orders for Reviews: *Monthly Review, Critical Review, Annual Register, New Annual Register, British Critick, London Magazine, Analytical Review, London Medical Journal, Annals of Agriculture* (Young), *Philosophical Transactions, Transactions of the Society of London,* ditto of *Bath,* ditto of *Manchester,* ditto of *The Royal Society of Edinburgh.*

9 Thirteen most frequently quoted reviews: *Philosophical Transactions; Nicholson's Review; Philosophical Magazine; Trans. R. Soc. Edinburgh; Trans. R. Soc. Ireland; Manchester Memoirs; Medico-chirurgical Trans; Edinburgh Review; Annals of Philosophy; Trans. Soc. Adv. of Arts; Trans. Linnean Soc;*

Trans. American Soc. Phil.; *Trans. Geological Society.* This list shows that the *Bibliothèque britannique* did a great deal more for British science than literature.

10 Gold coin: There was a shortage of gold coin in France, partly as a result of repeated bankruptcies of the state, making all paper money / bankers' drafts at best highly suspect and frequently valueless. Consequently residents on the English southern coast saw 'guinea-running' as a risky, but potentially highly lucrative, form of smuggling.

11 Weymouth and Morlaix: Both are now known as holiday resorts. Morlaix has the benefit of a beautiful, forested hinterland. Weymouth in *Emma*, is the scene of the meeting between Frank Churchill and Jane Fairfax (her seduction?) and their secret engagement.

12 In Somerset House, The Strand, London.

13 Musical soirée. Letter 70, dated 18.04.11 and letter 71, dated 25.04.11, in *Jane Austen's Letters*, ed Deirdre Le Faye, OUP 1996.

14 *Nous périrons*: 'Freedom for the individual, political freedom, freedom for the press, we will achieve these three aims for the nation, or die in the attempt.' Letter of 17.11.1788 by J.J. Duval d'Eprémesnil to d'Antraigues, quoted in *La chute des aristocrats 1787–1792 La naissance de la droite* by Jacques de Saint-Victor, Perrin 1992.

15 Pamphlet: *Point d'Accommodement* (No Compromise) showed how the aristocrats' party had evolved from its first, liberal ideas into total opposition to reform, in contrast to many aristocrats still in France, who were working hard to achieve a constitutional monarch on the English model.

16 Hyde Park Gate: Letter 71, as above.

17 Joseph de Boffe died: There is no burial record for him, either in the parish of St. Anne, Soho, where his shop was, nor in the Huguenot registers for the year.

18 His son: There is a suggestion that the son may have started out in Basle. The *Tableau de libraires des principales villes d'Europe* for 1804 lists: J.S. Deboffe Bâle / Deboffe Londres. An enquiry to the Basle city archives produced nothing, but a finger-tip search through the records may reveal the clinching detail.

19 Transport Office: This was in Somerset House, off the Strand. The building is now better known for housing the Courtauld and Gilbert collections and rotating exhibitions from The Hermitage, St Petersburg. Also in the run up to Christmas part of the courtyard is turned into a very popular ice-skating rink.

20 An associate: B.C. Crocker was possibly a fan-maker, for a fan-maker of that name paid parish rates in Sarjeant's Inn in 1822, that is a few years after Deboffe gave up Nassau Street.

In Geneva – the City

At first blush Geneva does not spring to mind as a prime holiday destination. But if your mind is on literature there is Voltaire in one direction along the lake, Byron and the Shelleys in another, Rousseau in the city itself and also at its centre a publishing venture, *la Bibliothèque britannique*, born of revolutionary turmoil. By a happy accident that magazine brought Jane Austen to the Continent.

If you are in Geneva, climb the hill to the Vieille Ville, Place Bourg de Four, where there are several restaurants, a very helpful bookshop and a good *patisserie*. Restored, take the Rue de l'Hôtel de Ville, to the north-west. You will pass the opening to the neo-classical Cathedral of St Pierre on the right; ahead at the wider T-junction, the Hôtel de Ville is on your left and several ancient cannon on the right. Turn *left* down the short Rue R.H. Fazy. It ends in a classical portico framing, against a leafy background, the statue of the patriot, diplomat and literary editor of the *Bibliothèque britannique*, Charles Pictet de Rochemont. There is another pleasant café just the far side of the portico on the left, particularly agreeable at lunch time on a sunny, spring day. But if sustenance is not a priority, turn *right* into the Rue de Granges, *la belle addresse* of Geneva, fine eighteenth century town houses, sober in their grey stone. Stop to glance at number 14, home of F.G. Maurice, the business partner of the *Bibliothèque britannique* and where it was printed. Continue as the street curves to the right, slides down the hill and is renamed Grand Mazel, past its fountain, ending in another T-junction. The present number 19 was the site of the popular reading room owned by J.J. Paschoud, who in 1822 printed a translation of *Pride and Prejudice* without cuts. Turn *right* up the Grand' Rue with its attractive shops especially the Maison des Amateurs du Livre and you will return to the cannon. Altogether a 20 minute stroll unless window shopping detains you.

THE CITY

What was it about Geneva that made the city conducive to Jane
Austen's ethos and view of human behaviour? Let us, like Elizabeth
Bennet, make it 'our business to be satisfied'[1] with *un peu d'histoire*, as
the green Michelin guides used to say, on the way to better understanding for ourselves as in the event it was for her.

In the latter half of the 18th century Geneva was a magnet, rather
like Hong Kong in the thirty years before the 2001 handover to
China. It consisted of the city proper with some surrounding territory and more in separate holdings along both sides of the lake,
similar to the Hong Kong archipelago. The city state was a republic,
unusually well run by a small ruling class and taxes were low. It was
extremely prosperous through high-skilled trades in clock and
watch-making, jewellery and printed cottons; it had extensive commercial connections with England, France and the various parts of
as yet disunited Germany and Italy; its banks, owned and managed
by a small group of inter-related families, also had flourishing
branches outside the city's territories – the Banque Schmidtmeyer,
for instance, had a branch in London, the Banque Mallet in Paris.
The zenith of Geneva's prosperity was around 1760 to 1785.

For all the strength of its far-flung commercial interests Geneva,
as a political entity, formed part of the very loose Swiss confederation. Its separate component parts viewed each other with some
suspicion. The glue that held them however elastically, was, apart
from geography, the Protestant religion; here Geneva, the cradle of
Calvinism, the extreme form of continental Protestantism, was
thought to lead.

In the context of literature this had contradictory effects; for instance there was no theatre in the city until 1783 – the year that
20,000 lived off watch and clockmaking – allegedly, gossip said,
because the male city councillors did not want their womenfolk corrupted by drama. On the other hand the ideas of the Enlightenment, with its secular emphasis, were given a very fair hearing.

The heroes of the Enlightenment, the promoters of the *Encyclopédie* (the first attempt at a summary of all Western knowledge) were sheltered here. Voltaire, for one, spent many years in and around Geneva, staying for part of the time in a beautiful house, Les Délices, (open to the public in summer and well worth a visit). What with the heavy hand of censorship in France, many French authors and publishers often found it more prudent to publish through a friendly house in Geneva and have the copies carried more or less secretly across the frontier. Such was the case with the *Encyclopédie*.

Overall, in an intellectually liberal climate, there was no great enthusiasm for literature. However, in neighbouring Lausanne literature flourished, especially among women. It was at least a hobby promoting the social acceptability of its practitioners. But Geneva preferred the sciences, two nascent ones in particular – meteorology and the study of high mountains. (Remember, Humboldt, the Prussian–born explorer and natural scientist, had not yet travelled to central and South America, let alone published his definitive findings on climate, oceanography and geology.)

Some miles north, on the edge of another lake, Neufchatel, then a Prussian dependency, harboured the 'Neufchatel set' of young Englishmen on their Grand Tour, including Jane Austen's brother Edward. They came to observe a country brought to popular attention in England with Abraham Stanyan's *An Account of Switzerland*, written in 1714, to admire the fine buildings and cleanliness of Rousseau's birthplace (marked by a plaque at 40 Grand' Rue) and Voltaire's sanctuary, to check out the prosperity of its industry and commerce, and the high level of literacy of the population, to converse with the cultivated and, if the historian Edward Gibbon's experiences in Lausanne[2] are anything to go by, to dance, flirt, gamble and get drunk.

Significantly, in the second half of the 18th century 90% of the population of the city of Geneva (40% of the city–state, including all its villages) was literate. This had been achieved through the efforts of the local church – its *Société des Catéchumènes* [Society of Confirmation Candidates], started in 1736 – it provided sound primary education for both sexes with the aim of allowing pupils to benefit from religious instruction, in the first instance to make Bible reading easy. These classes were open also to the children of the *domiciliés*, resident foreigners, most of them attracted by the opportunities for work and education. Inspectors reported on the ten classes, five for boys and five for girls, with 65 to 80 pupils apiece. Very few were unable to read, the illiterate being mostly the children of the incomers, who, as such, had no political rights.

In this they were not alone and the differences in political status were the focus for periodic rowdy dissatisfaction in an otherwise most attractive city state. The population was divided between two major groups – the first, the oligarchs, were *bourgeois de Genève* (burghers) and *citoyens* (citizens); they, that is the males, had political rights of voting and sitting on governing councils, worked in a professional capacity in well-paid jobs and controlled the levers of power, both economic and political.

The second, much more numerous group of *habitants* (inhabitants) and *natifs* (natives, ie, born within the city territories) were also considered nationals – with the *domiciliés*, they lived in the suburbs, worked in less skilled trades for low pay and had no political rights. For them moderate taxes and good government were not enough. Periodic riots led to minor concessions – political rights were marginally widened after each but the newly enfranchised did not have sufficient leverage to bring about more far-reaching reforms.

1782 saw the first major crisis – the disenfranchised, having formed their own political party, *les Représentants*, led large-scale rioting that undermined the ruling council. In a rush, 460 of the *Représentants* were admitted to full political rights, a *Conseil représentant* (representative council) of heads of propertied families was set up and economic equality for all was proclaimed. This amounted to a proper revolution and for a few months the revolutionaries were in power. Of course the bourgeois oligarchs fought back; with the help of troops from Berne,[3] Piedmont-Sardinia, (that is, northwestern Italy) and France, the old order was restored but with some powers ceded to France, this being preferred by the bourgeois to 'pure democracy'. The ensuing repression closed down all clubs (these were predominantly political, as in France at the same period) and prominent Genevan liberals like François d'Ivernois and Mallet du Pan, emigrated to France. There they stood for an alternative, reforming government for Geneva, not for revolutionary democracy. In Paris they regrouped to support Mirabeau, the French liberal who in 1789 tried to set up such a reforming government for France.

In the meantime in Geneva fewer pamphlets were published, some journals closed, some changed their names, but the city continued substantially prosperous and certainly literate. Its Bibliothèque Publique, ancestor of the present admirable Bibliothèque Publique et Universitaire, had 30,000 books as early as 1761; every family had a Bible, artisans had a few books, more prosperous families had private libraries; Rousseau, Voltaire, Montesquieu, the *Encyclopédie*, Locke,[4] were found in them more often than Calvin. And there were lending libraries.

Readers of Jane Austen's letters will remember her reference[5] to the local library in Chawton, and how much better it was than the one in the neighbouring village of Steventon. Books were owned in common and passed around a circle of neighbours. A more formal and substantial version was the subscription library with a fixed location. (A descendant of such a library, the *Société de Lecture*, exists to this day in Geneva, in a beautiful building, 11 Grand' Rue.) These were part of a Europe-wide development flourishing from the second half of the eighteenth century. They flourished particularly in Germany, Holland, France, countries with a prosperous middle-class with leisure on its hands. Since these libraries were open to women, they were an excellent focus for socialising. You will remember in *Pride and Prejudice*, when wild, giddy Lydia is off

the parental leash in Brighton, she reports returning from the library where officers had attended her and Mrs Forster.[6]

So the entrepreneurs moved in – a subscription library, with a
section of novels for ladies, looked like a reliable if modest money-
spinner, all the more necessary after the considerable losses
Genevans had suffered in the wake of successive financial crises in
France during 1787-1788. The last was also a year of poor harvest in
France. The price of bread rocketed, and by January 1789 panic and
riots in Geneva forced the oligarchs' bourgeois party to try for closer
co-operation with the *Représentants*. Nothing much happened – the
bourgeois stayed in control of the operational council (*Petit Conseil*)
and refused to grant to all born on Genevan soil the same limited
rights as the *natifs* had. In July in Paris the Bastille was stormed,
starting what is known as *the* French Revolution – never mind the
first effort by the French-speaking Genevans in 1782 or the several
that followed the 1789 revolution in France.

Early in 1790 an optimistic twenty-two year old Genevan, J.J.
Paschoud, opened his *cabinet littéraire*, that is, lending library with
fixed reading room, on the corner of Grand Rue and la Pelisserie, in
what was the heart of the booksellers' and printers' area. Further, he
published a catalogue of the 1600 books on offer, in alphabetical
order of title. While this was not unprecedented, it shows the confidence young Paschoud had in the maintenance of civil order and
sustained reading habits of his fellow Genevans. Two of them in
particular, neighbours across the road in Grand' Rue, Paschoud was
to be associated with for many years. They were two of the three
brothers Pictet – the eldest, Marc-Auguste, (1752-1825) and the
next, Charles Pictet de Rochemont, (1755-1824).

(Because Genevan bourgeois families were highly inter-married,
younger sons added their wife's surname to their own to distinguish
them from their brothers and cousins.)

The City — Notes

1 *Pride and Prejudice*, vol.2 ch.19.

2 Edward Gibbon 1737-1794: He spent some ten years of his life in Lausanne and is remembered as the author of *The Decline and Fall of the Roman Empire*, published between 1776 and 1788. For a magisterial work it is a surprisingly easy read, by an author whose value for freedom and enlightenment led him to many sly jokes in beautifully crafted sentences.

3 Berne. That is the canton of Berne. The city of Berne is the capital of the Swiss Confederation that came into being in its present form only in 1815.

4 Rousseau 1712-1778, Voltaire 1694-1778, Montesquieu 1689-1755, John Locke 1632-1704, were four of the many writers who profoundly influenced the thinking of the 18th century, nudging it towards the rational spirit, absence of superstition, general scepticism and faith in religious tolerance; these are the hallmarks of the Enlightenment and its great monument, the *Encyclopédie*.

5 Her reference. Letter 78, 24 January 1813, in *Jane Austen's Letters*, edited by Deirdre Le Faye, OUP 1996.

6 Mrs Forster. *Pride and Prejudice*, vol. 2, ch.19.

The Pictet Brothers

(More history but Jane Austen comes into focus)

In 1790 the two older Pictet brothers, Marc–Auguste and Charles, were not doing well. Losses, stemming from the financial disarray in France, affected them sharply; their comfortable life–style was seriously undermined, since neither at that juncture had any means of lucrative employment. The family had been prosperously settled in Geneva since 1474; with bourgeois status came a tradition of public service and close connection with other similarly well–placed families – their mother's maiden name had been Dunant, the family of the subsequent founder of the Red Cross.

The eldest Pictet, Marc–Auguste, a sociable man with an easy, expansive manner, a lawyer by initial training, had spent 1775 (the year of Jane Austen's birth) travelling in France and England. He learnt English well; his chief contact in England being the astronomer Alexander Aubert, F.R.S. (also a man with Genevan connections). On his return home Marc–Auguste pursued his hobby as a scientist, and worked to such good effect that by 1786 he was professor of natural history at the Genevan *Académie*. Income was supplemented by taking young Englishmen to live with the family, while they studied and expanded their view of the world by contact with an alternative, soundly Protestant country.

On the other hand, Charles, the middle son, had been given an unconventional education. As a young boy he had been sent to the Reverend Martin Planta in the eastern canton of Grisons/Graubünden. Planta had visited England in 1750, partly to visit his brother Andrew, pastor to the German Lutheran church in London, and partly to see how the public schools were trying to reform themselves. On return he started taking in pupils at his vicarage in Zizers, just as the Reverend George Austen, Jane Austen's father, had done at Steventon. While both parsons' first object was to form the Christian principles of their charges (*Die jungen Leute erstlich zum Christentum zu bilden*), Planta then went on to prepare them for the political, economic, military and commercial professions (*sie hernach in dem politischen, Oekonomischen, Militar – und Kaufmannsberuf vorzubereiten*). The modernity of the enterprise lay in the frankly vocational orientation of the system on offer to the children of the prosperous.[1]

Planta did not want to overload his pupils' memory, but to get them thinking for themselves, and he wanted to make learning easy and agreeable. The syllabus laid heavy emphasis on modern languages taught by natives of the relevant countries – German, French, Italian with Latin; history included the history of Switzerland and of the area; similarly with geography, to include information about the economic activities of the region; nature study involved the care of plants; to maths and physics was added some chemistry in the final year; book-keeping, correct writing, spelling and handwriting, as well as music and singing, were part of the syllabus. Time was devoted daily to physical fitness – games or hikes in the mountains. If the weather was too bad for outdoor pursuits, the lads had a turner's workshop, glass cutting, paper-making, drawing, music-making, according to their choice. The school was run like the Roman Republic, with elections for the various offices that retained their Latin names (*consul, censor, praetor* etc). Uniform was compulsory. There were no lessons on Saturdays and Planta himself and his assistants were always on the spot.

This educational regime, so unusual by English standards of the time, was less so by local ones – in 1753 Edward Gibbon, banished to Lausanne by his irate father, was taught by his clergyman host modern history and how to analyse classic Latin and French texts. And in the twentieth century, about 100 kms to the north, the school at Salem, later transmogrified into Gordonstoun, offered what was, for its day, equally unconventional education.

Planta's regime was so well supported that one of the several Counts de Salis (a very large and well set-up family of local aristocrats) offered his castle at Haldenstein for the school to expand into. If you happen to be in Chur/Croire, an attractive city with the agreeable characteristic of smelling of pine trees first thing every morning, take the local bus or train one stop up the line to the village and climb up to the castle. It is a solid, turreted foursquare pile, with a large garden terrace overlooking the valley of the infant Rhine.

It is a place to sit over a drink and think of young Charles Pictet growing into a serious, thoughtful, almost melancholic young man, according to a biography published by a great-nephew in 1892. Family history is streaked with hagiography; Charles is described as tall, elegant, distinguished looking (his statue in the Promenade des Treilles in Geneva bears this out), with little change in facial expression, *une voix grave* (a measured voice).

> Mais sous ce dehors sévère . . .se cachait une imagination vive, des impulsions généreuses, une sensibilité presque féminine à certains égards, enfin de rares facultés de séduction.
> [But this austere appearance concealed a lively imagination, generous instincts, a sensibility almost feminine in some respects, in short, an unusually attractive personality]

To which he added *un coeur porté au devoir*, [devotion to duty], a sentiment that governs Anne Elliot of *Persuasion*.

In 1775, while his brother was in England, Charles went into the French army, the *division modèle* which intended to follow the Prussian example for discipline and response rapidity. It was not achieved, since only the two Swiss regiments responded to the training. So in 1786 he resigned his commission (had he seen, three years before the event, how the political horizon was shaping?) and returned to Geneva with the reputation of a great and thoughtful reader with well formed literary opinions, friendships among Parisian publishers and a considerable knowledge of agricultural practices.

He married Adelaïde-Sara de Rochemont. Her Protestant family originated in Burgundy[2] but felt threatened from 1685 when revocation of the Edict of Nantes had removed the last vestiges of toleration of Protestants in France.

Consequently, the Rochemonts, along with some 250,000 other French Protestants, escaped (death was the penalty for attempted emigration) in dribs and drabs. Some came to England (the silk weavers of Spitalfields are well known, but David Garrick, the actor's family, were wine–merchants), some to Holland, Prussia, even South Africa. On the way, Geneva was an obvious first port of call for many. In fact, French Protestants had been creeping over the frontier since 1662, when all Protestant churches in France were closed by royal decree. The histories of individual families in the region around Geneva, now the canton of Vaud, are full of escape stories to rival anything the second world war produced. But the Rochemonts, well set–up in Burgundy, had more to lose than most; they hoped, planned, delayed and did not arrive in Geneva until 1689.

The father settled the family and hurried off to join the Protestant William of Orange, the new king of England, who needed reliable officers for his army to fight the Catholic Stuarts,[3] supported by Catholic France, in Catholic Ireland. Rochemont *père* was one of 736 Huguenot officers in that army, forming what came to be known as *La brigade vengeressee* [the brigade of revenge]. They attacked their former persecutors and the indigenous Irish, their allies, with such skill and venom (after all, for any one of them captured, the death penalty was the only option) that King William's string of victories at the Boyne, Ness, etc, was ascribed by Swiss and French historians, to their *furie vengeresse* [the fury of their revenge].

Pause for a moment on the vision of King Billy's dirty work in Ireland being done by Frenchmen. Gear down from this mega offence against political correctness, to Adelaïde-Sara, who some hundred years later, perhaps fuelled by her ancestor's devotion to the Protestant English cause, did her noticeable bit for the victory of England against Napoleon, another French tyrant, and again, a Catholic, at least officially.

Upon marriage, Charles and Adelaïde lived in his country house

at Cartigny (now a suburb of Geneva); in 1787 came the first baby.
Charles published a detailed description of a Parisian home for
abandoned boys and submitted a model for a "*marmite économique*"
(a fuel efficient saucepan). This was a matter of recurring concern –
Rumford,[4] the founder of the British Institution, whose modern
fireplace Catherine is disconcerted to find in the drawing-room at
Northanger,[5] installed new kitchens in the foundlings' home in
Coram Fields[6] and designed cost-effective ways of feeding the
needy in both Munich and Geneva. Charles tried to start a pottery
genre anglais (this was the heyday of Wedgwood).

When that failed he bought some marshy land, and using un-
skilled labour, exploited its peat. He even found time for a two
months' visit to England, together with his elder brother, Marc-
Auguste, and another local friend. They carried a book titled
Beautés d'Angleterre, which led them to the Derbyshire moors and
Chatsworth.[7] They took in the Iron Bridge at Telford and a centre
for inoculation against smallpox in Chester, factories, mines, forges,
a few theatres and concerts. Marc-Auguste bought mineralogical
specimens and scientific instruments; he renewed social contacts
from his 75-76 journey and made new ones – Joseph Banks, the
botanist and president of the Royal Society,[8] Herschel the astronomer, Adam Smith the economist, Wedgwood the entrepreneur
of pottery and porcelain (referred to in *Northanger Abbey*), Wil-
berforce the abolitionist, Grenville the future foreign secretary and
his Oxford friend, William Wickham.

The last had been in Geneva in 1782, the time of its revolution,
ostensibly to study law, but he had an unofficial remit from the British government to keep an eye on developments and report back.
He turns up again, a few years later, as a diplomat and spymaster,
based in Berne. Finally, although there is no specific record, the
Pictets may well also have met Joseph Planta, foreign secretary of
the Royal Society and nephew of Charles' headmaster at
Haldenstein. Altogether it was a journey that added greatly to the
brothers' knowledge of England, its latest technological develop-

ments, and to their network of useful contacts, a form of capital that would be essential a few years later.

For political upheavals and their economic consequences turned the Pictets' fortunes from bad to worse – January 1789 saw bread riots in Geneva, July the taking of the Bastille in Paris. Charles was given the job of re-organising the city's militia and was anxious that the militiamen should remember they were citizens. In 1790, under the influence of events in France, the militia was renamed *garde nationale*, and one of the regiments took the analogy further by revolting against its officers. Charles was elected to be *auditeur de justice* – effectively he had to deal with rioting crowds. Still, peace was maintained sufficiently for young Paschoud to open his reading room a few doors down from Marc–Auguste's house, and the latter was appointed director of the observatory.

In the following year 1791, Kotzebuhe published his play *Das Kind der Liebe*, to be memorably translated by Mrs Inchbald and used explosively in *Mansfield Park*. Marc–Auguste had the satisfaction of being elected corresponding Fellow of The Royal Society, in recognition of his work as a practical astronomer, but financially he was ruined.

In January 1792 England was not at war with France, nor opposed to the country as such, but to its revolutionary (and later Napoleonic) government. The representative of that government, ambassador Chauvelin (familiar to readers of *The Scarlet Pimpernel* as both villain and fall guy) was forced to accept on to his staff Talleyrand, the wily bishop turned politician and turn–coat foreign secretary of both Napoleon and the subsequent restored monarchy. Lord Grenville, known to the Pictets from their 1787 visit, got in touch. In other words, Britain and France were keeping a very wary eye on each other, with the politenesses observed and the secret agents hard at work. For the latter, Switzerland was the ideal channel of communication, Geneva in particular with its long established and very close links with France and proximity to Neufchatel. This city (visited at some length by Edward Austen–Knight in 1786) was doubly valuable since it belonged to Prussia, a country that was neutral till the spring of 1792, and therefore a reliable bolt-hole. Genevan banks were crashing comprehensively, as, from August 1792, with France at war with Austria and Prussia, refugees poured in.

They were the lucky ones who avoided the September massacres. Worse followed – the Swiss soldiers guarding the French king, Louis XVI, were slaughtered when the palace was stormed by the revolutionary mob. The Genevans, indeed all Swiss and the rest of Europe, were appalled. A French army menaced Geneva from the south. Berne and Zurich sent 3,800 well equipped and disciplined troops (in contrast to the French), complete with battle song, to the tune of *Prinz Eugen der edle Ritter*, ending 'and you Frenchies, sort out your own country first, and when you're quiet and orderly, we'll be mates again'. [I translate freely]. There was a stand-off, a negotiated retreat for both sides, but France annexed Savoy, that is, it continued to threaten Geneva from the south. By November the French general, that is the enemy, was so disillusioned with his revolutionary masters that he retired to Switzerland. Charles Pictet, now the father of two children, retreated to Cartigny and kept his head down.

The year 1793 started with street riots in Geneva. The oligarchs, that is, the Pictets' caste, were evicted from all positions of power. Two committees took on the job of drafting a new constitution – 5000 Protestant males alone were to be given full civil rights. In the summer France was invaded on all sides; there were internal risings by the royalists (Balzac's novel, *Les Chouans* describes the main one) and Geneva was again threatened by the French. Financial disaster overtook all the inhabitants – the harvest had been poor, so food prices rocketed. I.O.U.s between merchants were meaningless and interest from France, formerly a significant source of income for many, took the form of valueless paper coupons. Yet money was needed – for the army, for the neediest (Geneva had a very active and well-managed *Société de Bienfaisance*), to recapitalise the grain market and re-invest in trade, particularly to employ the highly skilled, unemployed clockmakers. Also in the summer Robert Fitzgerald, the British Ambassador to the Swiss cantons, was informed that Marc-Auguste Pictet would supply intelligence but would accept no payment.

1794 was worse. Robert Fitzgerald was recalled and replaced as no more than *chargé d'affaires* to the Berne authorities, by William Wickham (also an acquaintance of the Pictets' from 1787), by now married to a Swiss girl, herself descended from banking families on both sides. He started setting up a network of informers and checking out an offer of peace.[9]

Nothing came of it, but Wickham came across the Comte d'Antraigues, a double, possibly triple agent, working for Russia, Spain, and anybody who would pay him. When in 1811 d'Antraigues was living in London in what looked like the quiet retirement of a French royalist refugee, Jane Austen, together with her brother Henry and his wife Eliza, met him. She thought him 'a very fine-looking man with quiet manners, good enough for an Englishman, and I believe a man of great Information and Taste. He has some fine paintings . . . If he would but speak English I would take to him!'[10]

Did he really not speak English? He must at least have understood it, since in 1807 Canning, the foreign secretary, had offered him the title and post of Director of British Intelligence.

However in 1794 in Geneva the two constitution-drafting committees transformed themselves into one revolutionary one and in July *une insurrection terroriste* took place. Charles was one of the many arrested, his brother-in-law, deemed to be an aristocrat, was shot with six others at Bastions, now a park at the foot of the ancient city wall, with the hospitable Bibliothèque Publique et Universitaire on its southern boundary. Pillage had gone with arrests, then confiscations, and then taxes, levied even on wives and minors (this was unprecedented). The rates of tax were based on the taxpayers' presumed political affiliations – 25% from patriots, 30% from reactionaries and 40% from aristocrats. Laughable as these rates are by recent UK standards, the arbitrariness of the collecting authorities made them alarming. In this turmoil, young Paschoud, all of 26 by now, opened a bookshop next to his lending library and Charles found time and concentration to translate Jedediah Morse's *American Geography* (first published in London in 1789) and get it published under the title of *Tableau de la situation actuelle des Etats-Unis d'Amerique d'après J. Morse et les meilleurs auteurs Americains*. Charles later disclaimed any formal intention of producing a book:

> 'Je cherchais des renseignements pour des projets que je formais vaguement sur l'avenir'
> [I was looking for information to back some vague plans for the future.]

The Pictet brothers were wondering whether to emigrate, even as far as the New World. In fact they had a connection in the New World – their youngest brother Marc–Louis Pictet. This very shadowy figure, referred to in the literature only as *capitaine au service d'Angleterre* acquires more substance from the Army Lists. He was successively ensign in 1770, lieutenant in 1773 and captain in 1778, in the 2nd battalion of the Sixtieth, Royal American Regiment of Foot. This regiment had been raised in the middle of the century 'under the patronage of HRH the Duke of Cumberland', then C. in. C. of the British Army, to be 'a body of Troops for the Service in North America, which was to be levied chiefly among German[11] colonists in the back Settlements of America and to be completed by Levies from Germany and Great Britain. The original Projector of this scheme is said to have been M. Von Harbot, a Gentleman of the Canton of Bern, who brought it forward through the interest which Colonel James Prévost[12] of Geneva, then a Captain of the Prince of Orange's Swiss Guards, had with the Princess of Orange, sister to the Duke of Cumberland.'[13]

The second battalion of the regiment was known to be so sympathetic to the insurgent colonists that during much of the war of American independence it was left cooling its heels in the West Indies. When the war ended in 1783, the battalions were gradually withdrawn to Montreal, there to form in 1790 the nucleus of the King's Royal Rifles.[14] From 1790 Marc-Louis Pictet's name (by now anglicised into Mark Pictet) is absent from the Army lists. Did he stay behind in the States, buying up cheaply land abandoned by settlers loyal to England? Did he settle in Canada with these same politically cleansed settlers? How did he prosper? Was he ever in a position to help his brothers, a point of some importance a few years later? He certainly outlived them by a good margin.

In the event, the Pictets stayed. Life had become calmer, both in Geneva and Paris, after the execution of Robespierre in July 94, despite financial failure yet again in both countries due to the French Republic's repeated bankruptcy. Besides they were considering a new idea put to them by Frederic Maurice, a friend and neighbour in the next street, Rue des Granges. Why not start a magazine devoted exclusively to giving French readers excerpts, summaries and analyses from the most respected scientific, technological and literary English publications? Marc–Auguste, as a typical Genevan scientist, was admirably capable of presenting specialised scientific material; Charles was known for his knowledge of agriculture, as a humanitarian and anyway a literary editor (on the strength of his translation of J. Morse) needs no specialised knowledge; finally Maurice, despite financial difficulties, had enough capital to start the enterprise.

It should produce a living wage for all three of them and with stringent economy enable Marc–Auguste to start repaying his considerable debts.

Marc–Auguste hesitated. Yes, Geneva, Neufchatel and Lausanne were used to a variety of gazettes and journals, so one more would not be out of the way, and one about English publications would have no competitors; yes, Maurice had contributed to the *Journal de Genève* and knew about the production of journals; yes, Charles was highly capable. Still – Marc–Auguste wrote a memo to himself, setting out the arguments for and against. Eventually the clinchers were – his wife's mood swings, driven by anxiety over the family's future (there were three daughters to provide for), and man's duty on this earth to work and struggle. Hardly Excelsior, just the Protestant work ethic, and none the worse for that. The journal was to be called *Bibliothèque britannique*.

The most attractive and remarkable qualities of the three editors, seen through the lens of the 20th century's upheavals, are their resilience and creative energy. For twenty years, in the face of repeated set-backs, they turned their hands to anything to make their new journal, and later their city, prosper. They succeeded beyond every expectation. Not only was Marc–Auguste debt-free by 1806, but Charles made a fortune out of one of the magazine's sidelines. The journal became so highly regarded that, at the final peace negotiations after the fall of Napoleon, its twenty–year success was one of the elements in re–establishing Geneva's international position. It continued, under one name or another, well into the 20th century, and in 1813 it introduced Jane Austen to continental Europe.

The Pictet Brothers — Notes

1 Children of the prosperous: In that respect Planta is not a precursor of Pestalozzi, who offered education weighted to manual skills, to the children of the poor.

2 Burgundy: The French province to the west of Switzerland, it had long been an independent kingdom, with territories that are now in Belgium and the Netherlands.

3 Stuarts: King James II, the last of the Stuart kings, had fled in 1688. Parliament had ratified his deposition and invited his daughter and son-in-law to take over instead. However in 1689 James II used a campaign in Ireland to attempt a comeback.

4 Rumford: Benjamin Thompson, count Rumford, was an American scientist with a strong practical bent, who divided much of his life between the capitals of Europe, until he married the widow of Lavoisier, the guillotined chemist. He then settled in France.

5 The drawing room at Northanger: *Northanger Abbey*, vol. 2. ch. 5.

6 Coram Fields: Near the present Russell Square tube station, was the site chosen for the London Foundling Hospital, incorporated by royal charter in 1739. It was started by Thomas Coram, a merchant sea captain, who had spent ten years in Massachusetts as a boat builder and farmer. He was helped by friends and sympathisers, among them William Hogarth, the painter, whose portrait of Captain Coram is one of his best. The building is open to the public.

7 Chatsworth: Near Bakewell in Derbyshire, rates three stars in the Michelin Guide to Great Britain, and deservedly so. The park and garden are the finest work of Capability Brown, the house is a baroque palace, the welcome to visitors exceptionally friendly. It makes for a splendid day out.

8 Royal Society: Its full title is The Royal Society of London for the Improving of Natural Knowledge, founded in 1662. Its publication, *Philosophical Transactions*, starting in 1665, was the first permanent scientific journal, and, as such, a regular source of material for the Pictet brothers when they started the *Bibliothèque britannique*. The Royal Society remains the world-class academy of science; membership denotes outstanding achievement.

9 Offer of peace: This had been worded by Mallet du Pan, one of the reforming Genevans who had moved to France in 1782, while the Genevan revolutionaries were briefly in power. In Paris he had been a prominent political journalist, writing even for the official paper *Mercure de France*, that figures in this Jane Austen story. He had found it prudent to return to Geneva, but was maintaining his efforts to unite the argumentative factions

of the French royalist opposition to the republican government.

10 Take to him: Letters 70 and 71 of April 1811, in *Jane Austen's Letters*, edited by Deirdre Le Faye, OUP 1996.

11 That is Protestants: Roman Catholics could not hold a commission in the British army until 1778.

12 Prévost was also the name of the Pictets' friend who travelled to England with them in 1787, and one of their closest subsequent collaborators.

13 Duke of Cumberland: Quoted in Appendix II of the Annals of the King's Royal Rifles, vol. 1, by Lewis Butler, Murray 1932. The other volumes are by S. Hare.

14 The King's Royal Rifles are known as the Green Jackets. Their uniform was changed as a consequence of their experiences during the American War of Independence. The traditional colour for British army uniforms was red, which made the soldiers sitting ducks for the insurgents, who operated like a guerrilla army for much of the time. The tactic had been learnt from the colonists' earlier fights with the local native tribes. The point is demonstrated in Charlotte Smith's *The Old Manor House*, 1793. Its hero joins the army, fights the insurgents, is rescued by a local tribe friendly to the British, and finally makes it to safety in Canada and back home to riches and the waiting heroine. Charlotte Smith is the only woman novelist of the period who uses a journey to the New World as more than a narrative device to remove a character from the scene for a longish period. This happens notably in *Mansfield Park* and Mrs Inchbald's *A Simple Story* (1791). The convention persists in French literature, for instance in Madame de Staël's *Corinne* 1807, and *La Nouvelle Héloïse* by J.J. Rousseau.

Bibliothéque Britannique

Starting a magazine in Geneva in 1795, and one based on English publications, was not so hare-brained as might first appear. The French wars had disrupted long established religious and commercial links between the two countries. (Geneva was one of the loosely associated Swiss cantons.) Scientists of the two had well-developed contacts and England's highly advanced technology was of the greatest interest to the Swiss. English visitors had been numerous and the Swiss diaspora in London growing by the month. The pragmatism of both cultures was another affinity, as well as admiration for each other's political liberty. In short Geneva and England were natural allies and had been so for many years.

The *Bibliothèque britannique*, given entirely to translations, filled a market niche – curiosity about England. It did not attempt intellectual debate (unlike the *Décades Philosophiques* of Paris founded only two years earlier); it aimed to provide a balanced mixture of articles, either straight translations or abstracts, on a variety of subjects, all of which had to be useful morally and/or practically; all had to be understandable to a mixed readership, with, if necessary, the more difficult and specialised subjects re-presented in an accessible manner.

What is now referred to as 'the public understanding of science' was one of the editors' aims. Definitely the contents were intended for serious thought; they had nothing fashionable or sensational about them; the probity of the individual (think of Elinor Dashwood in *Sense and Sensibility*) was supported, social responsibility expected and the improvement of man and his institutions seen as entirely possible for men of good will and good sense.

Events interfered – William Wickham, the British *chargé d'affaires*, had much support in Berne, where he was officially accredited. His Swiss wife joined him from London, bringing Foreign Office money to pay his network of informers – one of whom was Marc-Auguste, although he refused to be paid. But

Wickham was not managing to bring together the various French royalist parties to present a coherent and united opposition to revolutionary France, so he was increasingly being by-passed by Pitt, the prime minister, and Grenville (the Pictets' acquaintance from 1787) the foreign secretary, who dealt directly with agents in Paris. There Napoleon, put in command of the army of Italy, had no money to pay them – victory, with opportunity for pillage, was therefore essential. It came in May 1796, at Lodi.

Napoleon entered Milan and Geneva's independence became more precarious. Back in Steventon Jane Austen was writing the first draft of *Pride and Prejudice*. The editors of the new *Bibliothèque britannique* stuck to their Anglophilia but coded it:

> Le désir d'opposer à l'étude des théories, si séduisante pour les hommes ardents et légers mais si vaine dans ses resultats, l'étude des faits, seul guide capable de conduire à la verité.
> [The wish to counterbalance the examination of theories, so attractive to men more vehement than thoughtful, but so fruitless in practice, with an examination of facts, the only possible guide to truth.]

The difficulty lay in obtaining 'the facts', that is the latest English language publications – since March 1793 and the start of the war between Britain and France, the French had imposed a blockade on British goods, which included all English-language books and journals.

Consequently, the editors and their prospective readers were intellectually cut off from Britain, where also their political sympathies lay. By focusing on English publications, the *Bibliothèque britannique* would signal Anglo–Genevan understanding and resistance to Britain's enemy. The editors became less guarded in stating their desire to:

> dissiper à l'égard des moeurs, des institutions et resources d'Angleterre . . . une ignorance profonde, fruit de la haine nationale.
> [To dispel the profound ignorance, itself the result of national hatred, of the customs, institutions and resources of England.]

In their prospectus the editors let rip – England, untouched by revolutionary ideas, where, despite the war, institutions were stable, intellectual pursuits developing normally and trade flourishing, was to be admired; the new USA, with its respect for religion and morality and down–to–earth wisdom to base laws on time–tested models, was an example to be followed.

This was a singularly tactless opening salvo, not least because the cheapest passage for printed material from London to Geneva lay through France, where also the bulk of the future readership of the journal was likely to reside.

The official French publication *Mercure de France* (handled by Arthus Bertrand, who later published Jane Austen) laid into the editors. Friends and colleagues from the Parisian world of science urged caution, so in May 1796 the editors rowed back sufficiently for the *Bibliothèque britannique* to get off to a politically correct re–start. Effectively, they traded an undertaking to avoid politics for the safe and regular passage (or as safe and regular as the disorganised French postal services allowed) of printed material from London, without which their enterprise would founder.

While the editors stayed discreetly with their opposition to revolutionary ideology, what evolved was the format of the monthly journal – it split in two. One half, entitled *Sciences et Arts* grew an addition with separate page numbers titled *Agriculture*; a fortnight later came *Littérature*; each was the size of a slim paper-back. Since books were serialised (*Pride and Prejudice* and *Mansfield Park* came out in four instalments each) it was advantageous either to keep back numbers in a special folder, or to buy a year's numbers bound into one indexed volume.

The first two outspoken numbers had been printed by Luc Sestie, a well–set–up local printer. But while re–thinking the expressed politics of the editors, Maurice, the editor concerned with the daily organisation of the enterprise, decided to cut costs by assembling the printing, binding and distribution in the basement of his house, 14 Rue des Granges.

One press was bought; a few men employed and printing and proof-reading streamlined by the use of a trap door between the ground-floor study and the basement work room. What Maurice's family thought of the arrangement is not recorded. A print run of 500 was usual up to 1800. Copies were distributed by post, price depending on distance from the source (hence in 1797 Rumford, then in Munich, complained of the cost). Once agents had been established in Paris, bundles were sent by stage-coach at concessionary rates for local distribution.

At about this time Charles inherited, through his wife, an estate at Lancy, now a leafy suburb of Geneva surrounding the Bois de la Batie, the very large park that contains the zoo. These days it is a brief bus ride from Grand Rue and Rue des Granges; in the late 1790s it was totally in the country and there was enough land for Charles to experiment with the new ideas out of England, crops, husbandry or new tools. There is an anecdote of his being highly satisfied with a novel design of plough and inviting local farmers to view it. They were unimpressed until Charles took off his jacket, rolled up his sleeves and ploughed a few furrows. Whether it was the excellence of the plough or the sight of a gentleman in shirtsleeves being proficient at a peasant's trade, the farmers were won over. More to the point, Charles acquired some merino sheep. The wool of these highly valuable animals was exported, but they were reluctantly sold from Spain – Joseph Banks had spent several years assembling, sometimes in doubtful circumstances, a flock for George III.

However, early in the eighteenth century the King of Spain had given some to his Bourbon cousin, the King of France; these animals were kept in the *bergerie du roi*, the king's sheepfold, which like everything royal, was downgraded after 1789. Hence Charles was able to buy some rams and more ewes for a reasonable price and came by prime specimens of the breed. Under his management the sheep flourished and multiplied; gradually he established an extensive and highly lucrative trade as far afield as Hungary, (later, in his son's time, as far as the Crimea). Charles' wife, Adeläide, turned out to be an extremely skilful spinner of merino wool which she then turned into exquisite shawls. These remained rare, luxury items. Attempts to establish a local industry of high–grade merino textiles failed.

The year 1797, despite Napoleon's sweep through Italy, was sufficiently hopeful for Paschoud, established as book–seller to Madame de Staël and her even wealthier father, Jacques Necker, to branch out into publishing. He used the printer, Luc Sestie, who had produced the first two, politically outspoken, numbers of the *Bibliothèque britannique* and published whole books, parts of which had been analysed or serialised in the journal. Either the writer of the original article had to provide a translation of the whole, or Paschoud found a new translator, as happened in March 1822 when he published a translation of the unabridged text of *Pride and Pre-judice*.

Looking back on this period Charles was later to write:

> Nous étions surtout persuadés que la guerre ne tarderait pas à être terminée par une paix générale. Cette illusion nous fut utile – jamais, sans elle, nous n'aurions osé braver la défaveur des circonstances, et nous croirions encore à l'impossibilité de l'exécution.
>
> [Above all, we were convinced that the war would end shortly in a general peace settlement. We found this illusion useful – without it we would never have dared defy the obstructive adversities in our way, and we would still have believed it impossible to put our plans into action.]

The 'obstructive adversities' came in 1798: French troops in Lausanne and Berne, and the Republic of Geneva annexed into France. By the new treaty the city became the *chef-lieu* (admin-istrative capital) of the equally new Department of Leman; the city's population amounted to only 10% of the whole department and therefore, it could send only two representatives to the council of the department. Pictet, Maurice and their class, the former *bourgeois de Genève*, kept well clear of it, although all Genevans were declared French by birth. To this there was a handful of vindictive exceptions – François d'Ivernois and Jacques Mallet du Pan for instance, both known as vocal and distinctly anti–revolutionary constitutional reformers, were exiled and barred from ever becoming French citizens.

They fled to London, where the news of the 'destruction of the cradle of liberty' had been received with indignation. D'Ivernois became doyen of the Swiss diaspora and useful to the Pictets. Mallet du Pan continued his efforts on behalf of the royalist French opposition; William Wickham, the recently withdrawn British chargé d'affaires in Berne and spymaster, was now working in the Aliens Office, and he helped to settle the exiled families. This mitigated the evils of emigration, particularly serious in an age of limited travel, and its distressing long–term consequences, made much of in Balzac's *Le Lys dans la Vallée*. In the event Marc–Auguste, too, found it prudent to leave Geneva for a while, but this time he travelled at his journal's expense. He came to London and stayed with his nephew, Charles Lullin who was also a cousin of Wickham's Swiss wife. Charles Lullin had been found a job by Wickham as clerk for passports, which involved filing alien registers and keeping in touch with alien service agents working in the ports, in support of Customs officers. Hence Marc–Auguste had another tie with British intelligence and came by information about official and unofficial channels of communication between London and the continent, useful for the forwarding of supplies from London to Geneva. He found an extensive *colonie genévoise*, visited Lackington's bookshop (known as the Temple of the Muses) and the Foundling Hospital at Coram Fields where Rumford had installed an 'economic kitchen.' He attended to business for the *Bibliothèque britannique* and, on the return journey met Humboldt in Paris. Most usefully, he carried home Jenner's treatise on cow–pox. While some few vaccinations had sporadically taken place in Geneva since the 1750s:

C'est à la *Bibliothèque britannique* que revient l'honneur d'avoir, la première sur le continent, et celà de 1798, attiré l'attention sur les résultats obtenus en Angleterre par la méthode de Jenner.

[The *Bibliothèque britannique* had the honour of being the first publication on the continent to draw attention as early as 1798 to the
results obtained by Jenner's methods.]

Overall the *Bibliothèque britannique* did a great deal to disseminate
knowledge of British science, technology and agriculture. The last
was so popular that all articles on the subject were assembled into a
ten volume *Cours d'agriculture anglaise*, which sold very well
between 1808 and 1810.

Literature was harder to present successfully, largely because of
the difficulty of translation. Charles was aware of this:

> La partie la plus difficile de notre entreprise, et l'écueil que nous
> redoutons le plus, est la traduction ou l'analyse des ouvrages
> d'imagination; le génie de la langue et l'esprit de la nation Anglaise
> sont tellement essentiels au caractere de ces écrits, que ni la traduc-
> tion servile, ni l'imitation libre ne peuvent atteindre la plénitude
> d'effet des originaux.
>
> [The hardest part of our enterprise, the reef we most dread, is trans-
> lating or analysing works of the imagination; the genius of the lan-
> guage and the spirit of the English so essential to the identity of these
> works that neither a literal translation nor a free imitation can
> achieve the full effect of the originals.]

The reason for this is English literary language:

> La composition Anglaise a de certains caractères qui frappent le
> lecteur Français − tels sont la longueur des périodes, la suspension
> fréquente du sens par des idées accessoires, la recherche des ex-
> pressions qui font images, l'abus des épithètes, les tournures qui
> sentent l'effort, quelque choses enfin qui nous parait lâche, guindé ou
> obscur.
>
> [English writing has features that forcibly strike a French reader −
> the length of the sentences, the frequent interruptions of the main
> idea by secondary ones, the forced introduction of metaphors, over-
> use of descriptive terms, strained construction, in short something
> that seems to us lax, exaggerated or muddled.]

These difficulties notwithstanding, *Littérature* provided rich and
varied fare. The largest fraction was devoted to travel writing, such
as items by L.A. Necker on Scotland and the Western Isles; then

novels (Maria Edgeworth was a favourite, Mrs Barbauld, Fanny Burney, Mrs Chapone, Mrs Inchbald and Mrs Radcliffe all featured); history, economics and *mélanges* followed and education (Maria Edgeworth again) with *Practical Education*. Biography and philosophy brought up the rear. The book most extensively extracted from was Roscoe's *Life and Pontificate of Leo X*, closely followed by the eleven-part serialisation of Kerr's *History of Scotland in the Reign of Robert I*.

Novels were not despised (after all Maria Edgeworth was highly esteemed) but they were something like loss-leaders designed to attract the less committed readers (mothers and daughters most likely) in the hope of strengthening their morals while leading them to more substantial and improving fare. This was standard for the period – you will recall the description of the accomplished woman in *Pride and Prejudice*, vol. 1, ch. 8 – Miss Bingley has her list on which Darcy comments, 'to all this she must yet add something more substantial, in the improvement of her mind by extensive reading.'

Amongst novels Charles had distinct preferences:

> Comme les combinaisons possibles de vieux chateaux, de souterrains et de phantomes doivent être bientôt epuisées, et qu'on se blase enfin sur ces sortes d'émotions, on doit croire qu'un genre plus gai remplacera bientôt cette noire manie.
>
> [Surely by now the variations possible on old castles, underground passages and ghosts must be nearly exhausted, and we are at length tired of the feelings they excite, so we must believe that soon a more cheerful genre will replace this funereal craze.]

The French phrase for gothic novel is *roman noir*, direct ancestor of *film noir*. Because of the nature of the material, the monthly numbers of *Littérature* contained a third more pages than *Sciences et Arts* or *Agriculture*. This meant that each month a great deal of text had to be translated to a deadline. The *Bibliothèque britannique*, as a family business, did not have the funds, especially in its early years, to farm out the task to specialist translators. So the work was done, literally, in-house – Charles's wife, the super-spinner Adelaïde, who took to it with enthusiasm, Marc–Auguste's two elder daughters, Marie and Caroline, who were of an age to help from the start; Charles's elder daughter, Amélie, is said to have been the most gifted. A visitor to Lancy at the start of the new century describes the activity in the house – Charles dictating a translation, the girls' impressive concentration, good humour and command of English, Adelaïde in control. They loved their work and took pride in Napoleon's rebuke to the Genevans *'vous savez l'anglais trop bien.'*

The three editors of the *Bibliothèque britannique* soldiered on. Their Anglophilia reproached the French for annexing Geneva and countered anti–British propaganda that was, reasonably enough, unremitting in France. By the very fact of its existence, the journal was a declaration of intellectual independence, always a Genevan characteristic, and a distinctive counterbalance to the loss of political independence. It was the outward and visible sign of Genevan patriotism. The French authorities reckoned that tolerating it was the wiser course. Napoleon had to have something to show for his claim that he was not a philistine (he was even persuaded in 1812 to give permission for Humphry Davy to travel to France and Italy, to meet Ampère, Cuvier, Humboldt and Volta).[1] As a journal of the highest intellectual order the *Bibliothèque britannique* had supporters amongst scientists in France (Dolomieu the geologist, Chaptal the industrial chemist, Lacepède the naturalist, Lalande the astronomer), and from 1802 Marc–Auguste was by correspondence a member of the *Institut des Sciences*, comparable to his status in the Royal Society that had come his way some ten years earlier.

So no difficulties were put in the way of Marc–Auguste and two friends travelling to London in 1801. This time he stayed with Rumford, (still busy organising the very new Royal Institution) in the latter's house in Brompton Row, awash with labour–saving devices. He met Jenner and Humphry Davy (later President of the Royal Society and inventor of the miner's safety–lamp). He went to Ireland, saw the Giant's Causeway, met the eccentric Richard Kirwan (*'le Nestor des chimistes de la Grande Bretagne'*), moved on to

Co – Longford to visit Maria Edgeworth (Jane Austen was to send her a copy of *Emma*); *son père l'éteint* [her father suppresses her], which was obvious to all who knew 'the great Maria.' The list of Marc-Auguste's contacts shows the *Bibliothèque britannique*'s continued emphasis on science.

The war went on and on. Nevertheless, the number of subscribers to the journal increased, till by 1811 there were 627 of them. By now the arrival of the monthly parcel of publications sent from London was irregular, so source materials were sought in the German states. At the start of 1813, looking back on the previous year, Charles explained:

> Nous avons été assez régulièrement pourvus d'ouvrages originaux pendant l'année 1812. S'il y a des parties qui sont faibles en matériaux c'est qu'il y a disette dans le pays même d'où nous les tirons.
> [During the year 1812 we obtained original works fairly regularly. If there are under-represented areas it is because of a lack of corresponding material in the source country.]

The disconcerting implication is that after March 1813 *Pride and Prejudice* might not have merited translation and inclusion in the July, August, September and October numbers of the *Bibliothèque britannique* if enough other books had been available to choose from. After all, in 1811, when supplies from London were somewhat more plentiful, *Sense and Sensibility* never made it.

Bibliothèque britannique — Note

1 Volta: Humphry Davy, chemist and physicist, was researching electricity; Ampère was his French opposite number; the Italian, Volta, invented the electric battery; Cuvier was a zoologist and palaeontologist.

The Instalments Translated

So on 6th March 1813 a copy of *Pride and Prejudice* reached Marc–Auguste. He had been charged 13/6 (thirteen shillings and six pence) and 10% commission, 14/10 altogether (about 75 pence). There is no record of how soon it was decided to feature the book in *Littérature*, nor who adapted it for serial publication in four instalments, nor who translated it, but it is likely to have been one of the ladies of the family who 'spoke English too well'.

The opening fanfare is rendered:

C'est une verité reconnue qu'un jeune homme qui a de la fortune doit chercher à se marier.
[It is generally accepted that a young man with a fortune must seek to marry.]

The trumpet sounds with something of a hollow sound . . . When the Bennets first meet the Bingley party, the whole scene of the dance in the local assembly rooms is omitted, making the heroine's early antipathy to the hero incomprehensible. The Netherfield conversation about accomplished women omits Miss Bingley's contribution and Darcy's final comment is:

Vous dites fort bien Bingley – reprit Darcy – mais les vrais talents sont une chose très rare, et il est encore plus rare d'y voir réunis l'instruction, la modestie et les graces.
[You are quite right, Bingley, replied Darcy, but real talents are very rare, and it is even rarer to find them united with knowledge, modesty and a graceful manner.]

Some way from the original:

"All this she must possess," added Darcy, "and to all this she must yet add something more substantial, in the improvement of her mind by extensive reading."

But this version of Darcy's answer is probably influenced by the Genevan perception of a well brought–up woman.

Another conversation at Netherfield takes an unexpected turn – Darcy is describing himself to Elizabeth, (ch. 19):

> It has been the study of my life to avoid those weaknesses which
> often expose a strong understanding to ridicule.
> [J'ai du moins cherché à éviter les faiblesses qui peuvent rendre un
> galant homme ridicule.]

Darcy referring to himself as *un galant homme*? No.

There is the recurring difficulty with the word 'gentleman' but
this persists even in modern translations like Barbara Vierne's (1996
Edition Anatolia).

Nit-picking aside, it is obvious that before serialisation there was
no time to read the book, consider it as a whole, and only then
select and translate. Consequently, a greater proportion of conversation – easier to translate than reflection or analysis – gets to the
printed page, with expressions elided into their French approxima-
tion – 'I will only add 'God bless you',' becomes '*Agréez tous mes
voeux*'. Flattening the original significantly falsifies it. So does a
patriarchal transposition – Mr Bennet agrees to Elizabeth's marrying
Darcy only after being told what the latter has done for Lydia.
Omissions show up the characters in different lights – Wickham
loses all his charm, so his plausibility as a confidence trickster disap-
pears; Mrs Bennet's vulgarity is omitted. She emerges as an accept-
ably concerned mother, not a comic figure; Jane loses her status as a
suffering heroine; Bingley's sisters are scarcely irritants; Mr Bennet
is not a man of the Enlightenment.

What the serialisation retains is the Gardiners as guardian angels,
the ridiculous character of Lady Catherine and the marked contrast
between Charlotte Lucas and Mr Collins on one hand, and Elizabeth
and Darcy on the other. It brings out the vividness of Elizabeth's
reactions to situations with a choice of words for surprise. So, with
humour lost and the language planed flat, what appealed to the
readers?

The bourgeois setting for a start, highlighted by the nastiness of
the titled aristo Lady Catherine, but validated by the hero, himself
at the cusp between aristocrats and bourgeois, but siding with the
latter. The problem addressed is a very recognisable one – solved

by the heroine, who by her own efforts achieves significant improvement in her wealth, security and status. Although she may not be entirely within the polite conventions of Geneva, she clearly passes muster in England and certainly does not throw herself at the hero in the manner of Corinne, as described at length by Madame de Staël, the sporadic novelist who, when not being 'the conscience of Europe,' lived a few miles away on the north side of the lake.

The serialisation of *Pride and Prejudice* took up 121 pages of four numbers of *Littérature*. They were embedded amongst *A Grammar of the Malaysian Language*, by W Marsden FRS, a serious paper to the Royal Society of Edinburgh on a blind–deaf child, an article by J. Nield on the state of prisons in England, Scotland and Wales, the seventh instalment of the *History of Scotland in the Reign of Robert I.* by R. Kerr, notes on the population of England, accounts of journeys in the middle East, the interior of Brazil and Africa and a description of Caracas. There were some notes on the private life of modern Egyptians, others by the Rev. W.B. Daniel on hunting and fishing. Fiction–wise, *Pride and Prejudice* had to compete with the last instalment of *La Famille Irlandaise à Londres*, originally *The Absentee*, by Maria Edgeworth, which manages to read much like the happy ending of a conventional novel.

The trouble with serialising novels was how to bridge the gaps between the selected extracts. Linking passages summarising the intervening action were used, but this tactic was less than satisfactory because, as Charles explained, '*Ce refroidit toujours l'intérêt.*' This is not far from the hassle of remembering to program the VCR for the weekly instalment of a series. We can recover the whole only when the video is on sale. If readers of the *Bibliothèque britannique* wanted the whole, they had to wait till the end of the war when supplies of books from England re–started arriving regularly, or an enterprising publisher, like Paschoud in Geneva or Arthus Bertrand in Paris, published a more or less free translation of the unabridged text.

However unsatisfactory the serialised novels appear to us, the *Bibliothèque britannique*'s original readers liked them and must have

made their preferences known to the editors (after all, a nucleus of
them was resident in Geneva, on the editors' doorstep). In January
1815 the editors disclaim responsibility for including so many, in
their opinion, poor – novels.

> C'est à nos lecteurs à décider s'il eut mieux valu supprimer pour un
> temps ce genre d'ouvrage.
> [It is up to our readers to decide whether it would have been better
> to shun this type of writing for a time.]

However, by now the context was very optimistic – the war was at
an end, Napoleon defeated and imprisoned on Elba.

> De toutes parts renait un nouvel ordre, dont nous pouvons espérer de
> tirer quelque avantage. Les communications entre la Grande-
> Bretagne et le Continent sont devenues promptes et faciles, la France
> régénerée, loin de s'opposer à la circulation des lumières, fait pro-
> fessions de l'encourager.
> [Everywhere the new order has started. We may hope to take
> advantage of it. Communications between Great Britain and the Con-
> tinent have become quick and easy; France, reborn, is far from
> objecting to the spread of enlightenment and declares its support; in
> fact encourages it.]

Mansfield Park with its win (perhaps it is only a win on points) of
virtue over vice, clearly fitted this hopeful mood. The introduction
explains:

> Le succès assez général qu'a obtenu le roman *Pride and Prejudice*,
> *Orgueil et Préjugé*, nous engage à en extraire un second du même
> auteur. Nous reviendrons à la même méthode employeé précédem-
> ment pour quelques ouvrages du même genre; celle de remplir
> l'intervalle des scenes qui méritent d'être traduites en entier, par un
> recit abrégé qui fasse suivre le fil des évènements, et montre les per-
> sonnages les plus interessants sous divers points de vue où l'auteur a
> voulu les placer.
> [The fairly wide-spread success of the novel *Pride and Prejudice*
> leads us to feature another by the same author. We will return to the
> same technique used formerly for several works of the same kind;
> that is to fill the gaps between such scenes as deserve to be translated
> in full by an abbreviated narrative; this allows the reader to follow

the sequence of events and shows the most arresting characters in the various situations into which the author chose to place them.]

Notice that *Pride and Prejudice* is referred to as *roman*, something nearer a romance, or a 'rom com' of film categorisation. Serious novels, such as Maria Edgeworth's, were *contes*, accounts of events, although much later she described herself as 'a writer of romances by profession'. Compared to Austen, the Edgeworth translations contain fewer and shorter linking passages.

Viewing *Mansfield Park* as a succession of scenes accounts for the predominance of conversation in the fully translated sections (as is the case with the version of *Pride and Prejudice*). However, the complications of the plot lead to the same number of pages being devoted to the summarised story as to the straight translation.

Mansfield Park appeared flanked by instalments of Jeremy Bentham's *Reward and Punishment*, more of *The History of Scotland in the Reign of Robert I* and another entitled *History of the Abolition of Slavery*.[1] Abolition was the hot topic (not that reference to the slave trade in *Mansfield Park*, vol.2, ch.3 made it to the translated page). The editors were proud to include the letters of Monsieur Kizell '*un noir*' from Sierra Leone. How well they understood his predicament:

> Sans doute, une circonstance accidentelle, un trait, une nuance, une teinte particulière de la peau, devrait avoir rien de remarquable; mais on sait trop les suites cruelles qu'a entraînées cette simple diversité de couleur; et combien ne jouit-on pas de voir l'humanité reprendre enfin tous ses droits!
> [Surely an accidental condition, a feature, a shade of complexion should go quite unnoticed; but we know only too well the cruel consequences of this simple variation of colour and how greatly we now rejoice that the human race has finally come into all its rights.]

After that, a note on the formation of the Society for the Propagation of Christian Knowledge falls rather flat.

There is, however, a description of an ingenious *Machine arithmétique* that does the four operations of whole numbers and fractions. Numbers are entered, the machine starts whirring and sooner that it would take to do the sum on paper, a bell rings to indicate that the solution has been arrived at. The examining Commission of the Royal Society of Warsaw enthused:

> Tout ce que Pascal, Grillet, Schlott, Polerius et l'immortel Leibnitz ont imaginé en vue de cet objet se trouve réalisé par Abraham Stern, busy devising a machine destinée à la recherche des nombres premiers, [designed to discover prime numbers].[2]

It was one of several European attempts to construct an automatic calculator, to eliminate human error from mathematical tables. As applied science it fitted in well with the *Bibliothèque britannique*'s continued predominant interest in the sciences and recent search for material in German journals.

As to novels in English, Maria Edgeworth remained unrivalled:

> Quant au conte de Miss Edgeworth intitulé *Patronage*, nous n'avons qu'a regretter de n'avoir pu lui rendre toute la justice qu'il mérite. On y trouve, au plus haut degré, la justesse d'esprit, la finesse d'observation, l'adresse dans l'enchainement des circonstances qui distinguent cet auteur.
>
> [As to Miss Edgeworth's story titled *Patronage*, we can only regret that we are unable to do it the justice it deserves. It contains to the highest degree wise judgement, subtlety of observation, skill in depicting the skein of events and circumstances that are typical of this author.]

Patronage is not one of Maria Edgeworth's best. However, Jane Austen mentions, perhaps tongue in the cheek, liking them all (letter 108, 28.09.14) but it scarcely merits the encomium above. An instalment of *Waverley* next to it evokes no comment from the editors, though Jane Austen, in the same letter to her niece Anna, is quite clear in her high opinion of Scott's novels.

Again the translator of *Mansfield Park* is unknown. The talented Amélie Pictet de Rochemont could well have done it – she was twenty-four at the time, at home, for she married only after Charles', her father's, death. It certainly was not Charles, because immediately after the first abdication of Napoleon in 1814, Charles was sent as representative of Geneva to the first of the successive peace negotiations configuring the new map of Europe. Marc-Auguste grumbled:

> Je fais la part du travail de mon frère tandis qu'il fait la belle jambe au congrès de Vienne dont j'ai décliné la mission
> [I am doing my brother's share of the work while he's manoeuvring in Vienna, but I declined to go away on congress business.]

Charles met Talleyrand, the subtle foreign minister, first of Napoleon and then of the restored monarchy, and asked why the *Bibliothèque britannique*, that propaganda thorn in Napoleon's flesh, had been allowed to publish and expand its readership. The half-jocular reply was, 'If we'd suppressed you we'd have had a revolution on our hands.' The importance of this twenty-year-long intellectual irritant had been understood by the French authorities. It continued to be taken into account by the European Powers in their deliberations, as a symbol of the continuity of Geneva's specific integrity. It called for reward. Charles emerged as the most successful of the Swiss envoys – he persuaded the Kingdom of Sardinia to cede to Geneva territory to the south of the city, so now more of its scattered parishes were joined up. The road across the Simplon pass was opened to traffic with the other Swiss cantons. Finally the northern portion of Savoy, the province nearest Geneva controlled by Sardinia, was neutralised.

This inception of neutrality was of the highest importance. Charles built on it during the long, difficult negotiations after Napoleon's final exile to St Helena. Charles drafted the treaty by which, on 20th March 1815, the European powers recognized the permanent neutrality of Switzerland and guaranteed the integrity of its territory. Over the years up to our day that treaty has saved countless lives.

Next time we come to praise famous men, let us remember Charles Pictet de Rochemont. He served us well.

The Instalments Translated — Notes

1 The article seems to refer to agitation against slavery under the leadership of the Society for the Propagation of Christian Knowledge (founded 1698) together with Dissenters and the evangelical wing of the Church of England. District committees were being set up and the Rev. James Austen, Jane's eldest brother, was an active supporter in his diocese. *History of the Abolition of the African Slave Trade* had been published in 1808; Jane Austen must have read it, because in a letter of 24 January 1813 she mentions having been 'in love with Clarkson', referring to the anti-slavery context.

2 Prime numbers: Its nearest English counterpart was Babbage's 'Difference Engine' built to very exacting standards and abandoned in 1833. Models of it can be seen in the Science Museum, South Kensington, London, in the context of similar machines from France, Sweden and Germany.

Madame de Staël

Madame de Staël crops up in the Jane Austen story several times. To put her in context, she was the daughter of a devoted couple – Suzanne Curchod of Lausanne (the love of Edward Gibbon's life) and Jacques Necker of Geneva. He was a hugely successful banker, who became a director of the Compagnie des Indes and the Paris representative of the Republic of Geneva. Further, despite not being French, and a Calvinist (that is, not *la religion du roi*), King Louis XVI, when financial ruin stared France in the face, appointed him his director of finance. So home for the Neckers, together with their daughter, was in Paris; for a number of years Madame Necker's salon was the most brilliant of the capital and the little girl was allowed to spend much time in it listening to, and taking part in, adult conversation.

Madame de Genlis, the novelist whose ideas on education Emma quotes with approval in volume 3, chapter 17, frowned upon this. The bright youngster preferred precocious conversation to dolls. Naturally, she developed a taste for company, wit and admiration and devotion to her father. She grew into a rather plain, lumpy girl, exceptionally intelligent, brimming with ideas and lively feelings, generous, enthusiastic, unused to contradiction and the richest heiress of Europe. An exceptional husband had to be found for her, but the list of candidates was limited by her Calvinist faith, excluding all Roman Catholic suitors. After strictly hard–headed negotiations, at age 20 she married the handsome Baron de Staël, Swedish ambassador to Paris. Conjugal amity was the order of the day; Madame l'Ambassadrice, whose considerable charm negated the plainness of her person, had a salon that gradually overtook and superseded in brilliance that of her mother. This was insufficient for her restless imagination. She wanted to influence political events – after all, she had grown up with politics and her father was director general of the king's finances. But it could only be done through her husband, busy elsewhere, who was unwilling to fall in with her wishes.

There is a story of his making a mistress of Mademoiselle Clairon, the great actress resident in Rue Visconti, who herself, according to an earlier story, had taught his wife to act. Madame de Staël wanted passion and took the first of many lovers while her father's political fortunes waned, waxed and finally collapsed.

He retired to Switzerland; she stayed in Paris, convinced that as the daughter of the right-thinking former director of finance and herself a strong supporter of reform, she was entitled to continue guiding the destinies of France.

However, in June 1791 she was visiting her parents at their château in Coppet[1], and the Pictet brothers visited her. Charles wrote to a friend:

> J'arrive de Coppet où j'étais allé déjeuner avec mon frère et Bossier. Nous allions pour voir Madame de Staël et nous n'avons vu qu'elle. Elle a une dose d'esprit qui fait pardonner bien de choses, mais il est certain qu'elle porte l'extravagance un peu loin. Ses confidences sur ses amants, ses amis, son mari, sa mère, ont occupé une bonne partie du temps. Il est impossible d'être plus naïve qu'elle ne l'ait – on n'en pardonnerait pas la dixième partie à une autre. Mais elle est gaie, bonne enfant, extrèmement brillante, on ne voit que cela. Elle n'est pas rassurée sur l'état de la France, bien qu'elle persiste à regarder la contre-révolution à main armée comme impossible. Quand on la presse pour savoir d'elle comment tout cela finira, elle est embarrassée. Je le suis aussi, et mon opinion est qu'il faut s'en remettre à la bonne Providence.
>
> [I'm just back from Coppet, where I went for lunch with my brother and Bossier. We went to see Madame de Staël and saw her alone. She has such bright vitality that much is forgiven her, but she certainly goes some way beyond the limits. Much of the time was taken up by the low-down on her lovers, friends, husband, and mother. It is impossible to be more naïve than she is – no other person would be treated one tenth so indulgently. But she is merry, good-natured, her conversation dazzling – that's all you notice. She is not sanguine about the state France is in, although she still maintains that armed counter-revolution is impossible. When you press her for an opinion of how all this will finish, she has nothing to suggest. Neither have I, and think we must leave it to a kindly providence.]

Back in Paris, her salon continued to flourish, at first with visitors of wide-ranging political opinion. Gradually the constitutional monarchists were the majority and with events accelerating after the unsuccessful flight of the royal family in June 1791, the embassy building sheltered some of them. Eventually, even Madame de Staël found it expedient to make use of the exit visa that she had been granted. She left in the embassy carriage drawn by six horses and servants in ambassadorial livery. This did not ensure a safe journey – she was arrested, dragged back to Paris, shouted at by an abusive crowd and held in the Hôtel de Ville long enough to be extremely uncomfortable (she was six months pregnant). With difficulty she made it to Rolle, a small town on Lake Geneva about half-way between Geneva and Lausanne. Her second son was born there but she didn't stay long. Her lover, Narbonne, was in England. She joined him at Juniper Hall, a country house near Dorking rented by French émigrés, where Fanny Burney met her and was dazzled by her conversation. Dr Burney disapproved of the acquaintance, for accounts of Madame de Staël's love life had preceded her arrival. Again she did not stay long.

In spring 1793 she was back in Switzerland, her mother dead, unmourned by the daughter. She wrote a pamphlet hoping to save Queen Marie-Antoinette from the guillotine. It did not work, but de Staël money enabled a number of aristocrats to escape. They joined her émigré salon that included the fair-haired Swedish Count Ribbing, a character in Verdi's *Un Ballo in Maschera*, unable to return home because of his part in the plot against Gustav III, the subject of the opera.

Her next major lover was the red-haired Benjamin Constant. These days he is mainly remembered for his novel *Adolphe*, the story of an unbearable sexual attraction, a book very much worth reading, working the same vein as *Phèdre, Manon Lescaut, Le diable au corps*[2]. He had serious political ambitions and Madame de Staël hoped through him to influence events in France. The idea seemed feasible, for after the executions of Danton and Robespierre,

moderation was in the air. In fact, all she achieved was to be, herself, exiled from France. Napoleon could not abide her. She
returned with Benjamin Constant to Coppet.

The village of that name is on the north side of Lake Geneva,
readily accessible by both local train and the regular boats. If you
are in Geneva, the day is fine and a long afternoon free, take shipping from the main embarkation point by Parc Albion. The boats
chug along peacefully past the *Jet d'Eau*, the sailing boats loiter, and
if your eyes can rub out most of the buildings on both shores you
will be inside Turner's painting of Lake Geneva. A few tidy trees
shade the landing at Coppet, the stroll to the château is easy. The
first gravelled courtyard has low buildings on each side, a *corps de
logis* with steep roof and a wide doorway into the next one. The
second courtyard has buildings on three sides, the fourth only a
grille through which lawns, pool and large cedars seem to seep into
the house. No wonder Rousseau's feeling for nature surfaces so
frequently in Madame de Staël's writing.

The rooms are decidedly grand, both in proportion and furnishings. (Look out for remarkable Chinese prints in the ground-floor
dining-room.) This is no rural *pied-à-terre*, nor a prison, although
there were times when Madame de Staël viewed it as such. It was
the recuperative holiday destination for many of her friends, including Byron. They describe the delights, still extant, of the park,
of day-and-night-long conversation, and the dramatic performances given in the library.

Notably, in Racine's *Andromaque*, Madame de Staël took the part
of Hermione, the betrayed heroine; the beautiful Madame
Récamier,[3] a very close friend, took the title role of the enslaved
princess. Benjamin Constant, Madame de Staël's red-haired lover,
by now trying to detach himself from an exhausting relationship,
had to play the part of King Pyrrhus, the faithless lover of
Hermione. Unsurprisingly, he was less than commanding in the
speech in which he confirms to his newly discarded lover the
rumour of his change of heart. In reply, Madame de Staël's

character has a splendid range of well-known lines to throw at his head. She took full advantage of the sweep and staccato of the verse to castigate her departing lover with a fire and vehemence never previously seen in the part. The audience – all the local gentry had been invited – was amazed no less by the performance than by the self-revelation she allowed herself. Benjamin Constant left. The performances continued – *Phèdre* and some (un–actable) plays she wrote herself and made her children take part in. The audiences continued to crowd in to such an extent that the servants bringing refreshments had to go round the outside of the building and pass trays through the windows.

Had Jane Austen got wind of it through Eliza Austen, widow of a French aristocrat and wife of Jane's favourite brother Henry? Henry, who acted as his sister's agent, was a banker at the time, and some of his contacts may have been Genevan bankers in London. If, through them, he heard any stories about the authoress, Madame de Staël, he could have relayed them to his sister, also an authoress.

How far is it echoed by the episode of theatricals in *Mansfield Park*? The young prepare to put on a play already well known from the professional theatre, in which two actors, Henry Crawford and Maria Bertram (engaged to Mr Rushworth) use their parts to indicate their attraction for each other. Edmund Bertram, Maria's brother and an aspiring clergyman, is appalled to discover that many neighbours have been invited to the performance. Only the return of Sir Thomas Bertram, much earlier than expected, prevents Henry and Maria from publicising their feelings.

Much as we may laugh at or pity Madame de Staël (the fairies at her christening had signally failed to provide her with a sense of humour), as long as she had Coppet to return to she wrote ground-breaking works in that house, sustained by the immediate landscape, working from the experiences her inexhaustible intellectual curiosity led her to encompass. Her love life was a shambles, her attempts to conciliate Napoleon crass and in her non–fiction, her disregard for detail cavalier.

However, in politics she was on the side of the angels – she loved liberty; she loved France. She was a liberal opposed to all tyranny, foremost that of the Revolution and Napoleon. She complained, talked, wrote endlessly on the subject; to the end she wanted *Napoléon victorieux et mort*. In the process, she earned the epithet of 'the conscience of Europe.'

She considered the influence of feelings on the happiness of individuals and nations, the connection between literature and social institutions, the difference between Nordic and classical ideals, the balance between enthusiasm and clarity of reason and the intellectual ferment in Germany. She tried to lead the French to be open-minded about the contributions of other languages and other cultures, a perennially hard row to hoe in the country that gave us the term *chauvinisme*.

She also found time to write two long novels. The first was *Delphine*, in letter form, some fifteen characters contributing. So for dramatic orchestration this is a long way from Richardson's *Pamela*, and even Rousseau's *La Nouvelle Héloïse*. It covers two years, from the spring of 1790; the characters are distinctly Ancien Régime, bound by conventions, variously tied up in the usual amorous knots and related intrigues, at first seemingly immune to the events in the non-fictional world.

Gradually politics catches up with them and it all ends in tears. The novel is more absorbing than this flippant description might lead you to believe. It lends itself to only moderate skipping, but if you have the stamina for 1000 small paperback pages, it is a better read than *La Nouvelle Héloïse*. Being written only ten years after the events described, it also retains immediacy in the feel of a civilisation being swept away.

Madame de Staël, recently widowed and out of favour with Napoleon, decided to have the novel published first in Geneva. Later as an extant work, it would be easier to introduce into France with its much larger readership. She went to Paschoud, the publisher closely connected with the Pictets of the *Bibliothèque britannique* and whom she had known as her bookseller. A muddle ensued – Paschoud produced an edition in four volumes, which fits in with the overall length of the work. Madame de Staël, having divided the novel into six parts, each ending with a disaster, wanted it in three volumes. In a huff, she approached Maradan, the Parisian publisher in Rue Visconti, who was later to publish the unabridged *Pride and Prejudice*, and got him to produce a three volume edition within a few weeks of Paschoud's. Literary design was satisfied and the book a huge success.

Her second novel *Corinne* was the result of her visit to Italy in 1805. It came out in 1807, again triumphantly and was twice translated into English in the same year. Jane Austen read it either in English or French (Henry, her brother, in the biographical notice, tells us she had both French and Italian), and speaking with her fingers to the very deaf Mr Fitzhugh (letter 63, 23 to 28.12.08) she recommended him to read it. Why? It would have been a way of keeping in the swim, rather as we might recommend the new book by Germaine Greer. It is again a good, long read, useful for a man isolated by his disability. Much of it is travelogue, to compensate for the restraints of war, and the descriptions of particular monuments or landscapes would please any reader with half an eye for the picturesque.

There are several recaps, with examples, of the arguments relating political organisation to the literature and behaviour of the intelligentsia (the lower orders are uniformly attentive and well meaning), a few camouflaged swipes at Napoleon, the contrast between enthusiasm and reason, feminine and masculine, Mediterranean and Nordic, and there is the story line – Mills and Boon *par excellence*, no synopsis can do justice to the dollops of risibility in the avalanche of emotion. Madame de Staël throws into this book the sum total of her experience to date – her guilt at not reaching her father before he died, her continued and uncomprehending pain from the absconding of Benjamin Constant and others; her conviction of the amplitude of love:

Amour, suprême puissance du coeur, mystérieux enthousiasme qui
renferme en lui-même la poésie, l'héroisme et la religion.
[Love, the heart's supreme power, mysterious spirit that holds within
itself poetry, heroism and religion .]

Her feminism:

Chaque femme, comme chaque homme, ne doit-elle se frayer une
route d'après son caractère et ses talents?
[Does not every woman, like every man, have the duty of following
her own path as her character and talents direct?]

There are acclamations, premonitions, hesitations, recriminations,
pride, silences, doubts, regrets, miseries, and many almost pedago-
gic passages that explain, for instance, how the architecture of the
Pantheon in Rome produces its visual effect, or how Mrs Siddons, in
the character of Isabella (in Garrick's *Fatal Marriage*, one of the
peaks of her career) exemplifies the best English tragic acting. In
short it's a ragbag of a book, demanding from the reader rapid oscill-
ations between the willing suspension of disbelief and serious attention to some aesthetic, psychological or societal argument. Recommended.

A few years later Madame de Staël wrote *De l'Allemagne*, her
great apologia for the major civilisation often disregarded in France
of the period and its Romantic ideals. For once prudence guided her
and she ignored the violent nationalism that figured significantly in
German Romanticism. The book started printing in Paris, but
Napoleon, alert for his bête noire, found it anti-French and had the
whole run confiscated. Friends smuggled out one copy and the
manuscript. Madame de Staël was exiled from France yet again.
Back in Coppet she could not settle and before long was on the road
once more with her children and her new and secret husband.[4]
They travelled to Austria, Russia, Finland, Sweden and finally England during the autumn of 1813. John Murray (Jane Austen's future
publisher) published *De l'Allemagne*; she was fêted, although the
Tories found her too liberal, and Byron anti-Napoleonic rather
than truly liberal. James Macintosh, a prototype PR consultant,

squired her about town. She borrowed, the story goes, a copy of *Pride and Prejudice* from Henry Colburn, a bookseller of Albemarle Street, and dismissed it as *vulgaire*.

To do her justice, this is not to be translated as vulgar in the modern sense. It meant lacking elevation of expressed emotion, indifference to themes of wide concern in political or intellectual life. Fair enough, but there was a sequel.

According to Henry Austen:

> a nobleman (probably Lord Dudley, reputed to have been the best-read man in England) – personally unknown to Jane Austen – was desirous of her joining a literary circle in his house. He communicated his wish in the politest manner, through a mutual friend (obviously Henry)[5] adding, what his lordship doubtless thought would be an irresistible inducement, that the celebrated Madame de Staël would be of the party. Miss Austen immediately declined the invitation. To her truly delicate mind such a display would have given pain instead of pleasure.

To deconstruct that last sentence – Jane Austen, a gentlewoman totally opposed to self–promotion, especially in the guise of authoress – was she going to lend her reputation to enhance the triumphalism of that republican goer, the most notorious and least self–controlled woman in Europe, with her string of illegitimate children and a longer string of lovers? It was her money as much as her books that saved her from universal opprobrium. Huh! Besides, Jane hadn't a thing to wear.

Which emphatically Madame de Staël did. All descriptions of her mention the care she took over her appearance, turbans being a speciality, the odd lyre a useful prop. Alas, she wanted too much and once more put her foot in it. Came the end of the war and the *Bibliothèque britannique*'s good work for Britain recognised, she wrote to George III, mad and blind though he was, demanding that in recompense for their long efforts on Great Britain's behalf, Marc-Auguste, Charles and Maurice, the third business partner, should be given a pension of £500. On behalf of the King the British government was happy to oblige. The letter and draft duly arrived to the immense embarrassment of the trio. Of course it was a lot of money; of course they were going to refuse (although Marc–Auguste was said to have *pas de fortune*), but how? After much humming and hawing, they accepted on condition the money went to the Genevan *Société des Arts*.

Madame de Staël died in Paris 24 hours after Jane Austen had died in Winchester.

Madame de Staël — Notes

1 Coppet: Village on the north side of Lake Geneva.

2 *Adolphe*: The book came out in 1816, with the supplementary explanation – *anecdote trouvée dans les papiers d'un inconnu et publiée par M. Benjamin de Constant*. In other words, Constant disclaimed ownership of the text in terms used by Henry Mackenzie in *The Man of Feeling* and *Julia de Roubigné* some forty years earlier. While both men distance themselves from their narratives, Constant's is based on emotions he had painfully lived through, Mackenzie's are constructed as enquiries into sentiments based on theories of moral behaviour. Both are expressed in novels, a form of literature then seen as lacking seriousness. Since both men had public careers to protect (Constant in politics, Mackenzie as a lawyer) it was probably advisable to avoid the taint of having a side-line associated with frivolous reading matter.

3 Madame Récamier 1777-1849, very much in the thick of literary life, was also well known for her long and faithful friendship with Chateaubriand, the brilliance of her salon in the years 1815 to 1830, and the several portraits of her by David, Gérard, Chinard. A particularly graceful one has her sitting on a chaise-longue.

4 Albert-Jean Michel, known as John Rocca, twenty-two years her junior.

5 A mutual friend: There is a theory that Henry Austen invented this invitation. Even if it actually happened, it was less of a distinction than might appear – Madame de Staël was working her way through literary London, especially women writers. She had already bagged Amelia Opie, widow of the painter John Opie and author of *Adeline de Mowbray* (1805, based on the liaison between William Godwin and Mary Wollstonecraft) and Elizabeth Inchbald, dramatist, author of *A Simple Story*, (1791, a novel still worth reading and not only for its portrait of John Philip Kemble, the actor brother of Mrs Siddons). See Roger Manvell *Elizabeth Inchbald* – 'England's Principal Woman Dramatist and Independent Woman of Letters in 18th Century London' – A Biographical Study, University Press of America Inc. 1987.

To Paris — The Translator

Of the several early translators of Jane Austen into French, one is very well documented – Madame la baronne de Montolieu, to call her by her third and preferred name. She was born in Lausanne (less than forty miles from Geneva) in 1751, the untitled daughter of a pastor, as Elisabeth-Jeanne Pauline Polier de Bottens. At eighteen she married Benjamin Crousaz de Mézery, a surname that Gibbon aficionados may remember. It crops up when Gibbon, exiled by his father, enraged at the son's conversion to Rome, sent him off to Lausanne to sort out his ideas. The young man was finally re-convinced of the truths of Protestantism by following the system of logical thinking developed by an earlier member of the same Crousaz family (who also crops up in *La Nouvelle Héloïse*, scarcely a work devoted to logic). Edward Gibbon was re-admitted to his ancestral faith and inheritance at Christmas 1754. Some years later young Madame de Crousaz (no title) aged barely twenty-four, was left a widow with a son.

With the support of her extended family and friends in Lausanne, she was sufficiently in the swim to be a leading light in the literary diversions of the city and to mix with visiting foreigners. Madame de Genlis, (the novelist mentioned in *Emma*, vol.3, ch.17) became a friend, and Edward Gibbon, originally a friend of her husband, admitted to finding her dangerously attractive. Still, money was short. What was a respectable young widow to do? Exactly what Jane Austen did – write books. However, unlike Jane Austen, Madame de Crousaz started from a short story in a German compendium and expanded it into *Caroline de Lichtfield*, a two-volume novel. Granted, these are small (octavo) volumes (17 cm x 10½ cm), printed with decent margins, some 500 pages altogether, nearer the length of *Northanger Abbey* than most other novels of the period.

Gibbon and his friend Deyverdun advised on the manuscript and acted as agents. It was published in Paris in 1786 and was an immediate and lasting success. It was translated into English by Thomas Holcroft, the actor turned author, and then published in London by Robinson to equally good effect. Prints of scenes from it were soon on sale and Gibbon took a set back to the delighted Madame de Crousaz. Not that her name appeared on the title page. In that same year she re-married the widower baron Louis de Montolieu, a Protestant from Nimes,[1] but was widowed again in 1800. By this date, with the war in full swing and Switzerland firmly in the French sphere of influence, she had to turn full-time writer to support herself. She was hugely successful.

Of the forty-three titles credited to her in the 1878 *Dictionnaire Biographique des Genévois et des Vaudois* only nine are original, in the sense of being her own invention from start to finish as Jane Austen's novels are. All the rest are translations from English or German (for instance *Le Robinson Suisse*). Many are labelled *traduction libre*, as were both *Sense and Sensibility* in 1815 and *Persuasion* in 1821, becoming, in the process, *Raison et Sensibilité ou Deux Manières d'aimer* and *La Famille Elliot ou l'ancienne inclinaison*. For the last, the title page adds '*D'un Roman Posthume de Miss Jane Austen, auteur de Raison et Sensibilité, D'Orgueil et Préjugé, D'Emma, De Mansfield-Parc* etc' (*Northanger Abbey* did not get translated until 1824). Occasionally a text has been '*imité de l'anglais*' as with *Un An et Un Jour* of 1820. Not that the lady was much of a linguist, as was admitted in reference books as early as 1852 (*Nouvelle Biographie Générale* J.C.F. Hoeffer):

> Quant à ses traductions ou imitations de l'anglais et de l'allemand, on a remarqué avec raison que le charme répandu par elle sur tous ses écrits fait pardonner l'infidelité de ses versions, d'autant plus aisement qu'il ne s'agit pas d'ouvrages sérieux. Ces divers recueils ne sont pas entièrement originaux – ils renferment tous des limitations de l'allemand et de l'anglais, langues qu'elle ne possédait qu' imparfaitement.
>
> [As for the translations from English and German, it has been rightly said that the charm she endows all her writings with is ample to forgive the lack of precision in her versions, all the more readily since it is not a question of serious works. These miscellaneous compila-

tions are not entirely original; they are all constrained by features specific to German and English, languages of which her command was less than perfect.

Friends helped her out with the literal meaning of the original text that she then adapted to fit the conventions of the day. Consequently, for instance, to maintain patriarchal authority, Anne Elliot obtains her father's consent before allowing herself to be engaged to Wentworth. The beautiful, elegant and rich Mrs Willoughby remains only rich in the translation, to demonstrate the negative moral influence of fashionable London life. Yet at the time there were other translations much closer to the originals (the 1822 *Orgueil et Prévention* by Eloïse Perks, for one), pedestrian no doubt, but avoiding bolt-on incidents, copious weepings, strings of intrusive adjectives. So why did Madame de Montolieu get away with it? Partly because the originals were unread in France. Then because novels, being feminine literature, were not considered serious, so accuracy of translation was unnecessary. Also, because demand for novels was insatiable it had to be satisfied rapidly. Finally, Madame de Montolieu got away with it as a star writer on the strength of *Caroline de Lichtfield*.

Its opening is conventional enough – Caroline, an heiress aged fifteen, is translated from a rural retreat, where, being orphaned as tradition demands, she had been brought up by an elderly aunt, to the court of Frederic the Great. Thus the setting in Protestant Prussia eliminates the weapon of last resort available to parents of recalcitrant girls – sending off to a convent. So from the start the heroine has, at least in theory, a degree of freedom not available to heroines of, for instance, Madame de Souza, a French Roman Catholic and a very prolific and successful novelist of this same period. Psychologically, Caroline is a child:

> Un petit chien favori, la lecture d'un conte de Fées, avaient seuls le droit de l'intéresser et de l'émouvoir.
> [a favourite puppy, a fairy tale alone had the right to hold her attention and engage her feelings.]

Fairy tales were one of the most popular forms of eighteenth century reading matter, with *Les Contes Marins* alone weighing in at
twenty volumes in the Bibliothèque Nationale Française. Caroline,
this innocent, is told by her father, one of the king's ministers, that
the king has decreed she is to marry Count Walstein, highly
esteemed by the king and envoy to St Petersburg:

> Ton sort est fixé sans retour.
> [Your lot has been determined; there's no way of changing it.]

Walstein's return is delayed by illness, not that Caroline is informed,
which gives her time to demur:

> 'Cependant, je ne le connais pas, ce comte; si j'allais ne pas l'aimer?'
> 'Vous l'épouserez également, ma fille,' reprit vivement le Baron.
> 'Nous ne vous demandons que ce dont vous pouvez disposer, votre
> main et votre foi; pour votre coeur, il restera libre. Ni l'authorité
> royale, ni l'authorité paternelle, n'ont le pouvoir de le gêner.'
> ['But I don't know this count; suppose I don't like him?' 'You will
> marry him all the same,' said the baron (her father) quickly. 'We are
> asking of you only what you can control – your hand and your good
> faith. As to your heart, it remains free. Neither royal nor paternal
> authority can constrain it.']

Is that a hint that a story of adultery in high places, an early version
of *Madame De* ——, is to follow?[2]

Not twenty-five years after *La Nouvelle Héloïse*, the prime novel
of sensibility and sincerity still being reprinted, discussed and imitated. Caroline settles for welcoming the prospect of marriage
(there is a good description of a fifteen-year-old's capacity for
thought), imagining it to be a continuation of the parties she has
been attending at court, only squired by the one – delicious – dancing partner. Shock, horror when Walstein turns out to be stooped,
lame, scarred, minus one eye, wearing a horrible yellow-grey wig
and so old. (He is in fact thirty.) Caroline shrieks, scarpers, faints,
her corsets have to be unlaced (a sign of the extremity of emotional
trauma), she weeps and declares herself to be ill. Walstein half
believes her:

Il en sortit affligé de ce qui venait se passer. Ce n'est pas qu'il fut amoureux de Caroline, qu'à peine il avait entre-vue, mais ce marriage lui convenait à tant d'égards, qu'il y avait attaché l'idée du bonheur de sa vie; ensuite le roi le voulait.
[He left saddened by what had just happened. It's not that he was in love with Caroline, whom he had barely glimpsed, but this marriage suited him in so many respects that he had built round it the vision of a happy life for himself; besides, the king wanted it to take place.]

Caroline goes through the extremes of adolescent emotion (again a good description), cut short by her father who:

croyait de bonne foi, et d'après sa façon de penser, assurer son parfait bonheur par un aussi brilliant marriage, fait directement sous les auspices du Roi, et par l'ordre du Roi.
[He believed in good faith to his way of thinking that he was ensuring Caroline's perfect happiness by such a brilliant match, arranged expressly under the king's auspices and at the king's command.]

Hero, heroine and heroine's father are all under royal compulsion. The father, a highly ambitious man, has a particular motive for ensuring the marriage takes place – the king has declared his job is on the line because *un père aussi faible ne peut être bon ministre.* [Such a weak father cannot make a good minister.]
The father, telling Caroline that he will be shot if she refuses Walstein, further heightens tension. She capitulates, thinking only:

'Il (i.e. her father) me devra la vie', disait-elle avec une tendresse mêlée d'admiration pour elle-même, qui produisait une sensation assez douce; 'oui, mais à quel prix et avec qui vais-je passer la mienne.'
['He will owe me his life,' she repeated to herself, as affection for her father mixed with admiration for herself produced quite a pleasing sensation; 'yes, but at what price to me, and look at the man my life is to be spent with.']

Walstein insists on the marriage taking place secretly, on his estate just a week hence and Caroline uses the interval to hatch her plan. On the day, the king and two or three married couples of the nobility act as witnesses. Immediately after the ceremony Caroline unobtrusively hands Walstein a letter stating she is too young to

marry (the only permissible reason for delay) and wishes to return
to her rural retreat:

> 'Que j'attende là que ma raison ait fait assez de progrès pour me
> soumettre sans mourir aux liens que j'ai formés.'
> ['to await there for my reason to develop sufficiently and so allow me
> to submit without dying to the ties I have formed.']

This straight statement of the power of reason to control emotions
(in this case physical revulsion), is the familiar collision between
duty and personal inclination popularised by Corneille more than a
century earlier. So far, so traditional. What is new is Walstein's reaction. First he is astounded:

> 'Cette enfant si timide en apparence, et qui lui a paru si soumise, ose
> avoir une volonté et l'annoncer avec courage et fermeté.'
> ['This child, to all appearances so timid and so compliant, dares to
> have a will of her own and to express it firmly and fearlessly.']

Next he agrees to her wish, judging that his temporary sacrifice will
make him less odious to his bride:

> 'Je sens le prix de votre confiance en moi.'
> ['I appreciate what your trust in me entails.']

The king agrees to the arrangement on pragmatic grounds:

> 'Sa fortune est à vous, c'est l'essentiel; on vit toujours assez avec sa
> femme.'
> ['Her fortune belongs to you; that is the material point; more than
> enough time is spent with one's wife.']

But he insists upon total secrecy about the marriage without giving
his reasons:

> On a presumé qu'il avait craint que cette histoire ne répandit une
> forte ridicule sur son favori et peut-être sur son autorité.
> [It was assumed that, should the story get out, his (i.e. the king's)
> favourite (i.e. Walstein) would be much laughed at and his own
> authority possibly undermined.]

A pair of nifty sentences suggests the form taken by court gossip, but
in the event, the news management holds.

There follows the most believable section of the novel – a description of Caroline, back with her aunt in her otherwise solitary rural retreat, maturing physically and mentally, with the secret of her link to Walstein fermenting in the imagination. After the appropriate time–lapse comes the inevitable mega–coincidence – she meets the young man who, unknown to her, caused Walstein's lameness, loss of eye and scarred face. They fall in love; the lover discovers her secret and takes flight, but not before leaving her with letters, a diary and a miniature as incontrovertible proof of Walstein's goodness, sensibility and former physical attractiveness. Remorse kicks in to accelerate Caroline, sensitised by this apprentice–love, into emotional maturation. There's a journey, more fainting and unlaced corsets; she is very ill, delirious even and talkative with it. Walstein nurses her devotedly, proof of this devotion being that for a fortnight he doesn't take time out to change his clothes. Despite any olfactory obstacle, she recovers slowly, realizes she loves him dearly, but this time is genuinely too timid to say so; after a series of misunderstandings, renunciations and flights, she hot–foots after him to his estate. The reader is treated to a precise description of Walstein's restored physical attractiveness and a ladylike allusion to the success of the wedding night. In short, Mills and Boon in excelsis.

But there is more to it. For a start there is the aura of threat, the powerlessness of women only one degree more marked than that of men (though Caroline manages to take the initiative twice to further her private desires), the tentacles of royal power forcing the king's subjects into his moulds.

Frederic the Great is conventionally known as an enlightened despot. In this novel the despotism alone comes through. To avoid it, characters flee to England or plan self-imposed exile in the land of freedom, stability and prosperity. This is the same view of England as that informing the Pictet brothers as they established the *Bibliothèque britannique*, and kept it going for the long years of Napoleonic autocracy.

The account of the heroine growing up rings true, recognisable now, some two hundred years after the writing. A *bildungsroman* lurks in the text. If only the sentences had a little more spring to them, were built into more powerful paragraphs, and the author did not just abdicate at crucial points in the story:

> Nous n'éssayons pas de donner une idée des sentiments de Caroline àpres cette lecture, comment exprimer ce qui se passait dans un coeur partagé entre l'amour et le remords, l'admiration et peut-être même un peu de jalousie.
>
> [We will not attempt to describe what Caroline felt after reading (the letters, diary etc her would be lover had given her), her heart torn between love and guilt, admiration and perhaps even a touch of jealousy.]

A far cry from the description of Elizabeth Bennet's changing view of Darcy after she has read his letter of explanation. The treatment of Walstein is even more cursory:

> Il est inutile d'entrer dans le détail de tout ce qu'il souffrait pendant ces jours d'incertitude et de douleur.
>
> [It is unnecessary to go into particulars of all his suffering during these days of uncertainty and pain, (that is, the fortnight while Walstein was nursing the delirious Caroline.)]

Nevertheless, the book remains a page-turner, however precipitate the steps taken by the hero from his opinion that:

> L'amour honnête n'est autre chose qu'une vive amitié, fondée sur une estime réciproque et toujours exaltée par la différence des sexes.
> [Respectable love is no more than lively friendship based on mutual esteem and always increased by the difference between the sexes.]

A sentiment Jane Austen seems to have had in mind for Marianne Dashwood when she paired her off with Colonel Brandon changed to Walstein's later:

> 'J'aime avec autant plus de violence que je suis dun sexe qui n'a pas l'habitude de régler les mouvements d'une passion impétueuse; la mienne ne connait plus de bornes.'

['I am the more ardently in love for belonging to the sex that is not used to controlling the impulses of violent passion; mine is now limitless.']

Most striking is the fairy-tale quality of the whole. *Caroline de Lichtfield* is a direct descendant of *The Beauty and the Beast*. The 1756 classical text by Jeanne Leprince de Beaumont (itself a gentrified version of the much longer and rougher tale in *Les Contes Marins*) passed down to the novel the incident of the father of the heroine being constrained to deliver her to the Beast / Walstein, looking dreadful after his illness but expecting conjugal relations. In both the heroine is abstracted to a rural retreat and kept isolated with either very few other characters for company or none. In both, the heroine gradually comes to appreciate the Beast / Walstein through gratitude, esteem and lonely hours of thinking about him, much as Elizabeth Bennet also does. In both, the crisis is brought about by a journey out of the rural retreat/magic garden, leading to recognition by the heroine of the Beast's / Walstein's genuine tenderness of feeling for her, and her own more than tender feelings for him (more echoes of *Pride and Prejudice*).

Nowadays the reader may see it as a case of '*l'horreur renforce l'attrait*' and '*le danger paralyse, mais moins fort, il peut exciter le désir*' [horror strengthens the attraction; danger paralyses, but if less urgent, it can arouse desire], as Georges Bataille keeps exemplifying. But in the eighteenth century, French novels had taken to lengthy exploration of the self (six volumes to *La Nouvelle Héloïse* for one), which must include the body. So the Beast is changed into a handsome prince, much as Walstein recovers his health and attractiveness; looks are no longer an optional add-on to the Beasts's / Walstein's kindness, good sense and riches. These are no longer tales of explicit adaptation, like a century earlier Perrault's *Riquet à la houppe*, where the hero stays ugly and the question of sexual satisfaction does not arise.

Caroline de Lichtfield is a novel of contemporary manners; the reader, always the author's accomplice, adopts the sentimental mode, fully aware that the purpose of the book, as of the fairy tale, is to comfort very young girls about to be married to husbands not of their choosing. In countries, and at a period when the convent was the alternative, this was an important – and lucrative – subject for a novelist to address.

Jane Austen, being English and publishing sixty–three years after *Clarissa*, misses it entirely. There is no suggestion that any one of her female characters (granted mostly older than Caroline) is about to be married against her will. The judgment of Charlotte Lucas may be suspect, and Marianne Dashwood allows herself to settle for second best, but neither of them is frightened. Going through a catalogue of Austen female characters, none, bar possibly the two above, sounds as if she needs to 'close her eyes and think of the future of England.' Without heroines forced into arranged marriages and the consequent potential for conflict and its resolution, Jane Austen loses one significant point of contact with continental readers.

The widowed Madame de Montolieu, armed with the success of *Caroline de Lichtfield*, was in a strong position when she returned to writing. She translated from the German of August La Fontaine. She wrote some short moral stories and had them published in Geneva by Paschoud, the publisher who put out as complete books some that had been serialised in *Bibliothèque britannique*. He also had to cope with another aspiring novelist, the younger sister of Madame de Montolieu, while the lady herself moved on. By 1811 she was a regular contributor to *Mercure de France*, the official up–market journal *politique et littéraire*, published by Arthus Bertrand of 23 Rue Hautefeuille.

It came out weekly, and looking at a year's run for 1811, it is striking how detailed the accounts of English parliamentary debates are, in current terms much nearer Hansard[3] than parliamentary sketch writers having fun in *The Times*. Apart from the cringe–making poems on the birth of the King of Rome (Napoleon's son), it is a thoroughly serious journal. Most numbers have something on a science–based topic – non–European plants in Europe, '*une machine à plonger appelée Triton*,' (a diving bell called Triton), an eclipse of the moon very visible in Paris, or a comet in Ursa Major. The arts pages review books (Retif de la Bretonne,[4] for instance) and the pictures in the last Salon;[5] a think-piece about writing style, referring to *Corinne* or novels, in general, may be triggered by a review of a translation; *Clarissa* and *La Nouvelle Hélöise* are the models for epistolary novels and taken seriously, but with those two exceptions, women like novels, women can't get enough novels, so women unceasingly write new ones. Plays, an opera by Paesiello[6] given at court, are given attention and current events are briskly reported – in South America, an insurrection against Spain, the colonial power; the Governor of Egypt marching into Syria to attack the Wahabis; Mauritius and Reunion in British hands; losses to the British Baltic fleet inflicted by the Danes[7] and throughout the year the familiar running sore in the Balkans – Serbs fighting for independence from the Turks, and the Russians supporting their Orthodox Slav protégés with a 500 strong unit of Russian soldiers in a fortified part of Belgrade. Fortunately, *Dans les provinces illyriennes* (ie Dalmatia) *l'organisation française est complétement achevée*. Indeed, for many years the Napoleonic coastal road remained the best in the region.

In addition, some of the numbers contain free-standing short stories, moral, sentimental, exotic, written by ladies – *Nouvelle Arabe* by Antoinette Legroing in February, Madame de Genlis in September and two by Madame de Montolieu.

In March – *Le Petit Antoine et le Rouge-Gorge, imité de Starke*; in October, still sticking to small birds, *Le Serin de J.J. Rousseau* . This story, in edited form, used to be found in reading-books in French primary schools – the great man had been given the canary by Sophie; later his little neighbour and pupil Rosine had loved it too; but when Jean-Jacques had to leave the town, he gave the bird to Rosine to look after, with instructions that after his and its death, the bird was to be placed on his tomb. An editor's note states that a small box with a yellow bird in it had indeed been found on his tomb. Not that you will find a canary, with or without box, or any reference to this tale, if you visit the crypt of the Panthéon (not too far from the start of Walk Three), where Rousseau now lies.

Be that as it may, Madame de Montolieu capitalised on the Swissness she shared with J.J. Rousseau, and in 1815, on the strength of the third edition of *Caroline de Lichtfield* from Arthus Bertrand, persuaded him to publish also her version of *Sense and Sensibility* (*Raison et Sensibilité ou les deux manières d'aimer traduit librement de l'anglais par Mme Isabelle de Montolieu*).

Presumably Isabelle sounded a more convincing name for a lady author, or a more aristocratic one, for the 1828 re-print is by 'Mme la Baronne Isabelle de Montolieu.' Certainly it is a free translation, and a few changes are even admitted in the preface:

> A la fin où je me suis permis, suivant ma coutume, quelques légers changements que j'ai cru nécessaires.
> [Towards the end, where I took the liberty of making a few slight changes that I thought necessary.]

These are intended to spare the readers boredom induced by the great simplicity of the style. While she welcomes the departure from the Gothic and all its trappings, she emphasises the everyday ordinariness of the subject matter, the veracity of the characters and situation, then she hesitates:

> Perhaps the time has not yet come (in November 1815, five months after Waterloo) to bring out a book that ignores all the agitations we have gone through, a book without the slightest reference to political events. On top of the powerful sensations we have lived through, everything must seem insipid. Maybe our minds need a rest. After the events history has thrown our way and which were beyond anything the wildest fancy could imagine, an eventful novel would surely be unbearable. But an account of gentle, natural feelings, temporary distresses stemming from the most ordinary of life's events, a picture of talent, common sense and reason in all its perfection, will introduce new ideas and succeed by virtue of contrast. Only if the French have changed very considerably would they no longer occasionally need some light reading.

In 1815 Paris, Jane Austen was presented as a rest cure after twenty-six years of turmoil; it's not that far from the use of Jane Austen as escapism from the dreary juggernaut of our day.

To modern readers the changes made by Madame de Montolieu are risible; her version of *Sense and Sensibility* proves her ignorance of English and of different styles of novels. But such as it was, it sold sufficiently to have Arthus Bertrand publish a pretty accurate translation of *Emma* (accurate enough to raise a few smiles in the right places) in 1816, and *Persuasion* (aka *La Famille Elliot ou l'ancienne inclinaison*) in Montolieu's translation in 1821. They came out, like all novels, in blue, thin paper covers, the pages for the first reader to cut; so they come to us with pages of uneven size and fringed edges; because these books have been undisturbed for long months, the coarse-grained paper is full of tiny ruts and ridges, and the pages have to be prised apart gently. The librarians at the Bibliothèque Nationale Française are nonchalant enough about their copies to allow the reader to handle the 1828 edition of *La Famille Elliot* anywhere in the vast reading-rooms; while something rarer, or in a better binding, comes in an envelope and has to be read at *l'hémicycle*, that is the table nearest the librarians' island. The super-rare, like the Elöise Perks 1822 translation of *Pride and Prejudice*, is allowed only in the reverential hush of the *Salle Réserve*, which also gives access to *L'Enfer* (i.e. Hell), that is the 2,000 strong collection of erotic books. Jane Austen meets Don Giovanni (in the guise of Frank Churchill)? In fact twenty-four years separate the Mozart opera from the first edition of *Sense and Sensibility*.

The 1821 translation of *La Famille Elliot* is the first of Jane Austen's novels in French to carry her name. It is again a *traduction libre de l'anglais*, but this time *d'un roman posthume de Miss Jane Austen*, and it includes Henry Austen's *Biographical Notice*, translated with the usual unconcern for detail. It also has a *Note du traducteur* explaining how she had hesitated about including the *Biographical Notice*, thinking its praise over-generous. But, *un Anglais d'un mérite très distingué* [an Englishman of very high reputation] had assured her that far from exaggerating the wit and merits of Miss Jane Austen, the author of the notice had underestimated her achievement as the creator of a new type of novel, built on extreme simplicity of language and skill in holding the reader's attention solely through entirely believable development of the characters and faithful depiction of their emotions. Who could have been the *Anglais d'un mérite très distingué*, who had informed her? A contact through her publisher, Robinson? An English friend of the Swiss refugees in London? And why was she now willing to follow his opinion when her own, in the preface to *Raison et Sensibilité*, had been that the simplicity of the style dragged, and to avoid boring the reader she had to jazz up the translation, especially towards the end.

In 1815 she had judged the truth to nature of the daily round in *Raison et Sensibilité* excellent as a rest cure for an emotionally drained readership, exhausted by twenty-six years of revolution, terror, bankruptcy and war. In six years had her readership recovered so well that an endorsement from England, burdened only by deflation and victory, was needed to publish a story in which nothing much happens except that a girl falls down the stairs? Had Madame de Montolieu herself developed no opinions on the relative merits of different types of novel writing? It seems not. Perhaps she had no time or energy for opinions, because she continued writing relentlessly. 1824 saw her sequel to *The Swiss Family Robinson* aimed at children, but it may be proper to place all her writing into the section children's librarians label 'for older readers,' the equivalent in our day of something nearer 'Neighbours' than the three-parters by Stephen Poliakoff that the broadsheets applaud. She was immensely popular, the third most read novelist of the years 1815 to 1830. Strangest of all, her books were imported into England, by Dulau, a bookseller of 37 Soho Square, who had, on the same site, a lending library.[8] So *Raison et Sensibilité* and *La Famille Elliot* re-entered the land of their origin under the flag of Madame de Montolieu. Until well into the twentieth century nobody seems to have twigged, or if they did, it wasn't worth mentioning.

The Translator — Notes

1 Nimes: A delightful town north-west of Marseilles, with fine Roman monuments flanked by a Norman Foster glass building. Nimes had been predominantly Protestant and suffered greatly during persecutions of the Huguenots. The town's other claim to fame is as the original source of denim (De Nimes), for many years the staple of *bleus de travail* (blue denim for work), familiar, particularly from railway porters, up to the mid fifties.

2 *Madame De*: By Louise de Vilmorin, turned into a most elegant film by Max Ophuls.

3 Hansard: The official reports of proceedings in the Houses of Parliament give speeches verbatim.

4 Retif de la Bretonne: A most prolific writer, whose didactic romances are enlivened by accurately observed sketches of the underprivileged. If you can imagine parts of Mayhew's *London Labour and London Poor* interspersed into the novels of *The Lady's Magazine* (*pace* the chronology) you have a good idea of how he reads.

5 Salon. Drawing-Room: But since painters showed their new works in one of the drawing-rooms in the Louvre Palace (now museum), the word acquired its second meaning – exhibition, particularly one with official status. Which led to *Salon des Refusés*, exhibition of rejected pictures, in the first instance those by impressionist painters.

6 Paisiello: Neopolitan composer of well-turned, bubbly comic operas, whose *Barbiere di Seviglia* was heard by Mozart in Vienna before he wrote his own *Nozze di Figaro*. Napoleon was a great admirer. Paisiello spent some time in Paris; his last opera had orchestral accompaniment throughout.

7 Danes: This may have been wishful thinking, for although Denmark was in the Napoleonic camp in 1811, four years earlier the British navy had commandeered 33 of its ships, including the whole battle line, and sailed them off to British ports.

8 Library: Dulau, like Deboffe (see To Geneva) was a bookseller who supported French émigrés by publishing their texts. He specialised in religious subjects and hence printed the start of *Le Génie du Christianisme* for Chateaubriand, before the latter returned to France in 1800.

In Paris

And so to Paris, the pleasure promised at the start of this venture. Discard any atavistic guilt at the prospect of sheer indulgence. Recall all your hard-won exploratory information gleaned from the libraries, lakes and meadows of Switzerland. You are now ready to hit the literary ground running.

On second thoughts, you might as well first sit down with a coffee and croissant, or brandy, depending on the hour of the day, and get yourself organised. You could do worse than read to the end of this section.

The Paris walks add up to about 5 miles (8kms), tracking Jane Austen's publishers and printers around the streets and monuments, mostly on the Left Bank (Faubourg St Germain). Given comfortable shoes and enough daylight, the three walks together can be done in a day. But who would go to Paris just to pound pavements, however enticing their literary associations, and rush home again? So think week-end, preferably a long one, to allow for rain. Split the walking into sections, as shown on the three maps; fill in with some of the 'escapes lanes' suggested, or perhaps join the hordes on the *bateau mouche* (tourist boats, some with restaurant on board), or if the feet give out, sit in the Luxembourg gardens with your Austen paperback.

Don't worry if the rest of your party have gone off to Stade de France or Longchamp for the day. The proposed itineraries are 'so convenient for even solitary female walkers'[1]; should you briefly and improbably get lost, you are never far from an obvious landmark or metro station; places to sit, draw breath and re-orientate are everywhere. It may be better fun if, like Emma, you have a biddable walking companion, 'one whom' you could, as she did, 'summon any time to walk.' Failing such a 'lasting convenience' (as Elizabeth Bennet saw it) you will be, as I have been, perfectly safe. These streets hold no menace, only the irritation of too many tourists, while you and I are literary travellers.

You may want a map in addition to those in this book (where M
stands for metro station). The best, by far, is the Michelin 54 of
Paris, with street finder. On the hoof it has two disadvantages – it is
printed on heavy paper, making an alternative folding difficult, and
it is the size of a small spinnaker. Re-folding the map on a breezy
street corner, or while sitting at a small café table is not recommended. From experience, folding by consenting adults in private is
the only reliable advice.

If you look at the Michelin map you will see on it small daffodil-
yellow squares, with a number 1 to 18 in red, followed by E. This
stands for *arrondissement*, an administrative district, each with its
own town hall (*Mairie*), roughly equivalent to a borough. Nothing as
easy as the even-numbered ones on one bank of the Seine and the
odd-numbered ones on the other, which is strange since the rule
applies rigorously to house numbers. But not to worry. Our walks
are in only three districts – very properly, Walk One is in the
Premier Arrondissement, around the former royal and imperial
palace of the Louvre, on the Right (north) Bank. Walks Two and
Three are in the 5th and 6th *arrondissements*, on the south, Left
Bank (Rive Gauche). Historically the phrase Rive Gauche has been
associated with leftish politics and the intellectual heavy battalions.
But class consciousness seeps in – the 6th arrondissement covers the
area of the old, aristocratic Faubourg St Germain.

A faubourg was originally outside the city walls, an inhabited area
with its own parish church and such urban services as were available
from the Middle Ages onward. The best known faubourgs are – on
the Right Bank, Saint Antoine, with its revolutionary fervour
(where Monsieur et Madame Defarge of *The Tale of Two Cities* have
their base, the 1790s equivalent of *un p'tit zinc*); St Honoré, also on
the Right Bank, but linked by the Pont du Carousel to Faubourg St
Germain, centred on the church of St Germain des Prés on the Left
Bank. As you walk past the oldest buildings in the last, you will
sometimes see, near the blue and white name plate of the street,
another name cut into the stone, followed by FSG (Faubourg St

Germain). The second is the original, pre–nineteenth century name of the street, before Haussmann and his enthusiastic engineers got to work re–building the city (including the water and sewerage systems), providing it with street lighting, re–naming and re–numbering the newly configured streets.

One feature of the buildings may strike you by its frequency – the *porte–cochère*. This is a door on to the street, tall and wide enough to allow the passage of a carriage, giving on to a courtyard large enough to allow the carriage to turn round. Obviously the court-yards of some houses, like the ones in Rue de l'Eperon (Walk Two), would just about allow one carriage to be so manoeuvred. Others would accommodate more than one at a time, and the far side of the courtyard may be lined with a building quite different from the one facing the street – such is the wide courtyard of 27 Rue St Sulpice (Walk Three), with a graceful, one-storey, bow–fronted building at the back. Finally the grand *hotels* (an *hotel* is a kind of urban château), like the one at number 5 Rue des Grands–Augustins (Walk Three) make no bones about being princely edifices. In the shape of a hollow E, the open side of the E faces the street and is closed off from it with a curtain wall tall enough to deter intruders and low enough to allow passers–by to be impressed by the building behind; a huge wooden door in the middle of the curtain wall is the *porte–cochère*. Most of the courtyards remain cobbled and are gener-ally used as parking places, the buildings having long been divided into separate units.

Of course snobbery enters into it. André Gide in his autobio-graphy, tells how his newly–widowed mother, wanting to scale down to a more modest apartment, is persuaded by a sister–in–law to take one in a building with a *porte–cochère*; its absence would in-dicate a lack of status not to be stomached by a self–respecting bourgeois family. If this status–adequate building happens to be in a street of the old Faubourg St Germain, additional distinction is bestowed upon the flat–dweller; he's not merely one of the prosper-ous from the 16th *arrondissement* (near the Arc de Triomphe), in fact he may not be prosperous at all, but he doesn't care for show, he may be unconventional, raffish even, but he's into high thinking – not so much plain living – a contributor, however marginal, to the French intellectual and artistic ferment that nourishes the human race with ideas. In other words, a restaurant in the 6e may well be more expensive than one offering analogous dishes in the 5e. And that is without going to the stratospheric cost heights of any establishment marked with an ₰ on a little plaque, indicating approval from Brussels.

It is still worth while buying ten Metro tickets at a time, for although no longer stapled into the convenient *carnet* (*Mais il faut faire attention, Madame!*) it does save hassle.

A word of warning about maps of the metro – the colours of the lines tend to vary from one publication to another. Nor do the trains on a particular line have stanchions in the colour of the line, as happens increasingly in London. The metro lines are numbered on maps, and the trains and platforms should display the number. Look for the name of the final destination on each train. Also, when entering from the street, passengers often have to walk the length of the platform of one line in order to access the next, wanted, one.

Don't worry about getting lost in a metro station and looking foolish. You won't be alone – the number of travellers with perfect metropolitan French who sigh *Il manque une pancarte* [an extra label would help] is legion. Take it slowly and ask. If you can do it in anything like correctly accented French you will be complimented profusely and assured that it is *très rare* for the English – which, in this case, includes the Americans – to speak French *aussi bien que vous.*

In Paris — Note

1 Solitary female walkers – *Emma* vol. 1 ch. 2.

Walk One

Let's start at the top, near the Royal and Imperial Palace that is now the Louvre museum. The metro station you want is Palais Royal / Musée du Louvre, accessible via two lines – Number 1 Défense to Château de Vincennes, and number 7 La Courneuve to Villejuif / Aragon or Mairie d'Ivry (the line bifurcates at its southernmost end). As you surface on the Place du Palais Royal, the Louvre is behind you. Cross the Rue St Honoré and go to the *left*, towards Avenue de l'Opéra. Round the corner, in Rue Richelieu, you will come to the entrance of the Comédie Française, useful to identify if you are going to a performance later in your stay. But just short of its protruding bulk is a passage to the *right* that leads into the courtyard of the Palais Royal; a grid of striped columns of various heights, children playing leap-frog over the short ones. The mould formed by the rectangle of surrounding buildings is classically pillared, gardens are visible through the north colonnade and a sound of rushing water (one of the many underground streams of Paris) makes a steady background hum. You could be forgiven for wondering about the rush to symmetry and more symmetry and yet more symmetry so persistent in official France. Enjoy the warmth (it is a sheltered spot), the shadows adding their mote of dissent, and wander to the open colonnade that separates the pillared courtyard from the gardens. The three other sides of the garden rectangle are edged with arcades, with shops, restaurants and art galleries at ground level, apartments above, the first to be built specifically for letting. The developers were the heavily indebted Duc d'Orléans, cousin of the King Louis XVI, and his son, the Duc de Chartres. They did not get round to erecting permanent buildings on the fourth, south side. Instead, to maximise income, cheap one–storey wooden buildings were put up and the shops sub–let to sellers of the latest fashionable clothes, knick-knacks and books, mostly novels. Dentu,[1] the publisher and printer of the 1816 *Le Parc de Mansfield*, had a depot, a sales outlet, in the *galerie de bois*, and advertised it on

Jardin du Palais Royal
Palais Royal
Louvre
Cour Carrée
Rue de Rivoli
Rue du Louvre
Rue Etienne Marcel
Rue du Pont Neuf
Boulevard de Sébastopol
Rambuteau
Centre Georges Pompidou
Pont Neuf
Châtelet
Hotel de Ville
Conciergerie
Cité
Sainte Chapelle
St. Michel
Notre Dame
V.Y.
© 2004 Veronique Yapp

WALK ONE

the novel's title page. You can see a model of the *galerie de bois* at the Carnavalet, the museum of the City of Paris, one of the great delights of the city but well outside the area of these walks. If you are making a longer stay, do go; there is something for all ages and heights of brow, from the excellent print library to the well stocked shop.

The Palais Royal overall, and the *galerie de bois* in particular, remained during the restoration of the Bourbon monarchy (that is from 1815) a place of doubtful reputation, much frequented by soldiers of the victorious allied armies. A Rowlandson–style print, entitled *L'Embarras de choix ou les Anglais au Palais Royal* shows two English soldiers, precursors shape–wise of Abbot and Costello, choosing between four frisky girls dressed in the fashions associated with Jane Austen. Definitely more *Vanity Fair* than *Persuasion*, though Captain Tilney and Henry Crawford would have had no difficulty in that setting.

Wander round the Palais Royal, inspect the shop windows, note Le Grand Véfour, recall Colette and Cocteau who lived on the block, and Gérard de Nerval, who, with his serious and tranquil lobster on a satin leash, walked along the arcades.[2] On a summer Saturday you may run into a wedding lunch; any sunny day people work on their tans around the pool, sitting with faces up–turned; often sculpture shows are sited among the trees.

At the east end of the open colonnade, officially known as the Galerie d'Orléans, for their noble developer, is another exit; from it turn *right* into the Rue de Valois, to take you back to the Place du Palais Royal. On its east side you have Le Louvre des Antiquaires. A conglomerate of antique shops designed for conspicuous consumption and useful as a guide to the latest fashion in collecting, it is fun as long as you keep your sense of humour and a tight hold of your credit card. Look for a plaque in the north–east corner with Rue St Honoré that commemorates the long disappeared *salle de spectacle* (theatre), the site of Molière's triumphs. There, in February 1673 Molière was playing the title part in *Le Malade Imaginaire* – he was taken ill during the performance, managed to stagger home to Rue Richelieu and died a few hours later. If, with hypochondria confounded, you want a change, or it has come on to rain, you could turn *right* and take refuge in the Musée de la Mode et du Textile, in an arm of the Louvre overlooking the Jardin du Carousel. You are likely to have the place to yourself and will be able to enjoy, amongst much else, the beautiful shawls, cashmere and silk, like the one Henry Crawford's "quicker hand" placed round Fanny Price's reluctant shoulders. The same ticket will let you into the Musée des Arts Decoratifs and the new Musée de la Publicité.

If you are still staunch in the pursuit of Jane Austen, walk under cover straight into the Louvre's Cour Napoléon. The Pyramide immediately holds the eye. Much argument has beset this beautifully calculated addition to the Louvre. In every respect, in every season, at every hour it lightens, softens, enhances the huge palace. Why not stop in the arcaded restaurant, the Marly, immediately to your *left*? Sit and watch the pools, where the building's unyielding symmetry fragments in a continuous shiver. If you are exceptionally lucky you will see the glass being cleaned – a remotely controlled gizmo crawls systematically over the Pyramide to wash it. Children are fascinated by this, so it may be worth a photograph. Note the crowds, think of postponing your visit to the museum itself till well after lunch (it's cheaper after 15.30), and in your own good time stride past the polyglot snaking queue, eastward into the Cour Carrée.

This is sometimes described as the perfect summation of Renaissance architecture – indeed the dreadful symmetry in fawn stone for the building, grey for the cobbles and, on a sunny day, the palest eau–de–nil in the round pool, is splendid. If your luck still holds and the fountain is playing, you can take your turn to photograph through the spray the tip of the Pyramide beyond the arch.

The Cour Carrée itself dwarfs the little knots of tourists, many busily talking into their mobiles. It is a place to admire rather than feel welcome in.

Shrug off the impression of not being wanted; walk briskly to the arch on the east side and out. Look left and right; you will see a moat, notice the heavily barred windows on the ground floor. A prison and a palace? Cross the road, the Rue de l'Amiral Coligny, and look back at the Louvre. You will see the Colonnade, a magnificent stretch of pillars, glass, light and shadow, the sooty pigeons on its low reliefs like inkblots on a beautiful drawing. It was built by Claude Perrault, Le Vau and others, in part *pour épater les bourgeois* (to astound the lower orders), whose houses formed the fourth side of the present Place du Louvre[3] and were pulled down only much later. The literary grain in this architectural splendour comes from Claude Perrault,[4] the elder brother of the writer of fairy tales, Charles. Charles, a competent draftsman and inspector of public buildings, persuaded Claude, a physician and naturalist by first profession, to accompany him to lectures on architecture. The brothers sat through them jointly and once Bellini's designs for the Colonnade were abandoned (Christopher Wren complained about being allowed only a very short glance at them), as the story goes, jointly submitted their design for the Colonnade. Be that as it may, Claude is credited with the work. He went on to build l'Observatoire (on the Left Bank, outside the area of these walks), to translate Vitruvius and write copiously about both natural history and, as might be expected, classical columns. Charles, on the other hand, produced a propaganda piece *Le Siècle de Louis XIV*, which started a lengthy intellectual argument, *la Querelle des Anciens et des Modernes*. The famous fairy tales (there are only eleven of them) were written, theoretically, as a counterblast to the immoral tales of classical mythology. Their appeal, both to the general reader and the scholar, remains potent and paradoxical (much like that of Jane Austen's novels) – both deal in dreams and the fears behind dreams.

Glance over to St Germain l'Auxerrois, a church with a checkered history and an uneasy feel. This was the place where the bell for matins one August day in 1572 signalled the start of the St Bartholomew massacre of the Huguenots (Protestants). The frenzied mob having started with the nobles, went on to kill, chuck in the river, loot as many Protestants as it could lay hands on – of course unimpeded by the authorities. The bodies of the Protestants were washed up downstream, as the *bateau mouche* guide will tell you at the extremity of the circuit, pointing to a narrow spit of land with a few scraggy plants.

L'ABBAYE

DE NORTHANGER;

Traduit de l'anglais de JEANNE AUSTEN ,

AUTEUR D'ORGUEIL ET PRÉJUGÉ , DU PARC DE MANS-
FIELD , DE LA FAMILLE ELLIOT , DE LA NOUVELLE
EMMA , etc.

Par Mᵐᵉ. HYACINTHE DE F****.

TOME PREMIER.

PARIS,
PIGOREAU , Libraire , place Saint-Germain-
l'Auxerrois , nº. 20.

1824.

Fortunately Place du Louvre has more cheerful literary connections. At number 20 – the house has long since disappeared – was a *libraire* (book seller) called Pigoreau[5], specialising from 1804 in novels only. In 1824 his shop was selling *L'Abbaye de Northanger, traduit de l'Anglais de Jeanne Austen*. How would Jane Austen have taken to this one instance of the translation of her name? She is, however, acknowledged as the author of four named novels followed by 'etc', suggesting a string of publications, like those of the most popular French women novelists of the period. If only!

Pigoreau had had it printed by Hadamard in Lorraine. Compared to the other booksellers and printers of the period, a stroll away from each other, this 330km gap between Paris and Metz seems extraordinary. But it turns out that Pigoreau was not interested primarily in books. He was said to have married money and put it to work setting up and supplying *cabinets de lecture*, reading–rooms, popular throughout the country, indeed the continent. In short he was a business man. So in his travels, what easier than to find a printer to make him a favourable offer?

Balzac thought little of him, and characterised him in unflattering terms under the name of Doguereau, in *Illusions Perdues* of 1837. However Pigoreau does have a claim on our gratitude.

In 1824 he also put out a publisher's list, *Petite bibliographie biographico– romancière*, with a section for translations. Here all Jane Austen's novels are listed under her name.

At the end of the Place du Louvre take the diagonal Rue Perrault, which follows the line of the moat defending the 9th century Norman camp. Turn *right* into the Rue de Rivoli; you will be walking along the north frontage of 'La Samaritaine', a large middle–of–the–road department store, most distinguished for its architecture. Make for its main, east façade, on to Rue de la Monnaie. Recall the umpteen references to shopping in Jane Austen's letters and the mischievous description of the visit to Ford's in *Emma*. The Samaritaine's central hall is most attractive and best admired from the escalators to the 5th floor. There, and just to the *right* of the book section, is a floor–to–ceiling sheet of glass, giving an unbroken view of the roof of St Germain l'Auxerrois and its stubby tower (not the present tall bell–tower, that is a 19th century addition with a 38 bell carillon), from which the single bell for the St Bartholomew Day massacre was rung. Glimpse the Colonnade beyond. Go right up to the roof (lift and stairs) where a cold drink can be had in summer and up another short flight to the circular observatory. From here you have an unrivalled panorama of central Paris, with diagrams to indicate precisely what you are looking at. On a sunny day the city is pale silver, the outlines of the buildings a feathery blaze, the green patches scribbles from a luminous pen. Truly the City of Light – and to be accessed for free. Don't miss it. On the way down enjoy the huge peacock on the lift well and other light fittings; go out on the south, Seine side, and admire the elegant panels on each side of the door. You are facing the Pont Neuf (the first Paris bridge to be built without houses on it) and the point of the Ile de la Cité.

Cross over eastward to the start of the Quai de la Mégisserie. Originally this was the place where leather goods were sold. Thirty years ago there was a lively pet market here on Saturday evenings. Now few pet shops remain; it's mostly garden shops. Take the first *left* into Rue des Bourdonnais and the first *right* into Rue St Germain l'Auxerrois. Nothing visually to command your interest, unless a *Maternelle* [nursery school] next door to a Bistro à Vins makes you reflect on the difference between French and English building regulations. But in 1821, the then number 89 (no relationship to current numbers, for the street was shortened and re-numbered in 1883) housed Cordier, a printer and bookseller who also held auctions of remaindered books. Cordier's chief outlet was in Rue des Mathurins St Jacques (now named Rue Sommerard), behind the Cluny museum. At both outlets he stocked *La Famille Elliot (Persuasion)*, published by Arthus Bertrand, who was spreading his risk. Here Arthus Bertrand also had immediate access to recouping his losses, in case the book had to be remaindered. Clearly in 1821 Jane Austen was a doubtful seller. Yet seven years later she was worth re-publishing, by the same Arthus Bertrand, solo.

At the present number 18 a wine bar, Le Relais Chablisanais. At the original number 19 was For l'Evêque, a church prison that also cared for wrong-doers connected with the theatre. Notably, in 1781 it held for two days Mademoiselle Laguerre, who at the second performance of Piccinni's *Iphigénie en Tauride* walked on stage completely drunk and unrestrainedly puked over *la figurante qui l'aidait à se tenir un peu droite* [the actress who was helping her to stand up more or less straight.[6]]

At the junction turn *left* and immediately *right* into the Avenue Victoria, with more places to stop and rest. Your first bookish walk is now finished. You are at the Place du Théâtre Chatelet, with that theatre on your right (it has Sunday morning concerts) and the Théâtre de Ville opposite, also metro station Chatelet, a nodal point in the system.

If you want a rest from Jane Austen, you could now make for the Ile de la Cité. Cross by the Pont au Change. At week-ends it often sports a 'Golden Egyptian Mummy' on a tiny pedestal, with plastic begging bowl at its feet. You may wonder how the person inside manages to breathe – there is no discernible air pump, at most just a glimpse of a white T-shirt. If you drop coins into the bowl the 'mummy' will slowly bow to acknowledge. This is startling enough to unprepared adults; small children experience a moment of genuine fear.

As you reach the island, the forbidding Conciergerie is on the right. It was the most secure of all Paris prisons and much used during the Revolution – Queen Marie-Antoinette was held in it for the months before her execution. If you visit, you will see reconstructions of cells, with wax figures of the prisoners, lists of those executed by the guillotine (Lavoisier's, the great chemist's, name is easy to find), and a good slide show. It is a depressing place, its main benefit that the same ticket gives access to the Sainte Chapelle, on the same side of the Boulevard du Palais, but surrounded by law courts. Here the magnificence of the glass, the joy of the coloured light, the press of tourists remove all religious aura. You feel as if you'd come to the entrance of some huge and wonderful party. No wonder it was said in the Middle Ages to be like a 'gateway to heaven'.

If you wander further on the Ile de la Cité, just beyond the north side of Notre-Dame, that tinder box to Victor Hugo's imagination, a curved street to the *left*, Rue Chanoinesse, gives you a good impression of Paris in the 17th century, when Racine lived there. But if you walk on to the end of the Ile de la Cité and follow the Quai aux Fleurs to your *left*, you will first have a good view of the tip of the second island, the Ile St Louis, a most desirable enclave of domestic architecture, to your right. Next come the Victorian curlicues and fountains of the Hôtel de Ville (City Hall) on the north, Right Bank. You will walk past the site of the house where Abelard and Heloise lived. Does anyone these days read Helen Waddell, Alexander Pope or the letters between the lovers? (The Folio Society did an attractive edition in 1977.) They were translated from Latin, very freely, into the French of 1687, by Rabutin,

Comte de Bussy, a name that evokes views of a charming house in Burgundy rather than a literary connection. His efforts served to revive memories of the lovers in their tragic separation, and were used in 1761 by J.J. Rousseau to give a potent echo to his novel *La Nouvelle Heloïse*.

If you continue along the north side of the Ile de la Cité, you will go past the back of the Hôtel Dieu (hospital), then the beguiling flower market, and you will return to the Pont au Change.

Walk One — Notes

1 Dentu: See Palais Royal.

2 Gérard de Nerval: The fallibility of memory connects this most elusive of poets to the most incongruous of his eccentricities. He is also remembered for writing on little scraps of paper, that then had to be assembled into coherent poems, plays, articles (he was a noted journalist), novels, translations of Poe, Goethe's *Faust* (praised by the older man) and Kotzebue (like Mrs. Inchbald with *Lovers' Vows* a generation earlier, in time to wreak havoc in *Mansfield Park*). Nerval chose *Menschenhass und Reue* (Misanthropy and Remorse). Sheridan had translated it with great success as *The Stranger* in 1798, the time when Britain's war against France was at its height. In England attention to German authors could be attributed to cultural combat, over and above the interest their work excited by its quality. Besides "a thorough knowledge of modern languagese" in the plural, was specified by Caroline Bingley as the mark of accomplished women; while French remained the temporarily reviled essential, German was the patriotically approved choice.

These days, what writing do we associate with Nerval?

Je suis le ténebreux, le veuf, l'inconsolable, a sonnet of desolation popularised some years back by Swann and Flanders, in their two-hander *At the Drop of a Hat*.

3 Place du Louvre: St Germain l'Auxerrois – Place du Louvre, not prone to flooding, has a long history. It appears in the records first as the camp site chosen by Labienus, Julius Caesar's deputy, generally given the task of bringing up the baggage train, as those who cut their teeth on Caesar's *Gallic Wars* will remember. This time he had a proper job – to dislodge the stubborn Gauls (*les irréductibles Gaulois* of the Asterix books) from their natural stronghold on the Ile de la Cité. He achieved it by a ruse. The Roman soldiers were split into four groups – the first stayed in camp (future

Place du Louvre) noisily. The second, equally noisy, tried to sail upstream, in a feint. The two remaining groups slunk out of camp, quietly crossed the river further downstream, and started marching along the south (Left) Bank towards the Ile de la Cité. The Gauls realised they were being attacked from their rear, and led by their old chief, Camulogène in French, rushed off the island. The battle was on marshy ground and the Gauls, including their chieftain, slaughtered, something that never happens to the fictional Abraracourcix, the head of Asterix' tribe. For once, *ils ne sont pas fous, ces Romains*. Gaul went on to benefit from contact with a more advanced civilisation, though no doubt there were many at the time to disagree.

Christianity came with the Romans, and in due course a church was built on the site of the present St Germain l'Auxerrois. Then, the 9th century saw invasions by the Norsemen. They too wanted to control the Ile de la Cité, to enable their ships to sail upstream unmolested and to protect their eastern flank. They too camped on the site of the Place du Louvre, put the church to use as a fort and dug a moat along the line of the present Rue Perrault. However in 885 they failed to defeat the Romanised inhabitants of the island, who did not yet call themselves French.

The present medieval church was popular with French royalty from the time the court moved from the Ile de la Cité to the castle on the Louvre site. Its next historic milestone came in August 1572 when its bell for matins was the signal to start the government-inspired killing of Protestants (see Huguenots and Jansenists), the day known as the Massacre of St Barthélemy. The inhabitants of the town houses built on the outline of the former cloister (that is the present Place du Louvre), had a ringside view.

In 1784 came the next big change. To ease traffic (perhaps to exorcise ghosts?) eleven houses on the west side, nearest the century old Colonnade, were pulled down, so a good view of Perrault's addition to the palace was opened up. The newly accessible Place St Germain l'Auxerrois, as it was then called, became the favourite spot for acrobats, singers, jokers, fortune tellers, confidence tricksters, particularly merchants of ointments, theoretically curative of various skin ailments. At the height of the Revolution the forcibly deconsecrated church was used as a store for fodder and a different style of street theatre sprang up on the present Place de la Concorde – the guillotine, fed by the procession of tumbrils, held sway. But with exhaustion after the blood letting, something nearer normality returned and the entertainers trouped back (the scene, some years later, is suggested in *Les Enfants du Paradis*) and remained until 1854, when the whole area was redeveloped. In the first instance the remaining houses along the side nearest the Louvre were pulled down and the present unbroken view of the Colonnade obtained.

4 Claude Perrault: Another Perrault, Dominic, was the architect of the even larger Bibliothèque François Mitterand, upstream from the Jardin des Plantes and Gare d'Austerlitz. The outside looks like a kitchen table upside down, the inside is science fiction as much as trad library, only, unlike Star Trek, the SF gizmos don't always work.

5 Pigoreau: Before the wholesale clearance of Place St Germain l'Auxerrois / Place du Louvre had taken place a publisher named Pigoreau had his shop at number 20 with fascia of yellow letters on deep green background, if Balzac, writing in the 1830's in his *Illusions Perdues* (part 2 *Un grand homme de province à Paris*) is to be believed. In 1826 the anonymous Monsier A.I *** in his *Biographies des imprimeurs et libraires*, says of Pigoreau:

C'est un homme qui a amassé une petite fortune par ses grandes économies; il est père d'une nombreuse famille. Ce libraire jouit d'une bonne re putation.

[He is a respectable man who has made a small fortune by dint of stringent cost-cutting. He has a large family. He is a book-seller of sound reputation.]

Balzac describes him as an old man, dressed in the old-fashioned Empire style, with an equally old-fashioned watch 'as fat as an onion', and looking like a cross between a lecturer on literature and a tradesman. His attitude to authors was equally out of date:

Un homme du temps où les libraires souhaitaient tenir dans un grenier et sous clef Voltaire et Montesquieu mourant de faim.

[A man from the period when booksellers wished to keep Voltaire and Montesquieu locked in a garret and starving.]

Not that Lucien de Rubempré, the hero of Balzac's novel, is an established and much read author like the two real life ones, both dead long before the Revolution. Consequently Lucien is a safe subject for old Doguereau to exercise his cost-cutting on. In a passage reminiscent of chapter 2 of *Sense and Sensibility*, when Fanny talks John Dashwood out of doing anything for his half-sisters Elinor and Marianne, Doguereau, faced with a first novel worth 1000 francs to him, gradually reduces his offer to 200 francs. As a business man *qui fait des romans* [who commissions novels] he is seen as on a par with the booksellers in the *galerie de bois* in Palais Royal, that is the less weighty end of the book trade, in it for the money. A familiar writers' view of publishers.

6 For l'Evêque: Mademoiselle Laguerre just managed to get on stage for the second performance of Piccinni's *Iphigénie en Tauride* with the help of *la figurante qui l'aidait à se tenir un peu droite*, only for the unfortunate assistant to be vomited over. So Laguerre was hauled into For L'Evêque and held for two days, about right for sobering up. Piccinni, alas, is very small print in

any book on opera. He figures because his ornate style was going out of fashion by 1781, in contrast to Gluck, whose own *Iphigénie en Tauride* was recognised as naturalistic and modern, and is still performed. A series of squabbles developed between *les anciens et les modernes* / Gluckistes, echoing a similar argument in Perrault's day a century earlier, and of course, *les Gluckistese* won. Come the summer of 1999, in the courtyard of the Hôtel de Ville in Geneva, Piccinni's *Le finte gemelle* was performed, *l'opéra perdue pendant deux siècles* [the opera lost for two centuries], said the posters. All agog, the aficionados congregated and agreed its merit lay in its brevity.

A more glamorous customer was Mademoiselle Clairon who shone in tragic parts and created many in the now forgotten plays of Voltaire and Crébillon. Her voice was said to be particularly fine and her first great success was in Racine's *Phèdre*. She was exceptional in her pursuit of authenticity; it led her into research and the creation of costumes, each appropriate to the play, the country and the character being shown. In this totally new departure she was supported by her one-time lover, the actor Lekain, who created many of the heroes of Voltaire's plays. When Garrick met her in Paris in 1763, her lover was the mathematician d'Alembert, one of the most vigorous moving spirits behind the first attempt to record all knowledge known to west European man, the *Encyclopédie des sciences, des arts et des métiers*. Later she was mistress of the Swedish ambassador, de Staël. Her non-professional life was a gift to the scandal-sheets of her day, embryonic in muck-raking though they were.

Palais Royal and the Coméde Française

The large area covered by the gardens of the Palais Royal was, until the start of the seventeenth century, the site of two ditches scarcely deep enough to qualify as a moat, remnants of old defences. To the east were crowded town dwellings in a multitude of winding streets. As the population pressure on the capital increased, the old defensive structures were knocked down.[1] Cardinal Richelieu (think of the triple portrait by Ph. de Champaigne in the National Gallery, London), for eighteen years the centralising minister of Louis XIII, bought up houses, had the ground cleared and built himself the Hôtel Cardinal, later enlarged to Palais Cardinal, to face what is now the metro station Palais Royal—Musée du Louvre. This gave him a residence close to the king, whose Palais du Louvre was much smaller than the present museum. Richelieu also laid out formal gardens, with a pond (formerly the location of a defensive tower) as the focal point. In his will he wisely left the whole property to his sovereign.

But Louis XIII died just a year later in 1643. His widow, Anne d'Autriche (in fact a Spanish princess, sister of Philip IV – think of the succession of Velasquez portraits in the National Gallery and another one in Dulwich) took the opportunity to leave the old fashioned Louvre and move into Richelieu's modern residence, now renamed Palais Royal. The new king – he was only five when he moved in – liked playing in the garden and, so the story goes, at one point fell into the round pond and nearly drowned.

But in 1652, with the short–lived civil war (La Fronde) in France, the boy king Louis XIV moved back into the old uncomfortable Louvre, which, with a proper moat was readily defensible. In came Henrietta–Maria, widow of Charles I of Great Britain, herself a French princess. Her exile was shared by her daughter, Charles I's youngest, known as Henriette d'Angleterre.[2] The worries about Louis XIV's security may have been exacerbated by the very fine gardens of the Palais Royal that had been open to the public from as early as 1648. From the start they were greatly enjoyed as an important local amenity amid the surrounding malodorous streets. Gradually the palace itself fell out of favour sufficiently to be partly down-graded to an un-princely use – in 1660 a large space was allocated to a company of actors who had, the previous year, delighted the court and the city with a comedy *Les Précieuses Ridicules*. The dramatist and actor-manager was a new name in the capital – Molière. He had caught the eye of the king's brother, known as Monsieur (also duc d'Orléans[3]) and husband of Henriette d'Angleterre; he had first arranged for Molière's group to share a performance space in another royal building, the Petit-Bourbon, which had perforce been pulled down to make space for the Louvre colonnade. So Molière's company were glad to be given effectively a repairing lease on a part of the Palais-Royal. For a few years, while they rose in royal favour, (Louis XIV was a very accomplished dancer and took part in at least one dance-interlude in a Molière comedy), a tarpaulin kept the audience dry. But what the groundlings really appreciated, comfort-wise, was the novelty of fixed, raked benches.

Molière and his actors, actively encouraged by Henriette d'Angleterre-d'Orléans, continued at the Palais Royal, going from strength to strength; in 1665 the king showed his royal favour by renaming the company *Troupe du Roi* and modestly subsidising it, in recognition specifically of Molière's genius. All the dramatist's great pieces were performed, with music and ballet, both at Versailles for the king and his court, and at the Palais Royal for the usual public. Here, one night in 1673, Molière was taken ill on stage and died a few hours later, unshriven.[4]

The company lost its subsidy and had to move out of the Palais Royal in short order.[5] They now had to rent (a new drain on their resources) and chose a real tennis court (*Jeu de Paume*) on the corner of Rue Guénégaud and Rue Mazarine – a tablet marks the place. A few years previously the building had been converted to theatrical use with the injunction to *jouer et chanter en public ces représentations de pièces de musique appelées opéras* [to act and sing in public the musical shows called operas]. Further, by order of the king, himself highly interested in theatricals, Molière's company had to amalgamate with another.[6] A few years later, the king interfered again – Molière's combined group, specialising in comedies, had to amalgamate with their generously subsidised arch-rivals, the *Troupe Royale*; the latter's speciality was tragedy and Racine their star writer. The Comédie Française, the oldest acting company in the world, was born – with subsidy maintained to this day.[7]

Whatever the internal tensions of the new company, external objectors soon became vociferous. The University of Paris, being in the immediate vicinity of the theatre in Rue Guénégaud, objected to its corrupting influence on the students. Another move was demanded. The actors complied by buying another real tennis court, backing on to a bowling alley, just a block and a half further south in the present Rue de l'Ancienne Comédie. The site was cleared, an architect engaged and a theatre of stunning comfort and grandeur built. It was labelled *Hôtel des Comédiens entretenus par le Roi*, an unanswerable two-finger salute to the university and the incumbent of St Sulpice, in whose parish it stood, and who forbade all church processions to pass within sight of it.

The opening in April 1689 featured two plays by two star writers – Racine's *Phèdre* and Molière's *Le Médecin Malgré Lui*. It was a huge success. The new theatre and its nearest restaurant, Le Procope both prospered mightily. Over the next decades all the classic and new plays were performed there. In 1759 the prestige of the Comédie Française was such that it was possible to clear the stage of the three rows of benches reserved for aristocrats, who came to be seen and to gossip loudly.[8] The great tragic actresses of the eighteenth century (for instance Adrienne Lecouvreur, Voltaire's mistress and Mademoiselle Clairon, d'Alembert's mistress,) were members of the company and started the habit of luvvies linking up with fashionable intellectuals. Eventually a new theatre had to be built, on the site of the present Théâtre de l'Odéon and in 1782 the Comédie

Française moved in. The new star writer was Beaumarchais, whose
Mariage de Figaro was again hugely successful.[9]

The Palais Royal in the meantime remained a secondary royal
palace, with the court residing mainly at Versailles. At the start of
the eighteenth century, Philippe d'Orléans, regent for another boy-
king Louis XV, used it for magnificent entertainments, interspersed
with episodes of 'gambling and debauchery', as the history books
phrased it. In 1763 the part of the palace with Molière's former
theatre, burnt down. Louis XVI, pressed for money, got rid of the
property onto his cousin, another Philippe d'Orléans, himself
equally embarrassed and more particularly on behalf of his son, the
heavily indebted Louis–Philippe, future king of the French. The
d'Orléans, father and son, between them decided to recoup their
fortunes with a new type of development – porticos on four sides of
a rectangle (that is round the present gardens), with shops at ground
level and apartments to let above. Needless to say, the local residents objected strongly, since losing access to the gardens and the
overall reduction of open space, would significantly reduce the
value of their properties. As usual, no notice was taken of their
objections. The architect Victor Louis was appointed and building
went ahead.

As it turned out, the ground–floor could not be limited to shops;
the development, being a royal enclave, allowed access only to
shopkeepers who were also masters of their craft, for instance
cabinet makers. (Think of the furniture in the Wallace Collection, in
Manchester Square, London.) There simply weren't enough of
them willing to move. Obviously there were some – for instance at
number 42 prints and drawings were sold. But there was also a children's museum, a puppet theatre, another of shadow puppets that
maintained a high moral tone, a bath–house including *bain
dépilatoire*, a hotel, a club for Americans who owned property in the
Antilles, another for freemasons next door to their lodge, a police
station at number 8, gaming houses galore and any number of cafés
and restaurants, especially the Café Caveau. The latter had moved

from the Porte de Buci (the present carefour de Buci, Rue Mazarine, see Walk Three) to the more fashionable new development. With it came its regulars – painters like A.C.H. Vernet[10], writers and dramatists, who immediately gave artistic aura to the newest in-place.

With the two long sides and one short, northern side of the quadrangle built, money ran out. The short, undeveloped, southern side still had to contribute to the financial viability of the whole. So little wooden booths were put up, Galerie de Bois (there is both a painting and a model in the Musée Carnavalet). These were sub–let, mostly to sellers of fashionable clothes and knick–knacks, or to booksellers. Many in the trade used these ephemeral constructions for clandestine sales of subversive pamphlets – these attacked the privileges of the aristocracy and clergy, and demanded the recall of the three chambers of the French Estates General, as a preliminary to constitutional but far reaching reform. The camouflage for hatching sedition was provided by an influx of *filles du monde*; for them the new development was a most lucrative cruising area.

The cafés attracted their own specialised clientele – people gripped by the new–fangled craving for daily news, obtained not from official spokesmen, but from servants, inn–keepers, etc. The aficionados met daily, to record the latest on handwritten sheets passed from hand to hand. The word *journalisme* [*jour* meaning day] had been coined in 1778, and at the Palais Royal investigative journalism flourished. So a royal domain turned out to harbour a forcing house for revolutionary ideas. The disaffected thronged the gardens, the workers in the many separate enterprises joined in, and on 12 July 1789, a young man, Camille Desmoulins, harangued the assembled crowd, calling it to arms. Two days later the Bastille was stormed.

The duc d'Orléans, owner of the Palais Royal and cousin to the king, had to do something to protect his chunk of prime property. He got himself elected, as the junior member for Paris, to the brand new Legislative Assembly, developed as a result of the first revolutionary efforts. He announced that he had no family surname and asked 'the people of Paris' to think of one for him. They came up with Egalité. Notwithstanding, in 1791 the arcades forcibly changed hands. The following year, Philippe Egalité, still a member of the legislative assembly, voted for the death penalty on his first cousin, the deposed king Louis XVI, in whose gift the Palais Royal had been. The motion was carried by one vote. In 1793 Philippe Egalité was beheaded.

Revolutionary feeling was at its peak. Since gambling did not fit the image of political fervour, the gaming houses in the Palais Royal were closed.

They were re-opened in 1795. By 1806 in the arcades, the Café de Foy was the mecca for artists and Vernet back in his former haunts. A year later most of the wooden booths were taken over by pawnbrokers; the palace itself housed the Bourse de Commerce, where wholesalers of foodstuffs, wood etc operated, as well as the Tribunal de Commerce, where commercial cases – and some old scores – were settled. Come 1815 and the second fall of Napoleon, the Bourbon monarchy came back to its inheritance. Louis XVIII, the restored king, returned the Palais Royal to the Orléans branch of the family, and the booksellers, still fuelled by political agendas, were back in force. One of the booths was a sales outlet for Dentu, a powerful *libraire* with headquarters on the Left Bank.

J.G. Dentu had started out in 1794 as a printer who weathered the revolutionary and Napoleonic years by specialising in literary works by both French and foreign writers. In 1816 he published *Le Parc de Mansfield ou les trois cousines*. The subtitle suggests the commissioning editor had seen it as a triangular tale, perhaps reminiscent of another serious novel, Madame de Souza's *Eugénie et Mathilde*, *roman de l'émigration*[11], published in Paris in 1811, and dealing with the fortunes of three disparately brought up sisters. Dentu's main office and printing works was at 5 Rue Bonaparte, *ancien hôtel Persan*, that is a building formerly owned by an aristocratic family. There he also held meetings for the most highly regarded of his colleagues (*représentatifs les plus qualifiés*) in the various book trades. These led to the formation of the *Cercle de la Librairie*, first an association, later a conglomerate trade union, representing all the trades relative to books and the graphic arts. It has recently evolved into a company that specialises in books and IT of interest to librarians and publishers.

Dentu père and his eldest son were much harassed by the authorities, but according to the 1829 *Biographies des Imprimeurs et Libraires* by the anonymous Monsieur A. I***:

> Divers procès ont établi la réputation de ce libraire qui a fait une fortune que l'on dit colassale. Ses deux fils maintenant à la tête du commerce et jouissent de l'estime de ceux qui les connaissent.
> [Various court cases have established the reputation of this bookseller, who is said to have amassed a colossal fortune. His two sons now leading the enterprise enjoy the respect of those who know them.]

What, other than envy, did Monsieur A. I*** have against Dentu? Had he not been invited to any of the meetings prior to the formation of the *Cercle de la Librairie*? Or was it politics? For in 1815, at the restoration of the Bourbon monarchy, J.G. Dentu put his fortune behind an ultra-royalist daily, *Le Drapeau Blanc* (the French royal flag was fleur-de-lys on white ground). One of the writers for his paper was the influential priest, La Mennais, whose views, rejected by the then pope, evolved over forty years to end as a mixture of humanitarian socialism and mysticism. One of Dentu's sons, also a royalist, published Sterne's *A Sentimental Journey*. His other son specialised in books on historical subjects.

In the meantime the Palais Royal had reverted to being a royal residence. The main representative of the d'Orléans family, originally the much indebted Duc de Chartres, now d'Orléans, had moved in. He was in residence when in 1830, after another revolution and more deaths, he was summoned to the Hôtel de Ville (Town Hall) to be proclaimed King of the French. He had eighteen years of it before another revolution drove him out, to end his days in exile in Claremont, near Esher, Surrey.

In the 1870s, after the French defeat in the Franco-Prussian war and the excesses of the Commune, the buildings of the Palais Royal were restored to their present form (the gambling-houses had been closed earlier). These days, the palace houses the Conseil d'Etat, the supreme legal body for administrative matters, and the Ministry of Culture, never a backwater in France. The main stage of the Comédie Française, Salle Richelieu, abuts on the west side. Even if you reckon your French isn't up to a theatre show, its shop has good theatrical post cards.

Palais Royal and the Comédie Française — Notes

1 The lower portions of the old castle and city walls are visible in the basement of the Musée du Louvre, a fascinating walk over comfortable duckboards, leading to one end of the Ancient Egypt collection.

2 Henriette d'Angleterre: This astute and charming lady, Charles II's favourite sister Minette, had an attractive maid of honour, Louise de la Vallière – the latter was the young king's *maitresse en titre* for many years; she also managed to have her two children by Louis XIV recognised as legitimate.

3 Duc d'Orléans: Successive French royal families maintained the confusing convention of giving this title to the king's next brother. So you will find three of them in this book alone. Otherwise the best known one is Charles d'Orléans, the poet, who died in 1465, having spent the twenty-five years after Agincourt as a prisoner of war in England, buffing up his poetry in both languages. The king's next brother was referred to and addressed as Monsieur, as distinct from the king, for whom Monseigneur or Sire were usual.

4 Molière dead, unshriven: The usual prejudice against actors prevailed – their profession was deemed so sinful that, short of a death-bed confession and recantation of a lifetime's work, a Christian burial in consecrated ground was refused. This happened in Molière's case. Predictably a huge public rumpus followed. King Louis XIV intervened on behalf of his much admired playwright, actor and stage director, whose official position at court was that of *tapissier du roi* [the king's supervisor of upholstery and tapestry]. Grudgingly, the ecclesiastical authorities gave permission for a private funeral at 10pm, with four candles only. It was the end of February, so darkness, cold and, with luck, snow were expected to reinforce the insistence on the strictly limited number of mourners.

Needless to say, the opposite happened – a huge crowd, with candles and torches, assembled and Molière was given a send-off consistent with his greatness and popularity undiminished to our day. The Roman Catholic church maintained its interdict on burial of unshriven actors. Some sixty years after Molière, the actress Adrienne Lecouvreur (see Walk Three), who had brought straight-forward naturalism to her tragic parts, died, also precipitately. The disposal of her body in a communal pit, unaccompanied by even 'maimed rites', was watched by her lover, the great Voltaire. Nothing in his reserves of philosophy, literature or wit softened the bleakness of the moment.

5 Moving out of Palais Royal: The *sale de spectacle* of the Palais Royal, used by Molière's company, was handed over to the composer Lully, who had

the monopoly of presenting opera.

6 Amalgamating companies: This other company had been based in the Marais, the oldest residential part of Paris, round the present Place des Vosges.

7 Comédie: In France *comédie* is, classically, a piece written for the stage, not necessarily one intended to make the audience laugh. Consequently, a *comédien* was an actor, in either comic or tragic plays.

8 Gossip loudly: Ten years earlier, in London, David Garrick, himself of French émigré descent, had put an end to behind the stage access to any punter willing to pay.

9 Hugely successful: Was it despite or because of its attack on the privileges of the Ancien Régime? The operatic version by Mozart, first performed in 1786, is said to have the sound of revolutionary drums in its score. Yes, but disguised as mockery of one specific character and his small group of hangers–on. For real bite, get back to the text. You need read no further than Figaro's first soliloquy – Beaumarchais's views lack all ambiguity.

For all the publicity given to radical views, the actors of the Comédie Française were substantially monarchist. After all, that's where their privileges and money came from. However in 1789 it was thought prudent to rename the house Théâtre de la Nation. Did this give a false sense of security? A provocative play was chosen to be put on next (*Charles IV* by M.J. Chenier); it led to rows amongst the actors, the company split. The dissidents, the 'reds' went back to the Palais Royal – the 'reactionaries' stayed on the Left Bank and put on *L'Ami des Lois* by Laya. As its title implies it argued for liberty within the law and was a barely veiled attack on extremists, the Jacobin party in the Convention (ie parliament). The city council of Paris, a growing source of extremist power, suspended all performances. The outraged author took his case to parliament, which took time out from debating whether to execute the king Louis XVI, to rescind the suspension.

So, for a few more months, the remaining actors of the Comédie Française kept their theatre going. What finished them was a French adaptation of Goldoni's play based on Richardson's *Pamela*. All the actors were arrested but, instead of being taken to the familiar and hospitable For l'Evêque prison (see Walk One) they were split between two of the standard and very rough prisons.

A few months later, a few were released on condition of joining their former 'red' colleagues now at the Palais Royal. Of the remainder, two men and four women were allocated to the guillotine. However, something like a mock trial had to take place first and the documents for this had to be prepared by employees of the Committee of Public Safety. One of them, C.H.

Labussière, was a former actor, a cultivated and courageous man, who first managed to have the trial postponed for a few more months. Then papers got lost, others were mixed up. It all took a while, despite the urgent demands from the public prosecutor, the pitiless Fouquier-Tinville. In the nick of time, Robespierre, the instigator of the Terror, was himself arrested and executed. With the most violent phase of the Revolution effectively at an end the prisoners were released.

The freed actors rushed back to their Théâtre de la Nation and, barely a month later, put on a double bill. There was much applause, but the Comédie Française as such no longer existed. Many of its actors were scattered through the several other theatres of Paris, the audience was absent, the theatrical centre of gravity had shifted to the Right Bank. There was much to-ing and fro-ing – should the Comédie Française be re-formed, and if so, where should it be based? The answer to the second question came in the spring of 1799 – the house on the Left Bank, on the site of the present Théâtre de l'Odéon, burnt to the ground. Two months later the state-subsidised and largely state-controlled Comédie Française was re-constituted, with a pay roll of 52 actors (the normal number was 30). Its first double bill was *Le Cid* by Pierre Corneille, Racine's older rival, and *L'Ecole des Maris* by Molière, performed on the site, on the edge of the Palais Royal, it occupies today.

Over the two hundred years since its fortunes have varied. It did, and still does, put on the classics beautifully. For some years the rebuilt Théâtre de l'Odéon was its second house, for experimental, modern shows, and saw the triumphs of Madeleine Renaud and Jean-Louis Barrault (another actor who retained his prominence in *Les Enfants du Paradis*). Nowadays it has just the much smaller and prettier Théâtre du Vieux Colombier as a second house. It complains about inadequate subsidies and too much government interference. The actors complain about low pay and the difficulty of obtaining leave of absence for short periods to cover some lucrative film or TV contract. The company started touring only between the wars; one of its outstanding successes was the visit to London in spring 1939, not least because it also symbolized the alliance of two democracies facing Nazi Germany.

10 A.C.H. Vernet: Several of his modest sized canvases are in the Wallace Collection, Manchester Square, London. His better-known son, Horace Vernet, painted very large battle scenes, four of them in the National Gallery, Trafalgar Square.

11 *Eugénie et Mathilde*: see The Competition.

Huguenots, Jansenists, and the Tragedies of Racine

Libraries-full have been written on these related topics. What follows, very briefly and very roughly, is just enough to weld the seemingly disparate items of information, dotted through this book, into a coherent background and suggest two reasons why Jane Austen did not, and still does not enjoy a high reputation in France.

In the sixteenth century France was disfigured by *les guerres de religion* [the wars of religion], between the Catholics and the Calvinists, that is Protestants. The latter were nicknamed 'Huguenots'. The word is a corruption of *Eidgenossen*, the name of Genevans, Calvinists of course, who joined in the fight against the Catholic Duke of Savoy, the ruler of the separate country that threatened Geneva from the south. So home-grown religion and the political survival of the city-state were inextricably mixed from the start. In France Calvinists / Huguenots were most numerous in the south and west, mostly in towns, with their prosperity built on embryonic industries rather than land ownership.

By 1570, with various aristocratic houses fighting one another, ostensibly in the name of religion, peace would have to be imposed from above by a powerful king. There had been four kings in forty years and the next legitimate claimant was Henri, King of Navarre (in the Pyrenees, in the south-west of modern France), himself a Protestant / Huguenot. For the peace of the whole country, he had to marry Marguerite de Valois, the Catholic daughter of his cousin, the first of the four short-lived kings. This would have the additional benefit of uniting Navarre to France.

August 1572 and Protestants trooped into Paris, to celebrate the wedding of their champion and the expected consequence – peace. But they forgot the bride's mother, the formidable Catherine de Medici. This Florentine lady, widow of one and mother of three kings, and regent since 1560, had been astute enough two years earlier to negotiate a peace treaty with the Protestants. But the Protestant faction, by presenting also an alternative view of government, was too much of a threat to royal authority that Catherine had spent a lifetime defending. Here was an opportunity of strengthening it further, or rather of weakening the opposition – let's have all the Protestants in Paris killed. This was the massacre of St. Barthélemy / Bartholomew.

The bridegroom of a few days, Henri of Navarre, fled.[1] He took to the field with his Protestant allies and twice defeated the Catholic faction. Then, with peace for his enlarged kingdom in mind, he said *Paris vaut bien une messe* [Paris is worth a Catholic mass] and became a Catholic, the religion of the majority of his new subjects. Henri IV of France, as he became, was a pragmatist and bon–vivant; sanity and common sense were characteristic of his reign. He wanted every French family to have every Sunday *la poule au pot* [a chicken dinner]. Certainly the country prospered and *la petite marmite Henri IV* used to be a delicious chicken soup on the menu of Le Vert Galant, a beautiful restaurant in the Ile de la Cité, nearest Henri IV's statue.

Henri IV's true originality lay in passing the Edict of Nantes in 1595, a law to enshrine religious tolerance. This was the only example in Europe of tolerance guaranteed by law, although in the United (Dutch) Provinces it happened in practice. Consequently in France the flickers of religious wars petered out. Huguenots were allowed to continue worshipping openly in the towns where this had earlier been established more or less in private. Their access to law was put on an equal footing with that of Catholics. They were allowed to send delegates to the royal court, and these ambassadors from the *Eglises Réformées de France* had the ear of the king. Fine for them, and for peace, but Catholics saw the Edict of Nantes as a truce in a long war. It was only a question of time before another opportunity arose to renew hostilities openly.

It came soon enough. In 1615, Louis XIII, Henri IV's heir, married Anne of Austria, that is a Spanish princess; his sister married Philip IV of Spain (think Velasquez, as in the National Gallery or the Dulwich Gallery), the chief champion of Catholicism. In

France the Catholic aristocrats were ready. In 1627–28 Richelieu, the king's prime minister, successfully besieged La Rochelle, the Atlantic port and Protestant / Huguenot stronghold. The *Eglises Réformées de France* came to be regularly insulted by being called *Religion Prétendue Réformée*.

In 1650 the Protestants defended themselves, as they thought, by publishing *La Discipline des E.R.F.* It described the organisation – each parish sends its pastor and two lay members of the congregation to provincial synods, where decisions are taken by majority vote and passed on to the national synod that uses the same decision-making process. The Protestants hoped that this reasoned, bottom–up process would strike their Catholic opponents as benign in both intent and execution, an example worth serious consideration.

With hindsight their political naïvety was little short of criminal. Were they unaware that they were describing democracy? Anathema to the absolutist government of the under–age Louis XIV. Democracies were republics – look at Geneva and the United Provinces; worst of all look at England – only the year before, democracy under the name of Commonwealth, had beheaded the king, Charles I, who had seen himself as divinely appointed, much as the French monarch did.

Of course harassment of the Huguenots was stepped up. In 1662 Huguenot churches were closed and / or destroyed. Brutality came in the late spring of 1681, with *Les Dragonnades de Poitou*.[2] Quite simply a regiment of dragoons was sent to a province known for its many Huguenot families and the soldiers were billeted only on them. For a start the families had to feed them and their horses. The dragoons were encouraged to maltreat their hosts as much as possible short of rape and murder. So houses were damaged, poultry stolen, furniture broken, families deprived of sleep, kept standing – tactics familiar from the twentieth century. Once the family had recanted, the dragoons left to tackle more stubborn ones. In a few weeks 30,000 recantations had been obtained.

Word got out. Christian II, King of Denmark, offered asylum. So did Charles II of Great Britain and here Huguenots found conditions so favourable that they rapidly integrated. The city of Amsterdam was equally hospitable.

The French authorities retaliated. 1682 saw the publication of two lists – the first named the towns where Huguenots were not allowed to reside; the second named the occupations they were no longer allowed to follow. So in many cases fathers could no longer pass on a family business to their sons. What were they to do, but sell their properties at knock–down prices to gleeful Catholics? The money obtained was sent out (often through the good offices of the ambassador of the United Provinces), but even reflecting depressed selling prices, there was so much money draining out of France that a shortage of metal cash, much of it precious metal, ensued.

The French authorities pressed on. The Edict of Nantes was revoked in 1685. From then on Catholicism was mandatory, religion and citizenship were indivisible. From 1686 fleeing Huguenots had laws aimed specifically at them; anyone who helped them escape also risked death. Any remaining Huguenots were forcibly con-verted – the Host was literally forced down their gullets. They took to secret meetings in private houses. If discovered, the women were sent to prison, the men to the galleys and the pastors to death.

More offers of help came – the Elector of Brandenburg, ancestor of the formidable kings of Prussia in the next century, offered favourable conditions to Huguenot refugees knowing that as a group they were highly skilled, highly educated, highly entrepreneurial. Collections were made in England, in the United Provinces (notably by the Jews of Amsterdam) to help the most destitute. In the event France lost very little of its total population, but it was a hefty pro-portion of its most able and energetic. As a consequence, much of its former flourishing export trade – for instance, of hats and ribbons – moved out for good; the Prussian army was modernised, William of Orange, later King William III of Great Britain, was endowed with his *furia francesca*. Printing in Holland and Geneva greatly expanded, to the eventual benefit of the novel-reading public in the early nineteenth century.

But at the end of the seventeenth century the new printing capacity produced pamphlets; these attacked Louis XIV and his treatment of the Huguenots. Little of this opposition literature was read in France, much of it in Protestant Europe. It fuelled anti-French feeling, particularly in the French-speaking cantons of Switzerland; it helped turn opinion against the newly Catholic James II of Great Britain, dethroned three years later.[3] Longer term, it started the debate on national rights compared to human rights; on the common interests of neighbours, regardless of religion, as distinct from the interests of people sharing a religion; on the superiority of the voice of conscience, interpreted as the voice of God, over that of the church, any church and especially the Roman Catholic. In short, the ground was prepared for the themes tackled by the Enlightenment and its supreme expression, the *Encyclopédie* of 1751-1772.

As late as 1787, just two years before the Revolution, the government of Louis XVI, desperate for money and clutching at straws, passed an Edict of Tolerance of Protestants. A few hundred thousand allowed themselves to be identified. To this day, according to the latest Larousse, the figure is under one million (out of a total of just under 60 million). So Jane Austen's faith, that bedrock of her thinking, would have in France now scarcely any greater number of informed sympathisers than when her translated books first came out.

While the Protestants / Huguenots were being persecuted in a highly visible way, another group of individualists were harassed somewhat more subtly, again for ostensibly religious reasons. They were Catholics, followers of Jansenius, who believed in totally arbitrary predestination – God, the all-knowing Creator of all things visible and invisible, pre-destined the individual soul to salvation or the opposite, in expectation of the merits that will be attained; the individual may support the positive process by co-operating with the working of the Redeemer's grace on him, but in theory at least, there was not much left for him to do. As something to get excited about, it seems in our day pretty thin. But predestination was also an important plank of Calvinism, espoused by those pesky, in-dependent-minded Genevans just on the edge of France. Besides Jansenius added emphasis on the damage caused by original sin, acknowledged the power of lust, and stated unequivocally that the power of grace, through Christ the Redeemer, alone gave man free-dom. Again that dreaded concept – freedom.

Neither the Catholic Church (*la religion du roi*), nor the state, smarting after a dangerous civil war (*La Fronde*, 1648–1653), could cope with freedom for the instructed Christian, even less for power-hungry aristocrats (some of whom supported the Jansenists), let alone the prosperous burghers and the rabble beyond. The Jesuits and the Faculty of Theology of the Sorbonne led the intellectual opposition to the Jansenists. On the other hand, support for them was rife among the parish clergy, who had to be whipped into line by signing special declarations. The matter was further complicated by the Jansenists, heavily into learning and good works, running the best schools in the kingdom, with aristocrats queuing up to have their sons educated by them. Many of the Jansenists were learned, some more than brilliant (Pascal, the mathematician and physicist, notably); all lived in a simple, unostentatious way, many just outside the capital at Port Royal des Champs (south-west of Paris, between Versailles and Rambouillet), with another house near the present metro-station, Port-Royal. No Jansenists aspired to life at court, or any contribution to the glory of the Sun King, as Louis XIV, the absolutist monarch, was increasingly referred to.

So Jansenists were persecuted as and when Louis XIV's relations with the papacy, or his plans for war against the United Provinces, dictated. One step in the persecutions came in 1665 – the Jansenist nuns, unwilling to sign a renunciation of their particular slant on doctrine, were taken in by the police. This shocked large swathes of the capital's prosperous classes and, more to the point, also four bishops. Then, for the next dozen years things were a little easier.

However, as the Jansenists, deprived of influence in the church, started transforming themselves into a political party, Louis XIV restarted the persecutions. He died in 1715, and in the immediately following years the Jansenist party greatly increased its numbers amongst the laity as well as the clergy. The last got together under the four sympathising bishops and decided that the authority of the nation-wide church council ranked higher than that of the pope. You might say, in current EU-speak, they voted for subsidiarity. Even then it wasn't allowed – they were excommunicated.

But support for the Jansenists persisted. In answer, the Duc d'Orléans, regent for the boy-king Louis XV, insisted on further repression. A Papal Bull, the fifth promulgated against the Jansenists, became French law, and all dissenting clergy were deprived of their livings. Still Jansenism survived as a political ideology. It stood for the inviolable rights of the human conscience, another stream feeding the thinking of the eighteenth century philosophers of the Enlightenment. It nourished opposition to the absolutism developed first by Richelieu and then Louis XIV, and it surfaced at the Revolution among members of the first, reforming National Assembly of 1789.

There was yet another form of alternative religion Louis XIV would not tolerate – the mystical doctrine of Quietism. For its adherents, Christian perfection on this earth consists of passivity, to allow the confident soul to contemplate God without interruption. A relief, you'd think, to have at least one group without a political programme. You'd be wrong. Louis XIV would not tolerate this either, partly because its main exponent was the great preacher, Fénelon, who had been appointed tutor to the king's heir, Louis de France, Duc de Bourgogne. As a teaching aid for his pupil, Fénelon had written *Les Aventures de Télémaque*, full of suggestions on how to improve on Louis XIV. Fénelon was sent back to his bishopric and Louis XIV made sure the pope condemned Quietism.

In short, what had developed in France after the death, in 1610, of the pragmatic Henri IV, was absolutism. What the king said went, no argument, no alternative. (Remember, it was Louis XIV who described himself and his country with '*L'état, c'est moi.*') Everything that could be centralised was, everything that was particular, or different, (like Protestantism, or Jansenism or even Quietism), everything that lacked the uniformity demanded by the absolute monarch was at least enormously reduced, at best extirpated. Murder, exile and censorship were the crudest tools to achieve this. More widely, everything and everybody with the least hope of preferment or any role or influence in public life, had to stick by the rules and work for the glory of Louis XIV, the Sun King. And there was no local, tribal memory for Jane Austen of such a state of affairs, let alone one sustained for nearly two centuries.

With hindsight, it is obvious that damming up mildly divergent streams of opinion fed directly into the cataract of the Revolution. But reasonably enough, seventeenth century France had no one to imagine, let alone articulate such a prognosis. The dreadful warning of Charles I of Great Britain, who tried absolutism and got his head chopped off, went unheeded. It was unthinkable for the French, even then, to learn from an English example.

In the meantime, enter Jean Racine, the very clever orphan of a modest, provincial family. His grandparents, impressed by the Jansenists' good works, arranged for him to be educated at Port-Royal. Once there, he was treated with great kindness by his teachers; being physically small for his age, most of the other boys, many from aristocratic families, treated him with amused contempt. Right – he'll show them, he'll be a poet, the greatest of the age. Inordinately ambitious and with a nose for cruelty, he immediately realised that the king and the king only, was the arbiter of all the arts. The king liked plays, but the theatre was totally condemned by Jansenists. Too bad – he'd forget about his (free) education. He'd ally himself with the playwright most favoured by Louis XIV, Molière, ensconced in a royal palace, a man remarkable also for his directing skills; those were particularly important for a green dramatist with no idea of the demands of the stage. Molière was eager to nourish a new talent and put on Racine's first play *La Thébaïde*. Its moderate success was sufficient to justify the commission of another one. In November 1665 (the year the nuns of the Port-Royal were being imprisoned) came the warmly received *Alexandre*, and Racine promptly took his play and his talent to Molière's arch-rivals at the Théâtre de la Bourgogne. Racine thought their star actress more suited to the tragic heroines he had in mind. To ensure performances to his demanding standards he coached her line by line and made her his mistress.

Racine was attacked in print by an anonymous Jansenist; piqued, he replied. A second flourish from the same anonymous pen followed, and this time Racine thought better of it. He was busy writing *Andromaque*, which describes King Pyrrhus in the process of freeing himself from one intended bride in favour of a new one. The situation echoed that of the king – Louis XIV was transferring his favours from Madame de La Vallière to Madame de Montespan. Prudently, the actors were given better reviews than the author. The next tragedies, *Britannicus* and *Bérénice*, were on Roman themes; this was territory worked by Racine's older rival, Corneille, and, by trespassing on it, Racine made no friends. For a supremely adaptable man this caused no problem. He next tried his hand at a contemporary Turkish subject, *Bajazet*[4]; the geographical distance was intended to focus intensity and strangeness, much as the time gap to ancient Greece had done for his first three tragedies. It was another success.

Molière died in 1673 and Racine did not find it necessary to attend the funeral. The excuse was, he was busy with *Iphigénie en Aulide*. With it he struck gold in a big way – the set was by Vigarine, the most fashionable Italian decorator of the day; the first performance was slotted into a particularly brilliant festival at Versailles. The king and the court with him were open in their admiration and much affected by the theme of a sacrificial victim willingly accepting her fate. If some had different opinions, they kept quiet, for Racine, totally taken over by his success in pleasing the king, was too much of a favourite to be openly attacked. His enemies had to make do with praising the star actress, Racine's new mistress.

His last tragedy, *Phèdre*, had more to contend with. The potential audience was developing a taste for opera: with its music, sets and special effects, actors were almost expendable. The king was off to war, fighting the United Provinces, so there was no first performance at court, to give the play the boost of royal approval. Finally the Duchesse de Bouillon headed the anti-Racine cabal by commissioning another new play for the same night and buying up seats and boxes for her supporters to shout down *Phèdre*. It worked all the more effectively as the star part was taken by Racine's mistress, an actress insufficiently weighty to express the murderous violence of a woman both guilty and acknowledging her guilt.

Racine retired hurt. What had he done with his plays? Had he poisoned souls rather than bodies? Had he confused his perception of the tragic figure, immobilised by the cruelty of fate in a desert of fire, with his sense of the divine? In his plays evil comes from instinct, from deep-seated weakness and fear; the cruelty it leads to is never part of ambition, of that thirst for *la gloire*, hall-mark of the Sun King; the resulting violence destroys the virtuous and the wicked indifferently.

What is love except the fascination, the rapture of seeing the other body, always wanted, seldom obtained? The characters, locked into the limits of their situations, have only two choices – flight or speech. And how they speak! Remember Phèdre, consumed by her incestuous passion for her step-son, Hyppolitus. She comes on stage, nurturing her secret guilt. Her first disclosure to a sympathetic friend, shows her still in control, even narcissistic. The second, furious one, to Hyppolitus himself, forges an indissoluble, magic bond between them. The last disclosure to her husband, the king, is a plain, official statement, up to a point corrective. The only course left to her is flight – into death.

Did Jane Austen ever read the play, or any of Racine's? She owned a copy of Ariosto, and her sister Cassandra had a complete set of Racine. The latter is much easier – a vocabulary of about 1000 words, a limited number of constructions, unmistakably way-marked by subjunctives, the plot familiar from mythology and the magnificent sweep of the alexandrines. Love and betrayal are the same the world over; Racine scaled them to the triumphalist court of the Sun King, Jane Austen to the country houses of dishonourable or weak young men. Crucially, she presented her characters as capable of life-defining choices. Racine's are born into Jansenist pre-destination. As Anouilh said much later, the spring, once wound up, has to unwind itself, regardless.

With time *Phèdre* changed from a *succès d'estime* to a sure-fire draw, the preferred vehicle for ambitious French actresses. What *Hamlet* is for the English-speaking theatre, *Phèdre* became for the French. No wonder French actresses are remembered for their success in the part – Feuillère in the twentieth century, Sarah Bernhardt of the golden voice in the nineteenth, Lecouvreur and Clairon in the eighteenth.

Racine was appointed historiographer to the king, which gave frequent proximity to him. A room at Versailles, a sign of exceptional favour, followed, as well as the job of reading aloud to Louis XIV; this was to be expected of a king into middle age, always interested in the arts, and – if Chateaubriand is to be believed – effectively illiterate.

More surprising in our day, Racine married, declaring *Ni l'amour ni l'intérêt n'eurent aucune part à mon choix.* [Neither love nor interest (i.e. control of his wife's fortune) had anything to do with my choice.] So why bother? Fear of death? Scarcely – he had made his peace with Port-Royal immediately after *Phèdre* was put on. Loneliness? His work kept him with other courtiers in the King's entourage, very busy and away from home. More like persistent ambition, to present the appropriate persona of a courtier with such access to the king, that even the polite knock before entering was no longer required. Also the mood at court had changed. The king's second, morganatic wife, Madame de Maintenon, had originally been a Calvinist and remained very devout. She had started a school for the daughters of impoverished noblemen and for their benefit asked Racine to write two religious plays[5] for the girls to act. Of course he obliged, and went on to prepare, very carefully, an edition of his plays. He lived *une existence bourgeoise vouée à ses sept enfants et la piété la plus austère* [he lived in bourgeois style, devoted to his seven children and the strictest piety]. Had Jansenism got the upper hand or was it yet another adaptation to the demands of the coercive king?

Huguenots, Jansenists and the Tragedies of Racine — Notes

1 The bridegroom of a few days: The marriage, of course, fell apart. In due course Henri married again, and after he had become king he was personally on good terms with Marguérite de Valois, the first wife, referred to, in French, as *La Reine Margot*.

2 *Dragonnade de Poitou*: Dragoons were mounted soldiers, armed with muskets. Poitou is the province inland from La Rochelle. It had been part of Eleanor de Aquitaine's dowry and therefore belonged to England in the twelfth century. It remains largely rural and cognac is its best known product.

3 James II of Great Britain dethroned: This happened in 1688. James II's daughter Mary and her husband, William of Orange, Stadholder of the United Provinces and himself a grandson of Charles I, became joint Protestant sovereigns of Great Britain.

4 *Bajazet*: This was first performed in 1672 and was of interest because the Ottoman Empire, precursors of modern Turkey, had conquered only three years earlier the island of Crete, long a Venetian, that is Christian, dependency. The Ottoman Empire was an ever-present danger throughout the seventeenth century, culminating in a long and very evenly balanced siege of Vienna in 1683, well within Racine's lifetime.

5 Two religious plays: *Esther* in 1689 and *Athalie* in 1691.

WALK TWO

Notre Dame

Quai de Montebello

Place Maubert

Rue Lagrange

Rue de la Bûcherie

St. Julien le Pauvre

Rue des Écoles

Quai Saint Michel

Rue Saint Jacques

St. Séverin

St. Michel

Rue Cluny

Boulevard Saint Michel

Musée Cluny

Quai des Grands Augustins

Place St. André des Arts

Rue Zuger

Boulevard Saint Germain

Rue de l'École de Médecine

Université

Rue des Grands Augustins

© 2004 Veronique Plapp

Walk Two

Make for Maubert–Mutualité, on metro line 10, St Cloud to Auster-litz. Place Maubert has the usual complement of cafés and a market on Saturday mornings. Cross Boulevard St Germain and turn *left* into Rue Lagrange, named for the mathematician, a wide street leading to the river. Ignore Rue des Anglais, the first on the *left*, although it was traditionally the preferred location for *les étudiants de la langue d'Angleterre* and turn *right* into the Rue Hôtel Colbert. Until 1887 there was a large house, *hôtel particulier* (a kind of urban château) on the corner, which had its heyday during the Empire, when it belonged to the Isserlis family.

The family's fall from grace paralleled that of Napoleon and by 1816 a printer named Lébégu was installed. In the spring of 1816 he printed *La Nouvelle Emma, ou les Caractères Anglais du Siècle* for Arthus Bertrand (see below).

Try to catch a glimpse of the pretty courtyard of number 4; num-bers 8 and 10 housed the early medical faculty; 11 and 12 date from the seventeenth century and number 13 housed in 1768 a bookshop called 'Au bout du Monde'. In London, 'The World's End' is a pub.

At the cross roads the modern Hôtel Colbert (literally a hotel, built in a hollow E filled with greenery) is on the right. On the *left* corner into Rue de la Bucherie is a fine eighteenth century building with a cupola and two Venetian windows facing north and east. It is the Théâtre Anatomique and replaces a 1617 building of the same purpose. (The upper interior is visible through the window facing Rue Hôtel Colbert; the light is better in the morning from this, east, side.) Its internal space is taken up by a circular chamber with tiers of steeply raked seats for the public viewing of dissections. It was put up in 1745, by Winslow, a Dane who spent his working life in Paris and died, a much honoured old gentleman, in 1760.

Numbers 13 and 15 Rue de la Bucherie,[1] on the same side, were occupied by the Ecole de Médicine until 1775. Continue along the Rue de la Bucherie to the T junction again with Rue Lagrange. On the right is the Pont au Double, to take you directly to the west door of Notre Dame, in no way part of the Jane Austen itinerary but rampant with literary and musical associations; and beyond it is Quai aux Fleurs with, at number 9, memories of Héloïse and Abelard.

Cross the road and you are in Square Viviani – gravel, benches, fragments of medieval buildings and trees, including the oldest in Paris, a Robinia, (false acacia, Papilionaceae) of 1601; supported and pampered, it screens the north wall of St Julien le Pauvre. The gun-metal stone holds a surprise – a pared down Norman interior, with shadows cast by fat columns, is interrupted by an iconostasis. On Sundays a blaze of hanging lights flares the gold background of the icons, the carved wood flickers, a crumb of the gorgeous East held in fee by dark stone and byzantine plain song. The building is now used by one part of the Greek Orthodox Church, its Melchite branch. On weekdays St Julien is a quiet place to light a candle (top tier for good health of the living, lower tier for repose of souls of the dead), rest the feet and day dream. Even the irrepressible Cornelia Otis Skinner, in *Our Hearts were Young and Gay* (1944 in England) mentions its power to induce reflection.

Back in the short Rue St Julien le Pauvre, turn *right* towards the river for the classic view of Notre Dame and then, keeping close to the buildings, turn *left*. You will come to a bookshop called Shakespeare and Company (featured in Richard Linklater's 2004 *Before Sunset*), on that spot since 1964. It opens late, stays open till all hours and is the one European-language bookshop in Paris where no French books are to be had. There are paperbacks galore (mostly second-hand), arranged in no discernible order inside and in the boxes and shelves outside. For serendipity it has few equals. If you buy a book it will be stamped 'Shakespeare and Company – kilometre zero – Sylvia Beach Whitman Foundation'. Shakespeare and Company has another advantage – next to it is a restaurant and then a corner café, both with tables out of doors sheltered from passers-by with waist-high greenery. So you can immediately sit and enjoy your book, looking up from it only for your drink and the view.

The Petit–Pont ahead right is scarcely a bridge – you have to lean over to see the narrowest arm of the Seine flowing under it. To continue the walk look for the zebra crossing, to cross Rue St Jacques (originally a Roman road) and go straight into Rue de la Huchette, walking westward, with the traffic coming towards you. It is a narrow street now heavy with Greek restaurants. Number 11 on the south side, still a restaurant, used to be Le Bouillon de la Huchette, according to Huysmans *café anglais des pirotins et des étudiants*, where a helping of meat could be had for 4 sous and vegetables for 2. Was this the place frequented by Sydney Carton and Mr Stryver (*Tale of Two Cities*) when they were 'fellow students in Paris, picking up French and French law, and other French crumbs we didn't get much good of'? After all Rue des Anglais is close enough.

On the right is a narrow opening, Rue Chat Qui Pêche (there used to be a sign of a cat with a fishing rod), allegedly the narrowest street in Paris. It will just allow one motor bike to go down it, with care. It opens on to the river and if you look *left*, to number 19 Quai St Michel, a totally undistinguished building, you will see where, on the flimsy–looking attic floor, Matisse had his studio. From it he painted a series of unmistakable canvases – light concentrated on two goldfish in a bowl, refracted through its glass into the room, blazing again through the window, and on to the building on the opposite river bank, in an aureole of light.

Rue de la Huchette is, as the Americans say, very historic. In the late Middle Ages its houses were known for their magnificence; ambassadors came up the river, anchored conveniently and were housed in splendour. Later it was the street where the best needles could be bought. (Jane Austen, who excelled at embroidery, would have appreciated that.)

On the façade of number 14, at the angle of Rue Chat Qui Pêche, there is an unobtrusive round medallion, with something like a handwritten letter Y in it. The same is also visible in the wrought iron protecting the first-floor windows. It is a rebus for a gizmo known as *lie-grègues*, sold on the spot and intended to hold together underpants and the skirt-like garments men wore in the fifteenth century. Ellision to i-grec (the French for the letter Y), was easy and that remained its name.

By the seventeenth century the street was known for its purveyors of roast meat and its cut-purses. In 1795 one room of number 10 was occupied by the young and penniless brigadier-general Bonaparte. He was in the habit of walking to Le Procope, just a stroll away, to have a cup of coffee and catch up on the news. Numbers 14, 16 and 18 are eighteenth century buildings, not that you'd recognise them as such at street level. But the pedestrianised Rue Xavier Privat on the left is much more convincing.

Also on the left, and easy to overlook, is the tiny Théâtre de la Huchette, a centre for avant-garde drama since before WW2. It presents the sort of plays we ran to see in greater comfort at the Royal Court in London. It is a shrine to Ionesco – there is a daily performance of *La Cantatrice Chauve* at 19 hr, now in its 43rd year (*The Mousetrap* is in its 52nd year). *La Leçon* an hour later and one more play at 21 hr. So the punters get their money's worth and, by day, parties of tourists crowd round the entrance while the guide gives a potted history of modern French drama.

Walk a few steps and on the right you will see the Hôtel du Mont Blanc, an establishment outwardly undistinguishable from its competitors. This is the hotel in a narrow street where Elliot Paul lived, as described in *The Last I saw of Paris*, so evocative of the period leading up to the Spanish Civil War.

Across the road from the Hôtel du Mont Blanc is the turn into Rue de la Harpe, named after a sign of King David playing the harp, to indicate the ancient synagogue now no more. Turn down it.

Verlaine, the symbolist poet, lived at number 6. His view was of number 3 opposite, the sort of apartment block a down-at-heels poet, in and out of psychiatric institutions, could not have aspired to. Nor did the view offer *les arbres si grêles* [such spindly trees], but *les hauts talons* [the high heels] struggling *avec les longues jupes* [with long skirts] were in evidence then as now.

Go to the crossing with Rue St Séverin, and there take a few steps to the *left*, the narrowest house in Paris, with a Japanese restaurant at ground level. The Abbé Prévost lived there while writing *Manon Lescaut*; he had a diagonal view of St Séverin, with enough minatory gargoyles to remind him of his calling.

Back to Rue de la Harpe and continue southward, past number 35 with its fine façade lightened by pretty wrought-iron, past the wider and more severe number 45 which, perhaps with a glance at Verlaine, is now a Centre Médico-psychologique for children, adolescents and their parents. In the eighteenth century it was the starting point for coaches travelling to Brittany and the Loire valley.

A few steps further is the junction with Boulevard St Germain. Across it is the metro station Cluny–Sorbonne and behind that the confused façade of the Cluny museum – the western part is gallo-roman, ruins of baths, the eastern part a medieval hotch–potch with highly decorated dormers in a steeply pitched roof. In summer the trees in front, part of a reproduction medieval garden, offer welcome shade. At any time the interior is full of medieval delights. So if it's started raining, or you are just fed up with streets, or a burger, ice cream or crêpe bretonne (all available immediately to the left as Rue de la Harpe joins Boulevard St Germain) hold no attractions, refresh the spirit with the poetic tapestries of the Lady of the Unicorn.

Having crossed the Boulevard St Germain, step *right* into Boulevard St Michel, keeping the Cluny museum on your left. Much of the original Rue de la Harpe was absorbed into Boulevard St Michel in 1855, which itself, together with Boulevard du Palais on the Ile de la Cité and the Boulevard Sebastopol on the Right Bank, was intended as the capital's main south–north thoroughfare. So the original number 80 Rue de la Harpe disappeared, and with it the premises of the printer d'Hautel, who in 1815 printed *Raison et Sensibilité* for Arthus Bertrand. Behind the Cluny glance left into

Rue Sommerard, these days a boring street with several useful hotels, but with a more picturesque past.[2]

Cross the Boulevard St Michel at the traffic lights a short way up the slope, then walk westward down the Rue de l'Ecole de Médicine. On the left, a tablet on number 5 proclaims it to be where Sarah Bernhardt, the super-star with the golden voice (there's a description of her in Proust's *Du Côté de chez Swann*) was born. The entrance is through the big wooden doors into a cobbled courtyard and the building now houses the English Department of the Sorbonne Nouvelle.

Across the courtyard, that is to the right of the big wooden doors as you enter, is another building with a cupola, with copies of parts of the Parthenon frieze decorating the exterior walls. This was started in 1691[3] as a *théâtre anatomique*, but in the early eighteenth century was absorbed into a free drawing school for 1500 students. What served for viewing dissections was also apt for life classes.

The next building along, after the T-junction with Rue Hautefeuille, is the refectory of the former Cordeliers monastery. The great doors are clearly visible and beyond them is a small door on to an easy circular staircase. This leads to the Association du Couvent des Cordeliers – Association pour la Promotion des Arts du 20e Siècle. So look around for a poster, for there may be an exhibition in the old refectory; it's the easiest way of having a look inside.

The former Cordeliers' refectory is surrounded by more parts of the university medical faculty, its Ecole Pratique. On the other side of the street is a fine portico-ed building built round a courtyard. It is the 'new' school of medicine, built in the eighteenth century. If its door nearest Rue Hautefeuille is open, or if you peer through the glass, you will see the dignified sale d'inscription.

Turn and face the Rue d'Hautefeuille. At its junction with Rue Ecole de Médicine there is a large building with a turret, the whole covering three sides of the square, the side facing the street closed off by a tall curtain wall and large wooden doors. As you face it, its right, southern wing, on its street frontage and almost at peeking

level, is broken by several small windows, one of them the usual
French *oeuil de boeuf*. Here Arthus Bertrand had his bookshop and
publishing house. He twice published *Raison et Sensibilité* (1815 and
1828) and *La Famille Elliot*, but stuck with just one edition of *La
Nouvelle Emma* (1816).

RAISON ET **SENSIBILITÉ,** OU LES DEUX MANIÈRES D'AIMER. TRADUIT LIBREMENT DE L'ANGLAIS, PAR Mme ISABELLE DE MONTOLIEU. TOME PREMIER, A PARIS, CHEZ ARTHUS-BERTRAND, LIBRAIRE, RUE HAUTEFEUILLE, N°. 23. 1815.	LA **FAMILLE ELLIOT,** ou L'ANCIENNE INCLINATION; Traduction libre de l'Anglais D'UN ROMAN POSTHUME DE MISS JANE AUSTEN, AUTEUR DE RAISON ET SENSIBILITÉ, D'EMMA, etc. PAR Mme. LA BARONNE ISABELLE DE MONTOLIEU. *NOUVELLE ÉDITION,* ORNÉE DE FIGURES. TOME PREMIER. PARIS, ARTHUS BERTRAND, LIBRAIRE, ÉDITEUR DU VOYAGE AUTOUR DU MONDE, PAR LE CAP. DUPERREY, Rue Hautefeuille, n°. 12. 1828.

Now follow the Rue Hautefeuille (a street dating back to Roman
Paris / Lutetia Parisiorum), north, back to Boulevard St Germain,
keeping the back of Université de Paris V on your left. Cross it to
the other arm of Rue Hautefeuille; after its crossing with Rue
Serpente (cinema at corner) it becomes more interesting. Number 16
was rented by a succession of *libraires* (booksellers / publishers);
number 18, dating from the early seventeenth century, housed
another, called Deterville, between 1806 and 1842, a long stretch for
a publishing house in those days. Number 5, with its pretty cor-
belled turret, has a glamorous history – it started as the medieval
town house of the abbots of Fécamp (an incongruous connection for

modern travellers, who know Fécamp as a holiday resort within 'very easy distance', as Darcy might say, of Channel ports) and was rebuilt in Renaissance style to give it two staircases with fine wrought–iron, sash windows and a mansard roof. For a while it was grand enough to be lived in by Diane de Poitiers,[4] mistress of King Henri II of France; she figures largely in *La Princesse de Clèves* and exudes silky menace in the Delannoy film with Jean Marais and Marina Vlady. Number 4 is a seventeenth century building with an oval staircase and more fine wrought iron; number 3, built before 1779, has another staircase worth looking at. Try ringing doorbells and asking for a peek, all along this section.

You are now at the end of Rue Hautefeuille, in the Place St André des Arts. Turn *left*, past several restaurants and into Rue Suger, another old street known from 1290 to 1844 as Rue du Cimetière St André des Arts. By the later eighteenth century the lay inhabitants of the houses facing Rue de l'Eperon and overlooking the cemetery, were complaining about the smell emanating from it. However the priests of St André des Arts, a large and rich foundation that maintained its prosperity from the Middle Ages until well into the eighteenth century, did not.

Number 1 Rue Suger housed the Sisters of Providence, noticeable for their habits made of sacking, which gave them the popular name of *Sachettes*. Numbers 3 and 5 had long been used as students' accommodation; in 1763 these mini halls of residence were amalgamated into one, the Collège Louis le Grand. J.K. Huysman (see above) whose writing developed from naturalism to aestheticism to medievalism (*A Rebours* is the most readable) was born in number 9. Number 11 has the original and very fine *porte cochère* guarding the entry to the now non–existent premises of Cogez *libraire*. In 1816 Cogez joined Arthus Bertrand in publishing and selling *La Nouvelle Emma*, a form of co–operation often practised at the time for individual books. Arthus Bertrand is documented as collaborating in this way to benefit Jane Austen's novel; it suggests that the initial sales of *Raison et Sensibilité* had not gone too well and

Arthus Bertrand was spreading his risk on *La Nouvelle Emma*. Similarly in London in 1811, *Sense and Sensibility*, printed at the author's
expense, had been sold by Egerton of Whitehall alone. But in 1813,
when it came to *Pride and Prejudice*, which Egerton had bought out-
right for £110, some copies were sold through Longman's, who, in
their turn, had no compunction about including in the binding a leaf
or two of their own advertisements.

LA

NOUVELLE

EMMA,

OU

LES CARACTÈRES ANGLAIS

DU SIÈCLE,

PAR L'AUTEUR d'*Orgueil et Préjugé*, etc., etc.

TRADUIT DE L'ANGLAIS.

TOME PREMIER.

PARIS,

Chez { ARTHUS BERTRAND, LIBRAIRE, rue Hautefeuille, n° 23.
COGEZ, LIBRAIRE, rue du Cime-tière Saint-André-des-Arts, n° 11.

1816.

LA

FAMILLE ELLIOT,

OU

L'ANCIENNE INCLINATION,

TRADUCTION LIBRE DE L'ANGLAIS

D'UN ROMAN POSTHUME DE MISS JANE AUSTEN,
AUTEUR DE *RAISON ET SENSIBILITÉ*, D'OR-
GUEIL ET PRÉJUGÉ, D'EMMA, DE MANS-
FIELD-PARC, etc.

PAR M.me DE MONTOLIEU.

AVEC FIGURES.

TOME PREMIER.

A PARIS,

CHEZ ARTHUS BERTRAND, LIBRAIRE,
RUE HAUTEFEUILLE, N.° 23.

1821.

At the end of the Rue Suger one block of the Lycée Fénelon is on
the left and the greater part of it on the other side of the T junction
with Rue de l'Eperon (named for the long defunct sign of a spur).
Find number 7 – *c'est une très vieille maison et puis on est dans la
cimetière romain* [it's a very old house, and besides we are in the
Roman cemetery] one of its occupants explained. Go in and have a
look at the courtyard – it gives you a good idea of what a mid–eighteenth century unpretentious town house was like. The present
building superseded an earlier gatehouse, second entrance to the

smelly Cimetière St André des Arts. Up to the Revolution, numbers 5 and 7 had been the administrative offices for the parish and other property owned by St André des Arts. After confiscation of church property in late 1789, a printing works was set up on the ground floor of number 7, owned and run by Madame Huzard; she ran the business with continued success, for in 1828 she printed for Arthus Bertrand – no more than a hop, skip and jump away in Rue Hautefeuille, *Raison et Sensibilité* and *La Famille Elliot*. But she did not live over the shop. Perhaps to avoid the exhalations from the cemetery, she lived on the other side, at number 10, a mid–eighteenth century building, originally owned by Monsieur Lafosse, *employé aux petites écuries du roi* [working in the king's lesser stables]. The equestrian connection persisted – the long–lived Monsieur Huzard, the printer's husband, was a well–known veterinarian; hence books generally needed by students at the veterinary school, were sold on the spot. Madame Huzard is listed as a specialist bookseller in the 1804 equivalent of the Publishers' Yearbook, the *Tableau des Libraires, Imprimeurs et Editeurs de Livres des principales Villes de l'Europe*.

As the nineteenth century progressed, number 10 took on a more literary flavour. In 1873 Theodore de Banville, who had been a friend of Baudelaire, moved in. He too was a poet, an undemanding one but sufficiently dextrous to try his hand at marrying the classical and romantic styles. He turns up in anthologies with the odd, easy, agreeable quickie. His more talented friends flocked to number 10 on Sundays, when he kept open house – Alphonse Daudet, whose *Lettres de Mon Moulin* retain their charm in the teeth of Provençal tourist guides pointing to several disparate windmills; François Coppet, whose best efforts for the underclass (*Les Humbles*) are irremediably sentimental to modern readers; Mallarmé who fussed exhaustively over English spelling and pronunciation but still found time to produce exquisite poetry and, with his *L'Après-midi d'un Faune*, jolted first Manet and later Debussy into work of the most sumptuous elegance, and then Nijinsky into his most erotic.

Rue de l'Eperon is short. At its northern end, at the T junction with Rue St André des Arts, you are faced by an apartment block of 1867, by T & G Ramand, the inscription informs us. The decorations by 'Roussel Sculpt' include figure heads with varied facial expressions. Turn *left* and then first *right* into Rue des Grands Augustins, leading to the river. Tall, pale houses and then on the right at number 7, a much grander version of Arthus Bertrand's establishment in Rue Hautefeuille. In one corner of that large building Picasso had his studio during the war, and the short film of him at work, made by Brassai, was shot on this location.[5]

Walk on to the end of the street. At the Quai des Grands Augustins take your life in your hands, or wait forever for the traffic to stop, and cross to the river side. Ahead you will have a fine view of the Ile de la Cité and, if you look down, of the cobbled river banks with occasional fishermen, the recurrent film image of Paris. Turning back, look at the row of undistinguished buildings except for one beauty, on the corner with Rue Seguir, number 35, with raked roof and large, attractive windows. Others like it lined the Quai des Augustins in the early nineteenth century, and, according to the *Tableau de Libraires*, many housed booksellers, including Arthus Bertrand. Why did he leave? Did his lease come to an end? Was he offered a better price at Rue Hautefeuille? Did he inherit the property? Whatever, by 1815 he was ensconced half a mile further from the river.

Walk back upstream to the Place St Michel, with its domineering fountain, and your second bookish stroll is finished. You are ready to refresh the spirit in the Sante Chapelle a few steps away across the bridge, or work your way through the book and music shops of Place and Boulevard St Michel, or dive into the metro, or sit and draw breath.

Walk Two — Notes

1 Rue de la Bucherie: Literally 'the street of the log-pile'. The name derives from the Middle Ages, when tree trunks for construction or fuel were floated down-river to this point, hauled out of the water and stacked before being sold on.

2 Rue Sommerard: Is named for the enthusiast who installed his collection of medieval artefacts in the Hôtel de Cluny in 1833. In the Middle Ages the street held the mother house of *La Sainte Trinité de la Rédemption de Captifs*, whose members were recognisable for riding about on donkeys. The mother house included a sizeable chapel dedicated to St Mathurinus, big enough to accommodate the election of the Rector Magnificus responsible for the arts faculty of the university. Another part of the building was used by the university for its Salle de Parchemins.

3 In seventeenth century Paris, to be a medical doctor the candidate had to start with an ordinary first degree *maitre des arts*. This was followed by two years of extra study. Then, if he was aged 22 or over, of good character (*bonnes moeurs*) and a Roman Catholic, he could embark on two years' work in hospitals, with exams along the way, and a thesis. The final practical exam lasting a week was followed by a fairly easy written exam. Only after all these hurdles had been satisfactorily passed was the title of doctor conferred at a solemn swearing-in ceremony.

4 Diane de Poitiers: You may remember a portrait of her having her nipple pinched by her sister while they share a bath. This curious blend of art and porn is possibly the best known example of the early French school of painting.

5 The film was shown in 2001 at the Brassai exhibition at the Hayward Gallery on London's South Bank. He is best known for his photos of Paris graffiti and has to his credit one book on Proust – *Marcel Proust sous l'emprise de la photographie*, 1997 and two on Picasso – *Les Sculptures de Picasso*, 1948 text by D.H. Kahnweiler, *Conversations avec Picasso*, 1964.

Why the Left Bank?

When you look at the maps you will see that the walks from one of Jane Austen's publishers or printers to the next are largely on the Left (south) Bank. This is because booksellers were part of the university, and its home was the Latin Quarter on the Left Bank. The medieval city had grown on the remnants of the Roman city and Latin was the one language the international student body had in common.

The university, of course, long pre-dated printing. From the twelfth century, public lectures were given in the open air on the Ile de la Cité, Le Petit Pont and around St Julien le Pauvre, with students sitting on little bales of straw. The faculties of medicine, canon law and theology were under the tutelage of the Chapter of Notre Dame Cathedral, but St Julien was the parish church of students and masters of arts. It was also the venue for assemblies to elect delegates from the arts faculties, charged with electing the *Rector Magnificus*. In turn the *Prévôt des Marchands*, in charge of the municipal government of the city, had to go to St Julien and swear to respect the privileges of masters and students. In time the colleges (primarily halls of residence), moved away from the river and up the Montagne St Geneviève, but the elections continued at St Julien. However, in 1542 the choice of Rector did not suit the students; their displeasure was familiarly expressed – they trashed the church. The king, then François I, stepped in and had the elections moved to the chapel of St Mathurin in what is now Rue Sommerard.[1]

In the meantime, printing had started round the corner in Rue St Jacques, bookshops followed and the university and the government got in on the act. Printing works [*imprimeries*] and booksellers [*libraires*] could only operate under licence. Much later they protected themselves by forming professional associations.[2] As early as 1555 King Henri II of France introduced a law that nothing could be printed without the name of the printer on it. Control of printers

developed and by 1750 their numbers in Paris were limited to
eighty and they were subject to inspection as well as licence.
Libraires, with their *brevets* [licences] were associated with the university. Anyone wishing to join them had to have a first degree
(*maitrise*), know Greek and Latin, produce a certificate of well-
conducted life (*bonne vie et bons moeurs*) and start with four con-
secutive years of work as an apprentice to an accredited *libraire*.
Three more years of *compagnonage* followed, then an exam, and, if
passed, a solemn swearing in before the brevet was obtained. By
1744 only *libraires* were allowed to sell books. They were seen as responsible and reputable members of the university of Paris, separated from the *arts mécaniques* [the printers], supported, maintained and confirmed in the rights, freedoms, prerogatives and
privileges of the university.

It added up to respectable bourgeois status for the monopolist
libraires well before the revolution of 1789. The booksellers' names
guaranteed the quality of publications because, as professionals, they
were known both for their loyalty and learning. They formed a
syndicate governed by a council (*Direction de la librairie*) and elected
their most learned and influential members to serve on it. The
council settled, on a friendly basis, all arguments between members,
at no expense to the contestants. It also examined every manuscript
proposed for publication. If the manuscript was judged suitable,
further advice was given as to format, printing style, number of
copies; arrangements were made for booksellers to take so many
copies each,[3] and this extended considerably the range of titles
carried by any one shop. However, the individual *libraire* was not
bound to follow the advice from the council; it had no veto, which
weakened its role as a preventative censor. Printers were the weak-
est link in the censorship chain. Although licensed and inspected, it
was always possible, if risky, to run off an unauthorised pamphlet or
poster on an *hollandaise*, [a light, easily assembled, table-top press],
or even set up an unofficial printing works. The space required for
such an operation was no more than the sitting room of a standard

house in a modest London square. You can check this for yourself if you extend your stroll in Geneva – from Place Bourg–le–Four walk along Rue E Dumont; number 16 on the right is the little house – with marble plaque – where the third impression of the thirty–five volume, *Encyclopédie ou Dictionnaire raisonné des sciences, des arts et des métiers* was printed, with Voltaire calling frequently to keep an eye on progress.

The *colporteurs* were another source of unauthorised literature. Forget Autolycus – these peddlers carried printed matter only. Their staples were almanacs, devotional texts, fairy tales, sentimental novels, practical guides to farming, all used to hide pamphlets printed abroad. These attacked the government, the clergy, or the conduct of the court, tilting opinion in favour of revolutionary ideas. The law regulating *colporteurs* was unclear. After all, the majority had been sellers of uncontroversial goods and one way and another they and the *bouquinistes* [sellers of second-hand books, much photographed along the Seine in Paris] went on being harassed by inspectors well into the nineteenth century. But at no stage were they a threat to the serious *libraires*, whose licences, binding them to the Left Bank, were valuable assets to be inherited or sold, and who prided themselves on their specialisms (*classiques, art militaire, école vétérinaire*) and their connection with the university, proclaimed by premises skirting its buildings.

Their monopoly was not absolute. It was breached initially by a few men and women in straitened circumstances who set up an intermediary service; books collected from a licensed *libraire*, generally at a discount, were carried across the river to the Right Bank and sold house–to–house. This service (*courrier en libraire*) was popular because – according to a history of bookselling published in 1853 – buyers who would hesitate to ask a respectable, licensed bookseller for a title had no scruples instructing their servants to buy it at their own back door.[4] Be that as it may, book shops on the Right Bank rapidly followed, especially in the Palais Royal. They were joined by non–syndicated booksellers competing with the *libraires* on the Left Bank. This new breed sought out authors, pirated books, found cheap printers and sold any books they were asked for. They were generalists with something like an integrated operation, guided by profit rather than the ideas of the Enlightenment as expressed classically in the thirty-five volume *Encyclopédie*. And they swept the board on the Right Bank.

Legitimately imported books from abroad had long been a feature of the official trade's prosperity. Those from Geneva were particularly important between 1750 and the Revolution. Translations also. From England, *David Simple*, an extraordinarily boring book by Sarah Fielding, sister of Henry[5], was well received; the Abbé Prévost had stamina enough to translate *Pamela*, *Clarissa* and *Sir Charles Grandison*, *Clarissa* being much admired. 1787 saw Beckford's *Vathek*, a farrago of an 'Arabian tale' that had originally been written in French. These and other English novels in translation were well established by 1815 when *Raison et Sensibilité* came along.

Before that, the rush of revolutionary events had reduced the price of books to little more than the price of paper. The trade stagnated. Then in 1810 an imperial decree set up the *Direction de la librairie et imprimerie*. It raised hopes among the *libraires*, whose licence depended on proving *attachement au souverain* [loyalty to the sovereign, that is, Napoleon] and could be withdrawn on publication of a book contrary to morals, religion, the government. In the event the *libraires* were further circumscribed – their licence, the new rules stated, could no longer be traded without authorisation from the Ministry of the Interior. This decree was primarily intended to control the printers. Their number in Paris was limited to sixty; they could have a maximum of four presses apiece; each had to keep a list of every one of their printed items bigger than a visiting card; also clearance had to be obtained from the official censor before printing any particular text. A year later, a supplementary law had printers filling in forms in quintuplicate for each work printed, giving all bibliographical information including the number of copies for each title. All this was to be reproduced in a monthly journal called *Bibliographie de France*. In 1812, its first year of publication, 4,648 titles were listed. In 1814, the year of Napoleon's exile to Elba, the number dropped to 2,685.[6] All of Jane Austen's novels in translation eventually figured on its pages, including the 1822 version of *Orgueil et Préjugé*, printed in Geneva.

In 1814 the legitimate claimant to the French throne was nicknamed *Le Gros Monsieur* [the Fat Gentleman] – his obesity was due to a malfunction of the hips, so he could barely walk, even in the garden of Hartwell House, his home in exile in Buckinghamshire. Was he a subliminal model for the timorous Mr Woodhouse, who so rarely ventured beyond the shrubbery of Hartfield? After all, *Emma* was written between January 1814 and March 1815, a period that covers Louis XVIII trundling back to Paris, his good intentions publicised on posters (no name of printer visible) within a border of fleur–de–lys, the symbol of the Bourbon kings:

> Chère France!
> En la revoyant, mon Coeur
> est plein des plus doux sentiments!
> Nous n'apportons que l'oublie du passé
> la paix et le désir du bonheur des Français.
> Qu'ai-je du faire de plus que je n'aye fait?
> Est-ce ainsi qu'on rend le mal pour le bien?

> [Dear France, in seeing the country again my heart is filled with the tenderest feelings. We bring nothing but erasure of the past, peace and a wish for the happiness of French people. What more should I have done? Is this the way to return evil for good?]

Le bien being that Louis XVIII had agreed to govern within a constitutional framework.

Much good it did him. Ten months later, just as Jane Austen finished *Emma*, Napoleon escaped from Elba and was welcomed enthusiastically by sufficient numbers of French for the roller–coaster ride of the Hundred Days to follow. It ended in June 1815 with the battle of Waterloo. For the non-historian, the battle is brought to life by Byron, Scott, Chateaubriand, Thackeray, Stendhal, Victor Hugo, Georgette Heyer, A. Mallinson, Joanna Trollope. The subsequent peace that brings Captain Wentworth back to land, looking for a wife, gave France a second peace treaty, much less favourable than the first. In its wake came more than a million foreign soldiers quartered on French soil, a minor bout of killing in the south (*Terreur Blanche*, that is Royalists settling old scores with Republicans and Bonapartists) and a law *sur les discours et écrits séditieux* [seditious speech and writing].

It punished anything that reduced respect for the authority of the king. On the other hand, after March 1817 it was no longer necessary to obtain a licence before importing books from abroad. By that stage, international movement was fully re-established, as Jane Austen, in her last letter from Chawton tartly noted of Miss Bigg, 'frisked off, like half England, into Switzerland'.[7]

So the translations of Jane Austen's novels came out in the turmoil of the Bourbon restoration. Bankers and industrialists were coining it (see the second volume of *The Count of Monte Cristo*); their wives held lavish salons. Modest, aristocratic ones survived in the Faubourg St Germain (where much of our walking takes place). An intellectual salon, where the spirit of the Encyclopaedists lingered, was that of Madame de Rumford, widow first of Lavoisier, the guillotined chemist, and then of Count Rumford, the founder of the Royal Institution and inventor of the Rumford stove, that triumph of modernity that General Tilney had been proud to install in Northanger Abbey's common drawing room.

Between 1815 and 1830 it was very easy to obtain credit from printers and paper manufacturers. Consequently a number of new *libraires* set up, but unless they were well capitalised, or also printers like Dentu, or had a staple publication, like Arthus Bertrand with *Mercure de France*, they were in grave danger of bankruptcy. Fortunately this happened to none of Jane Austen's publishers. This didn't stop a few from trying again repeatedly. One of the failed booksellers defined the possibilities:

Libraire – bookseller, either *détaillant*, retail, or *antiquaire*, dealing in high quality second-hand books and book auctions;

Libraire-éditeur – a significantly capitalised venture that initiates and carries through to publication both new books and new editions of earlier, high-quality texts, all by *hommes de lettres et savants*;

Libraire-commissaire – suppliers of books, often at a discount, and other goods on demand from *cabinets de lectures* [lending libraries] and provincial booksellers.

The last aroused much indignation for pirating books published in the capital. Belgian publishing houses were particularly vilified as, being much better capitalised than the Paris ones; they could flood France with cheap editions, known as *éditions anglaises*. Small groups of Paris *libraires* joined to combat piracy, especially between 1826 and 1830, but with no appreciable success. A parallel argument went on about the *brevets d'imprimeur* [licence to print]. Benjamin Constant wanted them abolished; others didn't. It still remained, more or less of a formality, in 1862, despite years of debate conducted through a series of pamphlets.

Why the Left Bank? — Notes

1 St Mathurin, feast day 9 November: The chapel was part of the mother house of the community of the *Sainte Trinité de la Rédemption de Captifs*. This long-lost pile answered so well until right into the eighteenth century, that the university also used it as its *Salle de Parchemins*.

2 Professional association: Authors had to wait till 1791 and 1793 before their rights were recognised.

3 So many copies: A similar arrangement obtained in London — Egerton sold *Sense and Sensibility* and *Pride and Prejudice* through both Longman's in the Strand and Sherwood, Nealy & Jones. One of Egerton's outlets was a Military Library, that is, one specialising in texts on military subjects. There was no shortage of these after Napoleon's defeat at Waterloo in June 1815; certainly later the same year Egerton published with Booth, another London publisher, *Circumstantial Details of the Battle of Waterloo*. Possibly one contributory reason why, in late summer 1815, Jane Austen left Egerton for John Murray to have *Emma* published, was that Egerton was too busy with accounts of Napoleon's campaigns and final defeats.

4 This compares with the late 1960s and postal sales of *Fanny Hill, Memoirs of a Woman of Pleasure*, an eighteenth century text by John Cleland that wouldn't raise an eyebrow in the new millennium, unmentionable in Jane Austen's day.

5 Henry Fielding: In 1744 he wrote a preface to *David Simple*, 'a moral romance', and revised it for its second edition. It was an early shot at a novel of sensibility and asked the question, put more acutely by Mackenzie's *Man of Feeling* of 1771 — how far does the man of sensibility, with his family, suffer, because he is too foolish or too good for the selfish, everyday world?

6 Number dropped: In 1827, when all of Jane Austen's novels had come out in French at least once, the book trade was the responsibility of the Ministère de Police, and the number of titles listed had risen to 7,542.

7 Jane Austen's last letter from Chawton: Letter 159, dated 22 May 1817, in *Jane Austen's Letters*, edited by Deirdre Le Faye, OUP 1996.

Revolutionary Paris

French critics, notably Léonie Villard[1] starting in 1915, cannot understand how Jane Austen, living as she did through the years of the Revolution, managed to write contemporary novels without once referring to it. But for Jane Austen politics, as declared in *Northanger Abbey*[2], leads to silence and a change of topic. However the successive wars of the Revolution and its aftermath impact on the domestic scene she describes. There is at least one military or naval character in every one of her novels. The obvious example is *Mansfield Park*[3], where William is encouraged to talk about his experiences, to Henry Crawford's secret discomfiture, a neat instance of characterisation that includes moral judgement. Even in *Emma*[4], the nearest to paradisial in the realistic novel genre, the clubbable Mr Weston started out as Captain Weston, and Jane Fairfax is the orphan daughter of Lt Fairfax, an infantry officer who had died in action abroad; her prospects, even after the enlightened affection of her foster parents are anything but rosy before the fortuitous intervention of Frank Churchill. In *Pride and Prejudice*[5] the notorious camp near Brighton draws Lydia dangerously close to infamy for herself and her family. For the military men in *Northanger Abbey* and *Sense and Sensibility* their profession determines the timing of their presence in the action of each novel, with far-reaching consequences. By *Persuasion* the wars are over, the sailors ashore and able to take time over a choice of wife.

Even at a personal level the earlier Revolutionary years held a chilling reminder for Jane Austen — her first cousin and later her sister-in-law Eliza Hancock had first married a French officer loyal to Louis XVI, and who, like his king, had been guillotined. Equally you cannot walk through Paris without coming across the reminders of the Revolution of 1789. Most of us remember it sketchily, as the confused background to stories in print (*The Tale of Two Cities*, *The Scarlet Pimpernel*, *Sylvia's Lovers*), or film (again *The Tale of Two Cities*, *The Scarlet Pimpernel*, *Jefferson in Paris*), opera (*The Carmelites*,

Andrea Chenier), a wild, violent period that nevertheless turned out to be, in retrospect, 'A good thing'.[6] At the time, of course, it was anything but, and the characters who crop up along and around our walks died for the most part violently, all disappointed, all having started out with the usual hopes that fuel instigators of revolutions.

It started in the New World. 1783 was a high-water mark for French diplomacy – the American colonies, with French help, had won independence, Britain was soundly defeated, France had regained Tobago, St Lucia and Senegal. By 1786 common sense, if not friendliness, had led Britain's prime minister, Pitt the Younger, to sign a treaty with France, reducing duties on goods traded between the two countries. This particular easement scarcely affected the major worry of the French government – how to redeem 400,000,000 livres' worth of short term debt, due to be repaid between 1787 and 1797. Necker, the former director of finance, was recalled in 1788, a year of poor harvests. Was it a measure of open-mindedness or desperation for the *Conseil du Roi* [the government], to entrust so vital a task to a Protestant citizen of Geneva, albeit the most celebrated banker of his age?

In May 1789 the king, desperate for a solution to the country's financial problems, summoned – for the first time since 1614 – the Estates General. This was the French equivalent of a national parliament (provincial parliaments had been meeting for some years) and consisted of three chambers representing respectively the clergy, the aristocracy and the people, effectively the bourgeoisie, the last being numerically equal to the other two together. Hope of reform was unleashed, thwarted – were they going to vote by head (majority for the people) or by chamber (the *status quo*). On 20th June a majority of delegates assembled in the Tennis Court[7] attached to the royal palace in Paris. They swore an oath *de ne pas se séparer avant d'avoir donné une constitution à la France*. This was the first formal act of disobedience to the king and revolution was now inevitable. From 3rd July large groups started assembling in the gardens of the Palais Royal, that hive of newsmongering, political discussion and subversion. Necker, having tried and failed to solve the country's financial problems, was dismissed on 12th July.

On that day in the Palais Royal a huge crowd was addressed by a series of speakers, most notably Camille Desmoulins, a young barrister with his hat decorated by a green leaf to denote hope. His rhetoric inflamed the crowd. On 14 July it stormed the Bastille, released its seven prisoners and started the torrent of violence. Camille Desmoulins for his part flowered into the most effective pamphleteer (we would call him a spin doctor) of the Revolution – he found time to fall in love and marry, and join the influential *Club des Cordeliers* before his far-out ideas so alarmed the authorities that in 1791 his arrest was ordered. He went into hiding, and while on the run, met Danton one of the biggest hitters of the Revolution. A few weeks later, both had been pardoned, Danton elected to an important post in the Commune of Paris (theoretically just the town council, but with huge powers to affect the course of events) and the Desmoulins family were living in an apartment in 24 Rue de l'Odéon, a stone's throw from the *Club des Cordeliers*.

The meeting place of the club was in a building that still stands in the present Rue de l'Ecole de Médicine at number 15. From the street you see a large and a small gate, with a late medieval building behind. It is the former refectory, all that remains of the very extensive monastery of Les Cordeliers (Franciscan friars, who used a length of thin rope, *corde* – for a belt). From the fifteenth century it had been a well-known centre for medical learning – the *Confrérie de Saint Cosme et Saint Damien* (the saints known in the Greek Orthodox church as the 'unmercenary healers') were authorised to run a school of surgery in a dedicated building. The site included a hostel for relatives visiting the sick and a morgue for cadavers to be dissected for the instruction of students. Permission had been granted in 1691 for a purpose-built anatomical theatre, a beautiful building decorated with panels of classical sculpture (visible from the cobbled courtyard behind the *porte cochère* into number 11). However, by 1783 a large scale reform of the university had taken place

– the multiplicity of small *collèges* had been amalgamated into one, called Louis Le Grand; the medical school had been re-housed in the impressive pillared building on the north side of Rue de l'Ecole de Médicine that is immediately opposite the Cordeliers and the present school of surgery. This re-arrangement released space on the Cordeliers' site; some of it was allocated to an officially appointed group of engineers charged with creating an overall plan for the development of Paris. More was given to the Ancienne Ecole de Dessin (as the tablet on the wall calls it); this was free to its 1,500 students, who learnt a range of subjects from the drawing of flowers, animals and humans to arithmetic, architecture and ornamental sculpture.

In 1789 what remained of the monastery, along with all other analogous entities, was disestablished – in other words all assets seized by the revolutionary government and inmates driven out. (This happened throughout the territory of France.) So by 1790 it was easy to find a space in the building for meetings of the *Société des Droits de l'Homme et du Cityoyen* (Society of the Rights of Man and Citizen), a bit of a mouthful, colloquially transformed into *Le Club des Cordeliers*. At that stage there was no connection with *The Rights of Man*, written in English by Tom Paine,[8] that peripatetic revolutionary who divided his energies between America, Britain and France. For five years he too lived in Rue de l'Odéon, was even elected member of the National Convention, the name given to the national assembly charged to produce a new constitution after the dethronement of the king in August 1792. (The king's position and that of his queen Marie-Antoinette, an Austrian princess, had become untenable after the French revolutionary government declared war on Austria in April 1792.) In due course Louis XVI was arraigned for treason, found guilty and condemned to death. Tom Paine who, with Danton and Desmoulins, had opposed the execution of the king, was arrested for his pains and lucky enough to miss the guillotine. Eventually he fled back to America, where he died, sick and neglected, in 1809.

But for the few years between 1790 and 1794 the *Club des Cordeliers* was extremely influential. While its members were of the left, *Montagnard's* party[9], as opposed to the more moderate *Girondins*[10], they were not of the far left, the *Exagérés*. Besides, Danton, the founder of the club, was a highly effective war leader, although officially he was no more than Minister for Justice, with Desmoulins as his secretary. Danton was most successful in organising resistance to Austria (which had, in Queen Marie–Antoinette, an Austrian princess, an additional interest in defeating the Revolutionary armies), but at huge expense. All public money was not accounted for, a matter Danton dismissed by saying that great causes needed commensurate money to back them, and he had saved liberty and the Revolution rather than excelled at book–keeping. More controversially he did nothing (could do nothing?) to stop the First Terror, the September massacres of 1792. A rumour had arisen that a counter–revolutionary coup was being organised from inside Paris prisons. The mob countered this by breaking into the prisons, including that de l'Abbaye, next to St Germain des Prés, pulling the prisoners out of their cells and killing them in any way that came to hand, 1,200 of them in 24 hours. A short distance to the south–east, at the corner of the present Rue Cassette / Rue Vaugirard, a convent, St Joseph des Carmes, was used as a holding pen for some two hundred religious and a job lot of other citizens; a few days later they too were killed. In the same month Camille Desmoulins was elected to the National Convention as one of the delegates for Paris.

The war continued; Danton carried on with his successful efforts. In March 1793 he became head of the *Comité du Salut Public* [Committee for Public Safety], living all the while in an arcaded house where the Cour du Commerce St André joined the Rue de Boucheries, that is just about where his statue now stands, by the entrance to the metro station Odéon. His near neighbour in the Cour du Commerce was a carpenter named Schmidt, who had built the prototype of the guillotine, devised by Dr. Guillotin, as a rapid, reliable and humane means to apply the death penalty.

Then things started going wrong – a general, Dumouriez, previously successful, lost a battle, was relieved of his command and promptly took himself and some of his disaffected units over to the Austrians. In the fall–out, the *Girondins*, the moderate party in parliament, were driven out and left to cool their heels until they too were murdered during the second Great Terror in October 1793. But the knives were also out for Danton, the leader of the *Girondins*.

Robespierre, the Sea–Green–Incorruptible (and he was, to give him his due) was Danton's most prominent rival, but too devious to come out openly against him. Instead two henchmen were called for – the first was Saint-Just, member of the rival political club called Jacobins; the other was Marat.

The instant recollection of Marat is of his being killed in his bath; David's canvas captures the moment, like a news flash of icy lucidity. There was more to him – a doctor by training, he had qualified in Scotland after several years' sojourn in Britain. All his life he was fascinated by electricity and magnetism, all his life he attacked privilege, inequality, the despotism of state and church, all his life he demanded the redistribution of wealth and the right of the oppressed to punish the oppressors. As early as 1783 he wrote *Projet de la Déclaration des Droits de l'Homme*; in the summer of 1789 he started a journal *L'Ami du Peuple* (printed at number 9 Cour du Commerce St André, opposite the carpenter's shop where the guillotine was built). The journal attacked Necker, the director of finance (and father of Madame de Staël) of deliberately starving the population. His diatribes were so savage that he was summoned to appear before a tribunal.

Sensibly he fled – to England – and returned to Paris only in May 1790, to attack the moderate revolutionaries then in power, demand the arrest of the royal family, regret the lack of executions and call for five or six hundred of them, to achieve peace and good order for the progress of the revolution. He enjoined his readers to go about with torches, in readiness for politically correct arson, to chop the thumbs off *jadis nobles* (former aristocrats) and slice the tongues

of supporters of the clergy. *L'Ami du Peuple* was suspended and
Marat fled to England yet again. By August 1792 back in Paris,
member of the *Club des Cordeliers*, member of a supervisory committee (*Comité de la surveillance de la Commune*) he was also a member of the National Convention, siding with the *Montagnards*, calling
for revenge all round. During the September massacres, Tom Paine
was drafting his version of *The Rights of Man*; simultaneously Marat
started another journal (*Publiciste de la République Française*),
demanding the death of the king. Indeed he did force the vote
through – the king lost by one vote, the king's cousin, the Duc
d'Orléans voting for the execution.

Understandably Marat was immensely popular with the mob, the
sans culottes. To maintain his popularity at the start of 1793, when
inflation and hunger added to the generalised havoc, he called on
his supporters to pillage shops. The moderates in Parliament attacked him for incitement to violence, but the Revolutionary
Tribunal[11] acquitted him, and he was literally carried home in
triumph. For revenge, he joined Danton in driving the last of the
moderates out of the National Convention on 2 July 1793. After
that, ill health, a kind of generalised eczema, kept him at home in a
building on the site of the present number 20 Rue de l'Ecole de
Médecine. He had a first floor apartment (rent paid by his mistress,
a milliner from Burgundy) of two rooms, one with hip bath, facing
the courtyard, and three rooms, with five windows between them,
facing the street. His address was common knowledge so that, when
Charlotte Corday arrived from Caën in Normandy and took a room
in the present Rue Hérold on the Right Bank (a street still with
several small hotels), she could easily find out precisely where he
lived.

On July 13th she had a letter delivered to him – knowing his
amour pour la Patrie could she, please, come to tell him about the
unhappy events around Caën? To fill in time, she went to the Palais
Royal to shop in the east, Valois, galleries, and bought a stout
kitchen knife with an ebony handle. After lunch in her hotel, she

walked to the Rue de l'Ecole de Médecine, but was refused entry. Back in her hotel she wrote another letter to Marat, posted it. Dressed in a grey chalk-stripe dress, pink fichu and hat with revolutionary cockade and green ribbons, she walked once more to Marat's apartment.

A temporary hesitation, then at 19.30, back to Marat's door. This time she was allowed in. Alone with Marat in his bath, she stabbed him, pulled out the knife, laid it on a table and sat down to wait (remember the murder in *Les Enfants du Paradis*?). Mistress and neighbours rushed round, Charlotte was bundled to the nearest prison, l'Abbaye, next to St Germain des Prés, and a few hours later to the more secure Conciergerie on the Ile de la Cité.

The next day, the fourth anniversary of the storming of the Bastille, the body of *le divin Marat* was displayed in the former chapel of the Cordeliers. The painter, David, also a member of the National Convention, took the opportunity to make sketches. On July 16th Marat's funeral procession wound its way through the streets, canon firing the while. Simultaneously Charlotte, under interrogation, declared to the investigating magistrate that *Je n'ai pas tué un homme, mais une bête féroce* [I have not killed a man but a wild beast]. And who, in our day, would gainsay her? But on her last day, July 17th 1793, she appeared before the revolutionary tribunal at 8am and was sentenced to immediate decapitation. She remembered to thank her defence counsel, who had previously acted for Queen Marie-Antoinette, and asked him to settle her hotel bill. Sanson, the chief executioner, cut her hair, chestnut, very long and very beautiful. She asked to be allowed to keep her gloves on for the ride to the Place de la Révolution (present Place de la Concorde) and stood in the tumbril looking round Rue St Honoré that she had not seen before. Robespierre, Danton and Desmoulins hired windows on the route, to watch her go by. She is described as hurrying up the steps to the guillotine.

Before the month was out, Danton had lost his seat on the Committee of Public Safety. Seemingly unbothered – he had a new wife

– he took himself for a holiday in the country, leaving the field open for Robespierre to continue undermining him, since Danton and his supporters now passed for the moderate opposition. In October, with the Great Terror in full swing, Danton was back in town and trying to row back, he pushed Desmoulins into starting a new journal *Le vieux Cordelier*, to argue for an end to the blood-letting. Nothing doing. Robespierre and Saint-Just continued to work against him. At the end of March 1794 Danton was warned to flee. He stood his ground and was arrested, with Desmoulins, on 30th March.

At his public trial he defended himself so eloquently that the tide was beginning to turn in his favour. Robespierre could not allow this, so his side-kick Saint-Just and the public prosecutor Fouquier-Tinville (referred to in *The Scarlet Pimpernel*) asked for the accused to be outlawed, in effect condemned to immediate death. This was agreed, but for one farcical detail – Danton and Desmoulins refused categorically to be executed in the same batch as Fabre d'Eglantine, a cheerful writer of comedies who had been picked up on the same day as the other two, from his home in Rue Monsieur le Prince, on the west side of the Cordelier site.

Fabre d'Eglantine had written a charming poem, now turned into a nursery rhyme, *Il pleut, il pleut, bergère*, and despite no attested scientific knowledge, had been the recorder-rapporteur to the commission that remodelled the calendar along revolutionary lines. The year was to start at the autumn equinox, months to have thirty days apiece, and the extra days reserved for revolutionary festivals, rather like the Hobbits' extra days for 'merry-making'. The months were given new names, the ones now commonly remembered being *Thermidor* (July) for the lobster dish, and *Floréal* (May) for the big Paris flower show. Small revolutionary beer no doubt, but none the worse for that. What Danton and Desmoulins could not abide was the suspicion of financial irregularities that hung over Fabre d'Eglantine's dealings some years earlier, with the *Compagnie des Indes*, the French equivalent of the East India Company.

In the end revolutionary honour was satisfied – Danton, Desmoulins and twelve others were scheduled for execution on 5th April. In the tumbril, passing Robespierre's house, Danton called out *Robespierre, tu me suis* [Robespierre, you're next] – as indeed happened to him and Saint-Just barely four months later. Fabre d'Eglantine was executed on 6th April, and Desmoulins' much loved and loving wife, who dared voice her regret at his death, on 13th April.[12]

If you have found this section as dispiriting to read as it was to write, you may reflect that 20th century tyrants had little to invent. In this, as in so many respects, the French are an example to us all.

Revolutionary Paris — Notes

1 Léonie Villard *Jane Austen: sa vie et son oeuvre 1775-1817* Saint-Etienne, Société Anonyme de l'Imprimerie Mulcey 1915.
2 *Northanger Abbey*: vol. 1, ch. 14.
3 *Mansfield Park*: vol. 2, ch. 6.
4 *Emma*: vol. 2, ch. 2.
5 *Pride and Prejudice*: vol. 2, ch. 16 passim.
6 A Good Thing?: Arguably not least for the British government, since the Revolution led to Napoleon and his disastrous retreat from Moscow ended French domination of Europe.
7 Tennis Court: Jeu de Paume, at the north-east corner of the Tuileries Gardens, it was for many years the museum devoted to impressionist painters.
8 Tom Paine: The marble plaque on number 10 Rue de l'Odéon says: *Anglais de naissance, Americain d'adoption, Français par décret* [English by birth, American by adoption, French by decree] – bureaucracy then, as now, was pervasive in France – *il mit sa passion de la liberté au service de la Révolution, fut Député de la Convention et écrit les Droits de l'Homme* [he put his passion for liberty at the service of the Revolution, was member of parliament and wrote *The Rights of Man*]. And the coda – *Lorsque les opinions sont libres, la force de la verité finit toujours par l'emporter* [when opinions are free, the power of truth always in the end wins].
9 *Montagnards* because they sat on the *montagne* (mountain), that is the higher tiers of seats in the legislative chamber.
10 *Girondins* the moderate party, who favoured local control as distinct from Marat who, as leader of the *Jacobins*, would allow nothing except centralised government, prefiguring the current EU arguments about subsidiarity. Charlotte Corday was a *Girondin*.
11 Revolutionary Tribunal: a body set up in March 1793 for the summary trial of those accused of crimes against the state. It easily found a great many victims.
12 In 1795 yet another constitution established the Directory, which lasted for four years and was replaced by the military dictatorship of Napolen Bonaparte. Startlingly successful as a soldier, he found energy and time to force the confused society of 1799 into a framework of centralised order, with power retained by himself and passed down in strict hierarchical sequence.

Walk Three

You need the RER fraction of the metro. It is shown on maps with a thicker line, has letters instead of numbers and is separately labelled in the stations. From Charles de Gaulle airport a courtesy bus, *navette*, labelled *Paris par le train*, will take you to its start, a smooth operation apart from the difficulty of getting luggage through the barrier. If you arrive at the abominably ill-signposted Gare du Nord, make for the lowest metro level. It is generally platform 42 for RER going into town, but do check.

From Gare du Nord the third stop is Luxembourg. Take the exit for the gardens (the other is for Rue de l'Abbé de l'Epée). You have to cross the road from the metro exit and into what is definitely the most attractive of the Paris parks. Carry straight on to the octagonal pool, where you could hire a little boat to sail, or sit and read the paper or just enjoy the view.

With the pool on your left, walk towards the palace and on, leaving it on your left and the Fontaine de Médicis on your right. Stop to tease you eyes with the illusory flow of water uphill into the fountain – then carry on out of the gardens and into the Place Paul Claudel. You are now at the back of the Théâtre de l'Odéon (nowadays also known as Théâtre d'Europe). The front has the predictable pillared portico. The first theatre on the site opened in 1782, as the home of the Comédie Française. After WW2 it was remarkable for its production of modern plays and its superlative collection of historic costumes. The collection and the building suffered gravely during the student riots of 1968, but the restoration of the latter is now complete.

Walk down the Rue de l'Odéon. It has a number of pretty shops, galleries, expensive and formal bookshops – the kind that specialise in autographs and have limited opening hours. It's a far cry from the period between the wars when at number 7 (now a hairdresser and a bookshop) Adrienne Monier had a shop called La Maison des Amis du Livre, described by Claudel as *paradis des bouquins, librairie de*

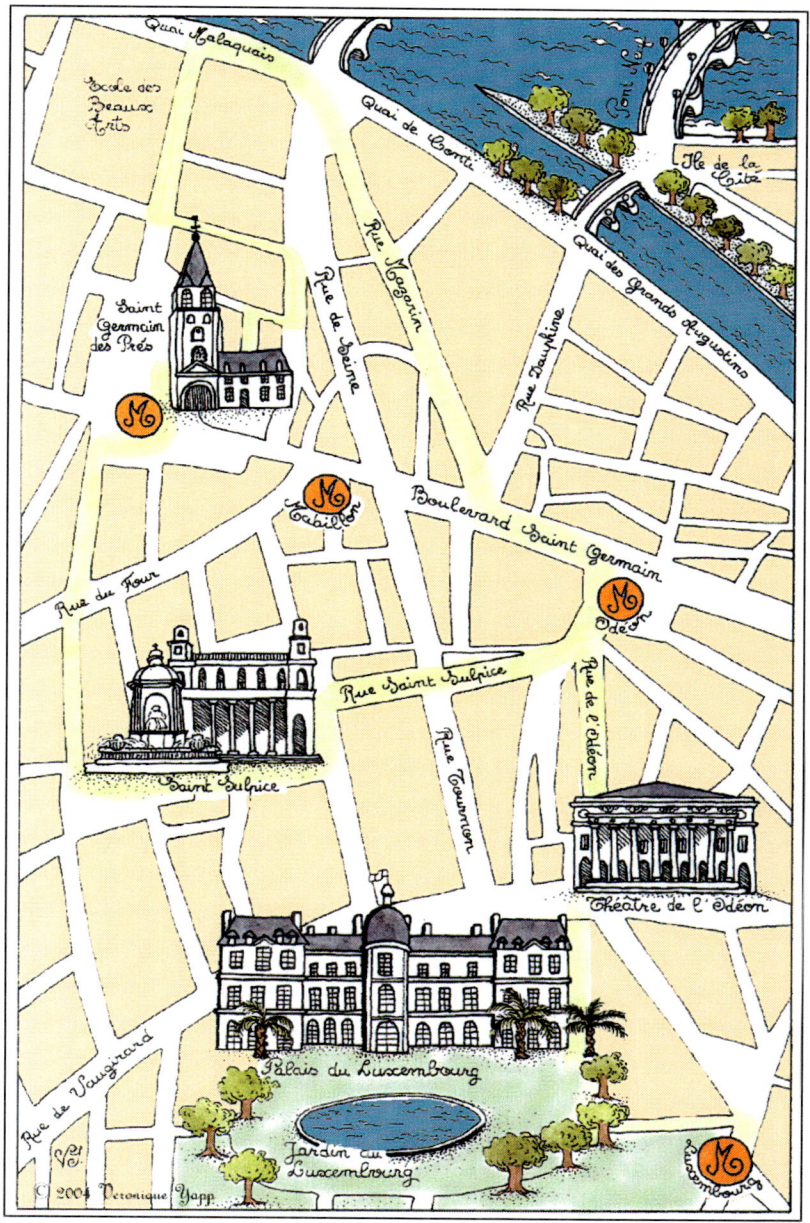

Quai Malaquais

Ecole des
Beaux
Arts

Quai de Conti

Ile de la
Cité

Quai des Grands Augustins

Rue Mazarine

Rue de Seine

Rue Dauphine

Saint
Germain
des Prés

Ⓜ

Ⓜ
Mabillon

Boulevard Saint Germain

Ⓜ
Odéon

Rue du Four

Rue Saint Sulpice

Rue de l'Odéon

Rue Tournon

Saint Sulpice

Théâtre de l'Odéon

Rue de Vaugirard

Palais du Luxembourg

Ⓜ
Luxembourg

Jardin du
Luxembourg

© 2004 Veronique Yapp

WALK THREE

neuf et d'occasion, cabinet de lecture, salon de thé [a bookfilled paradise, selling new and secondhand books, a reading room and a tea room].[1]

This nurturing spot was the scene for André Breton, Gide, Paul Valéry, Claudel himself, Aragon, Paul Eluard, Cocteau to give readings of their newest work.

Did this gregarious establishment inspire the present fashion for coffee bars in bookshops? It was certainly imitated by Sylvia Beach who, between 1929 and 1949, ran the original Shakespeare and Company across the road at number 12, now a jeweller. She befriended Eliot, Hemingway, Scott Fitzgerald, Ezra Pound and, most importantly, James Joyce. In 1920, that is before the publication of *Ulysses* in France, she introduced Joyce to Valéry Larbaud, a regular at number 7. Larbaud was an aesthete, critic, *homme de lettres*, who wrote the only inspired poem about travelling on a long distance train that I know. But his main call on our gratitude is that he was the staunchest advocate for *Ulysses*, in both English and French, and a long term supporter of Joyce.

Rue de l'Odéon ends in the Carrefour of the same name, a widening of the Boulevard St Germain with metro station, cinema, café and statue of Danton (on the site, it is said, of his drawing-room). These days Danton, a hero of the Revolution, is mostly remembered for *Il nous faut de l'audace, encore de l'audace et toujours de l'audace* [we must dare, and dare again and always dare]. More jaundiced hindsight sees him as a man of good intentions, who worked to unleash a hurricane, got scared, tried to rein back and had his head chopped off for his pains. Had Jane Austen heard of him? In 1794, one year into the war, was there a regular newspaper at Steventon for Jane to glance at? But she knew Eliza de Feuillide her cousin, future sister-in-law and traditionally model for Mary Crawford. Eliza had heard in February that her husband had been arrested in Paris and guillotined within hours of a fraudulent trial.

Turn your back on revolutionary Paris, face again the Théâtre de l'Odéon, and take the Rue St Sulpice to the *right*, westward. The

street is interesting rather than pretty – there's a highly decorated
porte-cochère at number 27. Across the road look at number 26,[2] a
house now divided into flats, but you can see how high the ceilings
are and how beautifully shaped the inside shutters, to fit the
rounded tops of the windows.

The church of St Sulpice, a large neo–classical pile some one hundred and fifty years in the building, is on your left. As you go in,
look out for the baroque holy water stoops – shell-shaped and with
crabs and squid for decoration. Then look around – on a summer
day the interior is unexpectedly light, giving the impression of total
openness. Where, in this tranquil lucidity, could the Abbé Prévost
have imagined the impassioned meeting between Manon Lescaut
and Des Grieux? Or Massanet find the crescendo rising to the lovers'
second elopement? The scene (Act 3, scene 2), as staged at Covent
Garden some thirty years ago, showed a shallow dull grey rectangle,
closed in with pilasters and heavy doors, to match the actual panel-
ling in the sacristy, totally at odds with the luminosity of the building. The only suggestion of violent feeling is in the first chapel on
the right, lush with Delacroix's murals. Note in *Jacob Wrestling with
the Angel* a beautiful still-life of Jacob's clobber in a graceful heap on
the grass.

St Sulpice holds another surprise. Walk up to the altar rails and
you will see, set in the marble floor, a metal rod spanning the
church from north to south. Above the rod, set high in the south
wall, you will see a narrow window, and opposite, on the north
wall, what looks like a funerary obelisk. In fact it is a gnomon (or
sun–dial pin), to go with the metal rod and an oval plate interrupting
it exactly below the high altar, half way between the gnomon and
the window. Depending where, on any particular day, the sun hits
the metal line, it is possible to calculate where, in its elliptical orbit,
the earth stands in relation to the sun. Ferret around a bit more and
you will find an inscribed marble slab to tell you that the whole was
assembled in 1714: Pro Nutatione Axios Terram
                     Obliquitate Eclipticae.[3]

It is one of several *meridiane* that were built into catholic churches, mostly in the seventeenth century. The ecclesiastical motive behind their construction was to have in cloudy northern latitudes a means of pin-pointing the spring equinox; then the date of Easter (on the first Sunday after the first full moon after the spring equinox) could be determined. The habitual spring cloud cover made them less reliable than the beautiful structures in the observatory in Jaipur, where the crisp shadows tell the time to the minute. Also, being restricted within a church, there is no feeling of moving through a landscape of abstract sculpture swathed in the pink and gold light of Rajasthan. But such as it is, here is scientific enquiry sponsored by the catholic church and housed inside St Sulpice, a parish that, unlike St Germain de Prés, has little truck with eucumenicism and specialises in the training of ordinands and missionaries. And yet, there is the suggestion that the present building stands on the site of an ancient temple of the sun.

As you come out of the church, on the right is the small Café de la Mairie, frequently used in films. Further right, number 6 has Yves St Laurent's windows adding wispy elegance to the beautiful eighteenth century building. The Place St Sulpice has a fountain commemorating four church worthies and the obligatory trees. In June this dusty space is transformed by the Foire St Germain, (the local fair). It has taken place, with interruptions, since 1176, and now consists of exhibitions, plays, concerts, children's activities, an antiques fair and a poetry fair (a small version of the Hay-on-Wye festival). The Foire spreads into the local town hall (Mairie du VIe), theatres, museums and into the Jardin du Luxembourg for the Fêtes du Sport, with food and drink to match. It's the greatest fun. Give it a go. A list of events is available from the local shops or the Mairie du VIe.

However, if you are in Paris during one of the other eleven months, there is nothing to distract you from walking on to the T junction with Rue Bonaparte. Look left. In Jane Austen's day this part of the Rue Bonaparte was known as Rue du Pot de Fer FSG, for

Faubourg St Germain.[4] Nothing of early nineteenth century left
now in this leg of the street but in 1821, number 14 housed a printer,
David, who printed *Orgueil et Prévention* for Maradan. This title,
askew from the usually accepted *Orgueil et Préjugé* was to distinguish
it from another translation of *Pride and Prejudice* published at the
same time by J.J. Paschoud printed in Geneva and sold in both
Geneva and Paris. Rue Pot de Fer FSG also had a very large book
warehouse which burned spectacularly in 1835. Scarcely had the
ashes cooled when punters came to scrabble for books, much as lat-
ter-day Londoners did after the Holland House library was bombed
in October 1940, the moment captured by Fox Photos.

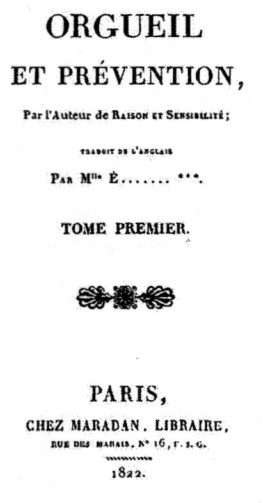

Turn *right* along the Rue Bonaparte, going north towards the
river. It is a street of attractive fashion shops. Cross the Rue du
Four, on to Boulevard St Germain and its metro station. Ahead on
the right is the church of St Germain des Prés, separated from the
pavement by a strip of shrubs dotted with a few statues.[5]

Walk round to the entrance of St Germain des Prés, the oldest church in Paris (though St Julien le Pauvre, in Walk Two, will dispute the title), notwithstanding much re-building, and described at length in all the guide books. It has a large congregation, to be seen hurrying towards it on Sunday mornings. Later, as the faithful spill out, they have a choice of three eateries – Les Deux Magots,[6] immediately across from the west door; Flore, long the home from home of Sartre and Beauvoir on the next corner with the Rue St Benoit, and across the road, the Brasserie Lipp, bright with ceramic birds. Stop for coffee or lunch and to admire the striding Zadkine abstract,[7] then head round the Place St Germain, under Sartre's erstwhile windows, to the north side of the church into the Rue de l'Abbaye (for St Germain was the chapel of a Benedictine abbey founded in the sixth century), stopping to look into the tiny Square L Prache.

Here among fragments of medieval sculpture, is Picasso's bulbous 'Head of a Woman, in homage to Apollinaire', another habitué of Flore from 1912. Perhaps it was intended as a joke – the heavy, jowly head to commemorate the most playful and delicate of the symbolist poets (or *fantaisiste* as he preferred to call himself) a few months after giving a lecture on *La Sculpture Aujourd'hui*.

Walk on. A few steps further on the same side is the Palais Abbatial, a calm sixteenth century building, its red brick surprising in a generally grey city. At the next narrow turn to the *left*, go into Rue Furstenberg; it widens into Place Furstenberg, a lovely, much photographed square, with four ornamental trees and a bronze street light, built on the outline of the main entrance courtyard of the original abbey. On the west side a *porte-cochère* opens into a cobbled courtyard, and on its left a steep staircase to the first floor Musée Delacroix. For seven years to his death, he lived and worked here, building himself a large studio to cover most of the garden. What remains is a gravelled patio edged with trees, their crowns trimmed into boxes. The location was convenient for St Sulpice and the Luxembourg library; the studio (later used briefly by Monet and

Bazille) and large apartment of well proportioned rooms, would be extremely comfortable. To modern eyes his pictures are often rhetorical, invariably filmic, but he was the most successful painter in the idiom of his day. Do visit the apartment. Though few of Delacroix's pictures and fewer of his furnishings remain, it is plausibly the scene where, come midnight, he confided in his journal paragraphs as absorbing and less choleric than Berlioz' better known memoirs.

At its north end, Rue Furstenberg joins Rue Jacob. Turn *right* to the junction with Rue de Seine. You will be facing number 57 Rue de Seine, with its *façade classée* [that is, a preservation order], an attractive building that housed the unhappy Baudelaire for a few months. Other houses worth a glance are – the seventeenth century number 41; 46 and 49 almost as old; 54 and 56 date from 1744. Number 60 is the Hôtel de la Louisianne – in *The Unquiet Grave* Cyril Connolly mentions it in one of his litanies of hotels and, at the end of WW2, Simone de Beauvoir lived there cheerfully enough, to judge by *La Force de l'Age*. Number 31 was occupied by George Sand during 1831, the year she was writing *Indiana*, the first novel she published under that pseudonym.

The whole street was re-numbered later in the nineteenth century, but in 1822 the then number 42 was the bookshop of J.J. Paschoud, the Swiss publisher, who had his main shop and reading room in Geneva's Grand' Rue. In the spring of 1822 he printed in Geneva, but sold in both Paris and Geneva, an unabridged version, translator unknown, of *Pride and Prejudice*, as *Orgueil et Préjugé*.

It's worth loitering in Rue de Seine. It has beguiling shop windows. Eventually make your way towards the river, going north, past the Rue Callot to the right, with a statue evocative of the painter / etcher.[9]

At the next corner on the left, number 26 was a well-established tavern by the early seventeenth century. Called 'Le Petit Maure', the building retains, just below first floor level, a roundel with a smiling, turbaned head. Now a gallery, in more expansive times *lieu de*

rendez-vous cher aux buveurs [a favourite meeting place for drinkers],
it was apostrophised in 1628:

> Sus! Allons chez la Coffier
> Ou bien au Petit Maure.
> Je vous veux tous defier
> De m'enivrer encore.
> [Come on, let's go to Coffier's or to The Moorish Boy.
> I want to defy you all to see me drunk].

It's as good a *chanson pour danser et boire* [a dancing and drinking
song] as any, the more piquant for being penned by Pierre Ballard,
of the family that held the monopoly for printing music from 1522.
The street on the left is now called Rue Visconti; it was Rue des
Marais FSG – the ground was subject to flooding – until the nineteenth century. It was built piecemeal – the oldest houses are numbers 14 and 15. After 1540 (numbers 5, 7 and 9 date from 1547) more
houses were added, each with a large garden. Being so out of the
way, so miasmal a spot, the justly apprehensive Huguenots chose to
live there, and in such numbers as to justify its nickname La Petite
Genève.[10]

Reasonably enough it was the venue for the first Huguenot
national synod in May 1559; seventy-two congregations were
represented and all passed off peacefully. But the continuing persecutions – for the university and Paris with it were implacably
catholic – made it necessary to confer again. A second synod was
called for October. This time it was raided; fortunately all but four
representatives fled to safety. Even after the massacre of Protestants
(the massacre of St Barthélemy, 22 August 1572), the street
remained a refuge for them. Bernard Palissy, the renowned potter,
lived there for a few years before 1586. That year, as a Huguenot,
he was taken to the Bastille, where he died a few years later, still imprisoned without a trial – a fate somewhat preferable to being burnt
at the stake for heresy.

With additional buildings, the street took on something of an ecu-
menical air. On the left, as you go westward to Rue Bonaparte,

number 11 belonged to the family of the Abbé Prévost, sound in *la religion du roi*, notwithstanding their picturesque relative and his questionable publications. Numbers 13 and 15 belonged to the Dames de la Visitation de Ste Marie, and were let out to well-conducted Catholics, so providing income for the order. Opposite, numbers 12 and 14 belonged in 1642 to the Duc de la Rochefoucauld – he of the *Maximes*, their brevity and worldliness handy for adolescents trying to appear cynical. Both have large doors, pretty courtyards and staircases, if you can get to them. It's worth ringing the bells in the hope of getting a brief look.

Numbers 17 and 19, nowadays Flammarion's bookshop, were built in 1826. Balzac lived for a year in a flat on the first floor, while on the ground floor he had a printing and publishing business. His backer and mistress was Madame de Berny; he describes her in his *Le Lys dans la Vallée* of 1835, a great Romantic novel, in the character of Madame de Mortsauf, a lady whose perfect self-control and sacrifice screen passion enough for half a dozen bodice rippers. As a publisher Balzac was a disaster, so his business was taken over by his mistress's son; young Berny published Stendhal's *Le Rouge et le Noir* in 1830, was inventive with typography and prospered. Another early inhabitant of the same building, but on the second floor, was Delacroix (see above). After him the studio was taken over by Paul Delaroche. His canvases in the Louvre are not much visited.[11] They look like stills from 1930's films, especially the best known *Les Enfants d'Edouard*, or the princes in the Tower, wearing black velvet and cowering on a four-poster with green hangings, a jaunty spaniel at their feet.

Number 21, nearly at the corner of Rue Bonaparte, has a *porte-cochère* tall enough to have encouraged a new design for coaches. Across from it is number 24, a tumbledown, graffiti-covered mess. To us, familiar with the manicured conservation of Stratford-on-Avon, it comes as a shock to discover it to be the house where Racine rented a large second floor apartment for the last seven years of his life, working on a careful edition of his works and where, in 1699, he died. The neglect is astounding, particularly since it was never forgotten as being Racine's house. In 1860 the magazine *Musée Universel* featured an article by Villonsens, including an illustration of the courtyard's vine, referred to as *la vigne de Racine*. Through much of the eighteenth century the greatest actress of the time (not that Garrick thought so) Mademoiselle Clairon, lived there. The first and best triumph of her career was the name part in *Phèdre*, Racine's last and greatest tragedy. The French Encyclopaedia sums her up:

> Elle porta l'art jusqu'à la perfection, sa diction était remarquable et son accent passioné
> [She brought her art to perfection, her delivery was outstanding and the voice passionately expressive.]

So you'd think the building deserved a second plaque. Or even a third. For the house, built in 1667, was owned by Mademoiselle de Joncoux, a learned writer of the Jansenist persuasion The orphan Racine had been brought up by the Jansenists at Port-Royal;[12] they totally condemned his writing of tragedies for public performance and he was only reconciled with them after giving up the theatre of passion and cruelty. By then, appointment as historiographer to king Louis XIV kept him solvent and networking brought him to the former Petite Genève.

Number 16, in the widest part of the street, was built in 1682, an unremarkable building with a wide porte-cochère, the windows and pitch of roof are the only clues to its period. In the early eighteenth century one of its larger than life denizens was another actress, Adrienne Lecouvreur; her portrait features on the pictorial section of the Comédie Française web site. The name rings a bell with opera buffs, although the 1902 opera by Cilea is not much performed, despite being easy on the ear and romantic in the extreme.[13] No plaque commemorates her either. But the building and the street, awash with real and imagined passion, is the entirely appropriate setting for Maradan, *libraire*, at this same number 16, to publish late in 1821 a new, unabridged translation of *Pride and Pre-*

judice as *Orgueil et Prévention*, the only Austen novel where Darcy's 'utmost force of passion' is openly articulated. The translation was by Eloïse Perks, *jeune anglaise élevée à Londres* [young English-woman, brought up in London]. That is the only clue to her identity. Was she a small-scale Becky Sharp with literary ambitions, lingering in Paris six years into the Bourbon restoration? The title page of her translation echoes the London one – it says *par l'auteur de Raison et Sensibilité*. However 'Miss Jane Austen' is named as author in the list from the publisher A.N. Pigoreau for December 1821 – *Emma, Mansfield Park, Sense and Sensibility* and *Persuasion*, translated by various hands under their several French titles, are mentioned in the rubric: *tous ces romans et le dernier surtout, ont eu le plus grand succès* [all these novels, and especially the last, have had the greatest success]. Yet no evidence of success has been found; only introductions, translator's notes and advertisements provide any comment before 1882. Ponder for a moment this extraordinary street, the concentration of talent that dreamt, fretted, hacked to convey its vision. The street offers nothing for the pleasure of look-ing, everything to the imagination.

At the west end of Rue Visconti turn *right* into Rue Bonaparte and walk north towards the river. On the right is the opening into Rue des Beaux Arts. Hop down to number 13, still a hotel but now expensive, where Oscar Wilde died at loggerheads with the décor – 'It's the wallpaper or me, one of us has to go.' More recently Jorge Luis Borges, the Argentine poet,[14] stayed there several times.

Resume your walk north. On the left, west side, is the Ecole des Beaux Arts, where Paul Delaroche taught and painted frescoes in the half circle of the main lecture hall, and Matisse and Raoult learnt their trade from that weird master, Moreau. Exhibitions – for instance of the work by final year prize winners – are held in the building, but in those cases the entrance, marked by a banner, is from Quai Malaquais. The rest of the building is also occasionally open to visitors. Try to get in (ask at the entrance) just for the mix-ture of architectural fragments, complete rooms, most of the chapel of the seventeenth century convent of the Petits Augustins, hugger-mugger with pieces of sculpture. The juxtaposition of styles and objects makes for an enlivening jumble of shapes.

LE PARC

DE MANSFIELD,

ou

LES TROIS COUSINES,

PAR L'AUTEUR DE RAISON ET SENSIBILITÉ, OU LES DEUX MANIÈRES D'AIMER; D'ORGUEIL ET PRÉJUGÉ, etc.

TRADUIT DE L'ANGLAIS,

PAR M. HENRI V*******N

TOME PREMIER.

———

PARIS,

J. G. DENTU, IMPRIMEUR-LIBRAIRE, rue des Petits-Augustins, n° 5 (ancien hôtel de Persan). 1816.

Almost at the end of Rue Bonaparte, at number five, is another large, hollow E building, the former Hôtel de Persan. Monge, the mathematician who went to Egypt with Napoleon's expedition and had a hand in founding two powerful bastions of the French elite, the Ecole Polytechnique and Ecole Normale Superieure, lived there, and where the painter Manet was born in 1832. The building was also large enough to accommodate Dentu, publisher and bookseller, and his printing press. In 1816 he brought out *Le Parc de Mansfield* translated by Henri Villemain.

Jane Austen was a minnow for his business, but for the progress of books and printing in the nineteenth century, Dentu was a most important figure.

You are now at the river, Quai Malaquais to your left. Look at number 9, and you will see a late nineteenth century entrance. But if you look at the elevation you will see that the proportions are those of an earlier building. This was the Hôtel de Transylvanie, a well known gambling den in the previous century. According to the plot of *Manon Lescaut*, that novel–within–a–novel by Abbé Prévost, it was where Des Grieux lost all his money. He and Manon were then arrested, put into chains and transported to the French New World colonies, that is Louisiana. Prévost goes on describe an entirely imaginary landscape, 'a desert in Louisiana', which is the scene of Manon's death, and very affecting both in the text and the opera by Puccini. Should you manage to get inside the building, climb up to the first floor just to see the beautiful doors leading into the gambling salon. If you are lucky enough to have friends in the attic floor flat, you will have magnificent views northward to the Louvre, or east to the Ile de la Cité.

Your third walk is now finished. You might like to walk downstream, to the Musée d'Orsay, to see Manet's portrait of Mallarmé and many impressionist delights. The d'Orsay also has one of the best museum shops in Paris. Or you might walk across the river on the pedestrian Pont des Arts and, if you are lucky, find an exhibition of sculpture on the bridge, before the pleasures of the Right (north) Bank claim you.

Or, if you can't tear yourself away from the Latin quarter, turn *right* as if you were going back to Rue de Seine. Just where the street reaches the back of the Institut de France – which you will know by its cupola – there is a small open space with a fountain by Evariste Fragonard, son of the better known painter of blushing girls. (Remember *The Swing* in the Wallace Collection in Manchester Square, London?) Walk past the fountain and take the fork into Rue Mazarine, leading you back towards metro Odéon on Boulevard St Germain. Carrefour de Buci was the site of one of the gates into the fourteenth century walled city and where, in 1792, nine priests were murdered to kick off the September massacres. Here the street changes its name to Rue de l'Ancienne Comédie, because on the site of number 14 the Comédie Française had its first custom built home. Opposite is Le Procope, now a restaurant but, traditionally, the first coffee shop in Paris. Voltaire and Napoleon patronised it, as well as George Sand, Balzac, Verlaine, Huysmans and Wilde. You will be able to admire the wall-paper with ribbons of revolutionary tri-colour. Bon Appetit!

Walk Three — Notes

1 Tea room: The similarly named shop in Geneva was modelled on it.

2 Number 26: In 1962 Georges Bataille died there, a depressing writer fixated on eroticism and mysticism. When he came up for air and considered the visual arts, he had sensible things to say, about the painter Manet for instance.

3 [To establish the fluctuations in the precessional movement of the earth's pole about the obliquity of the ecliptic.]

4 Faubourg St Germain was originally, like all the other faubourgs, outside the walls of the medieval city. FSG was added to the names of some of its streets until the large-scale re-modelling of the city in the nineteenth century. This distinguished them from streets with the same name in other parts of the expanding capital. In this particular case, there is, to this day, a Rue du Pot de Fer in the 5e arrondissement (the modern administrative district), south-east of St Sulpice. The current R Pot de Fer is distinguished twice over — by leading to the Ecole Normale Supérieure, one of the forcing houses of the French élite, and being described by George Orwell in *Down and Out in Paris and London*.

5 Statues: One of these is of Bernard Palissy, the Huguenot artist-potter, inventor of coloured glazes. He is known for dishes decorated with plants, fruit and animals modelled from life. Another of his innovations was to create moulds of these decorative items, so that they could readily be multiplied and combined as commissions demanded. A few of his colourful pieces can be found on the ground floor of the Victoria and Albert Museum, South Kensington, London.

6 Les Deux Magots: Two large oriental statues of squat, ugly characters (Magots) are to be seen inside the café. Between the wars it was patronised by then rising literary celebs, like James Joyce and Ernest Hemingway.

7 Zadkine: If you are into modern sculpture and have time, the Zadkine museum is at 100 bis Rue d'Assas, just to the west of the Luxembourg gardens. The small house and studio frame a delightful garden.

8 Apollinaire: Throughout his short life (he died in the 'flu pandemic of 1918, aged 28), he championed the avant-garde. His thirst for novelty included making a recording of his poems on wax cylinder, a sad, rhythmic sing-song, reminiscent of Yeats similarly recorded, and quite at variance with the typographical extravaganza of some of his poems, or *Les Mamelles de Tiresias*, quarried by Poulenc for a libretto and wittily staged by English National Opera, starting in 1979.

9 Callot: An early seventeenth century etcher and engraver of great verve and inventiveness. His series *Les Misères et Malheurs de Guerre* are pre-

cursors of the better-known *Disasters of War* by Goya, nearly two hundred years later.

10 La Petite Genève: Rue des Marais FSG was so nicknamed because the religion of the first group of inhabitants, Protestant Calvinism, came from Geneva (see Huguenots, Jansenists and the tragedies of Racine).

11 Paul Delaroche: In London's National Gallery in Trafalgar Square, you will find one of his large canvases, *The Death of Lady Jane Grey*, in a room full of smaller and more attractive pictures. One version of *Les Enfants d'Edouard* can be seen in the Wallace Collection, Manchester Square, London.

12 That is Port-Royal-des-Champs, now in ruins, a park on the D 91. Confusingly there is also a metro station called Port-Royal on RER line B, a line taken by travellers from London, going from Gare du Nord into the centre. It is one stop beyond Luxembourg, the metro station for the start of this walk.

13 Adrienne Lecouvreur: Adriana, as she is known in opera, was historically an actress – *l'une des premières à s'exprimer de façon naturelle et nuancée*. In other words, her style of speaking was the more naturalistic one of Garrick, rather than the older, declamatory style of Quin. Like Clairon, Lecouvreur's big success was with *Phèdre*. She was a friend and mistress of Voltaire, she championed his plays. Her many lovers included Maurice, Comte de Saxe, grandfather to George Sand the novelist, who, a hundred years later, lived round the corner in Rue de Seine. Maurice, a brilliantly successful general, was a rough diamond; Adrianne loved, humanised and civilised him. Cilea's opera, based on fact, has the familiar device of a performance within the performance – at a reception, Adriana is asked to give a recitation and chooses a passage from Act 3 scene 3 *Phèdre* to signal, by inference, the treachery of the mezzo-soprano (a short but telling part), who then poisons Adriana with the unusual device of a bunch of violets, their scent masking lethal exhalations. According to the stage directions the death takes place in Adriana's drawing room in Rue des Marais / Visconti, with the trees in their March greenery visible through the windows. Clearly the gardens in Rue des Marais / Visconti counted even in 1902. The four act opera has three attractive love duets for Adriana and Maurizio, the last enhanced by being part of the death scene.

14 Jorge Luis Borges: The poet is described in the 1998 Larousse biographical section as the re-writer of mythologies, nightmares and labyrinths, components of a real or imaginary library. Don't be put off. In the 1985 Penguin edition of his selected poems, with translations by several American poets, all are accessible (try *Chess* from *El otro, el mismo*), evocative, and even when veiled by English, often moving.

Le Luxembourg

The history of this beautiful garden and its lumpy palace weaves in and out of the literary concerns of our walks. It started in 1600 when Marie de Medici, the new queen of France and second wife of the pragmatic Henri IV, arrived from Florence to find the Louvre had not been prepared to receive her. Its smelly moats made a healthier Paris base desirable. However, she had to wait to be widowed after the 1610 assassination of her husband before she could realize her project. She had her eye on the Left Bank, on a house belonging to François de Luxembourg. This grandee had been ambassador extraordinary and had brought the condolences of James I of Great Britain, on the death of Henri IV. Counting on his loyalty, she borrowed his house for a fortnight and, two years later, bought it with its gardens and park. She moved in promptly with her children, the boy-king Louis XIII and his brother Gaston, the future duc d'Orléans. Since not all the rooms in the house were needed, she used some for a group of Greek and Turkish girls doing fine embroidery. She ordered tree planting to start at once and on the other side of Rue Vaugirard had an ice house and her numerous dogs, hens and other animals settled in great comfort. All her life she preferred animals to people – her documented indifference to her husband and coldness to her children look like a vestigial template for Lady Bertram in *Mansfield Park*.

So when work on the Luxembourg Palace started, Marie de Medici was Queen Mother and regent for her son Louis XIII. In contrast to her late husband, the common-sensical Henri IV, she greatly favoured the Catholic faction in France and, in external policy, Spain, its main champion. She was rash enough to intrigue against her son after his majority, to the extent of provoking a brief civil war. It took all the powers of her almoner, cardinal Richelieu,[1] to obtain her pardon and, come 1625, they were in residence side by side – she was in her almost finished palace, he in the Petit Luxembourg (that is the original house on the site) while his new home was being built on the site of the present Palais Royal, conveniently close to the king in the Louvre.

Richelieu's star was in the ascendant – the year before, at the Queen Mother's instigation, he had been appointed to the king's council. The Queen Mother planned to maintain her influence with the king through Richelieu, and certainly he was no protector of the Huguenots / Protestants – for instance he undertook successfully the siege of La Rochelle, a Huguenot stronghold on the Atlantic coast.[2] So the Queen Mother could relax and attend to her new palace[3] and garden – she added a grotto with statuary, now the Fontaine de Medicis; she had her animals and from 1627, her grand–daughter, the little Duchesse de Montpensier, daughter of her second son, Gaston Duc d'Orléans. This little girl is the only member of the family to whom the Queen Mother is described as showing affection.

Poor little girl, she needed it. Her mother, a mighty heiress, died in childbirth; her father, Gaston d'Orléans, was at best totally un-interested in her, except as France's richest heiress, through her dead mother, and he was managing his daughter's fortune. She lived in the Tuileries Palace, surrounded by waiting women who spoilt and flattered her. Little instruction came her way; she was con-stantly reminded of the grandeur of her birth and the size of her fortune; vanity and self-will went unmoderated by intelligence, but the king, Louis XIII and his wife, still childless, showed her much affection. She disliked Richelieu, the 'ogre', and was not alone. For Richelieu, once ensconced in the king's council, so to speak changed sides, and set about centralising and reinforcing the king's powers, effectively side-lining the Queen Mother. Piqued, the Queen Mother intrigued against her former chaplain, and one November morning in 1630 thought she had persuaded the king to dismiss Richelieu in disgrace. Her cronies and sundry enemies of Richelieu hurried round to congratulate her. But an evening proclamation re-stated Richelieu's position as the king's trusted first minister. This turn–around day became known as *la journée des dupes*. The Queen

Mother's cronies ran for cover; she could not, and so was exiled. The Luxembourg Palace, officially unoccupied, and the park – in those days four times as extensive as now – remained part of the royal estates, later assigned to the king's younger brother Gaston, duc d'Orléans and father of the young Duchesse de Montpensier.

Her colloquial title was La Grande Mademoiselle; she continued in the Tuileries Palace, except when summoned to court, in whichever royal castle it might be temporarily residing. In 1638 it was at St Germain–en–Laye, where, at long last, an heir to the kingdom was born. Immediately the idea was floated that the baby, the future Louis XIV, should marry La Grande Mademoiselle. This would have the advantage of transferring to the senior royal line the immense fortune of the junior and neutralize the continuing intrigues of Gaston d'Orléans, father of the proposed bride. La Grande Mademoiselle, aged all of eleven, delighted at the prospect of being queen of France and referred to the baby as *mon petit mari*. This was judged so totally inappropriate that she was sent away to Rueil-Malmaison and given a strict governess, in the hope of inculcating tact and modesty. Alas, she grew up to be sadly unattractive, romantic, ambitious and lacking judgement. Her father, with his new wife, was back at court and living in the Luxembourg palace, now known as Palais d'Orléans, a name retained till the Revolution. There, as the history books say, *il mena une vie d'intrigues, vie d'artiste et de bibliophile* [he led a life of intrigues, of an art lover and bibliophile].

The intrigues, against the king of course, were the real trouble. In 1642 Gaston d'Orléans was involved in the conspiracy against Richelieu, as led by Cinq-Mars, familiar from the novel of the same name by Alfred de Vigny, *le Walter Scott français*. At the last minute Gaston panicked, betrayed the conspiracy and saved his own neck. A few years later he was involved in *La Fronde des Princes*, a civil war against Louis XIV, aged 11. This time he sent his daughter to the town of Orleans, to establish the ascendancy of her father as head of the princely faction. A painting of her by Alfred Juhannot, a painter absent from the usual reference books, shows her as tall, stately, elegant with an almost Grecian profile. Ungenerous as the thought may be, the rule of thumb that in non-classical times a dead straight line from top of forehead to tip of nose denotes an IQ below average, seems to apply in this case. La Grande Mademoiselle was ostentatious in her support for the princes, who went on to attack Paris. The king's soldiers mounted a spirited counter attack, the princes had to run for it, and to cover their retreat she gave the order for the cannons of the Bastille, a royal fortress, to fire on the king's troops. End of her hopes of marrying Louis XIV.

As soon as order was even half restored, the king exiled Gaston d'Orléans and La Grande Mademoiselle from court. They were to live on one of their many estates in France. Gaston refused to have anything to do with his daughter, and she, casting about amongst her castles, settled on the least dilapidated Saint-Fargeau, between Paris and Auxerre. For the time being the Luxembourg palace was occupied only by flunkies, but the grounds were opened to the public and much enjoyed.

For five years La Grande Mademoiselle was in internal exile. She busied herself by getting Le Vau to remodel Saint-Fargeau, she wrote her memoirs, she took an interest in her estates (grossly mismanaged by her father), she received guests, she hunted with ardour, using her other castles in the area as hunting boxes.[4] Alas La Grande Mademoiselle lacked the inner resources invoked by Mrs Elton, so all these activities failed to keep boredom at bay. Away from court, life was an irritation. Even marriage to the exiled Charles II of Great Britain would have been an improvement. But, despite being penniless, he had shown no empressement for her and she had despised him for his lack of table manners (he had preferred beef and mutton to ortolans) and his lack of a kingdom.

Eventually Louis XIV relented and invited her back to court life. To show her gratitude she gave a splendid ball for him at the Palais d'Orléans (that is Luxembourg), where she was allowed to establish her own court. Marriage with the psychotic and sweaty king of

Portugal was proposed. She refused and was sent back to Saint-Fargeau where, having imperfectly drained the moat, she found herself living in a swamp. She sought permission to move to a healthier location and was allowed to go to Vernon, a small town very close to Monet's garden at Giverny. Swimming in the Seine was healthy enough but there was nowhere to walk. Again she was bored until the spring of 1664 when, grudgingly, she was allowed back to Paris, and she moved into the east wing[5] of the Luxembourg. By now she had learnt never to pass judgement on her cousin, the king Louis XIV – *Il est au dessus des autres* [he is above the others]. Court life was punctuated by a comet visible over Paris, the death of the king's mother (Anne d'Autriche who had been kind to her as a child), the disappointed hope of marrying the widower Holy Roman Emperor, the indignant refusal to marry the Duc de Savoie (a duke, forsooth!), the war to obtain the small eastern province of Franche-Comté, and the growing ascendancy of the king's new mistress, Madame de Montespan. In 1669 La Grande Mademoiselle organised large-scale festivities in the Luxembourg, including a performance of Molière's *Tartuffe*. This was something of a declaration of independence on her part, since the play – about the hypocrisy of the supposedly devout – had been denied all performance for five years.

Then, at the age of 42, she fell irremediably in love. She was desperate to feel, for once in her life, the sweet comfort of being loved by someone whom she thought worth loving. The not-so-unlucky man was Lauzun, a totally duplicitous courtier, whose overruling vanity sought two things only – the king's visible favour and money. He played her like a fish, poor stupid rich girl. She even obtained the king's permission to marry. But Lauzun's insistence on the particulars of the marriage settlement delayed its composition long enough for opponents of the marriage to regroup and persuade Louis XIV to withdraw his permission. Lauzun discovered that the king's mistress, Madame de Montespan, had led the opposition, and totally losing his cool, taxed her with this and insulted her. Louis

XIV demanded an apology; Lauzun sent in a justification. Result –
ten years' solitary confinement in Pignerol, an isolated prison in
Piedmont, to which he was escorted by Monsieur d'Artagnan,
nephew of Dumas' model for the hero of *Les Trois Mousquetaires*.

La Grande Mademoiselle, still based in the east wing of the
Luxembourg, was beside herself. For the best part of ten years she
tried everything to get Lauzun freed. The price was very steep – she
had to cede to the king's son by Madame de Montespan her two
most valuable properties. Under protest, she paid up. Lauzun was
freed, initially to go to a spa, to restore his health. To anchor his
affection, as she thought, La Grande Mademoiselle made over to
him Saint-Fargeau and a few other of her estates. By February 1682
Lauzun was back in Paris, showing no affection for her, but visiting
all the royals and his former enemies, in an ostentatious display of
forgive and forget. However, one item was embedded in his
memory – the remaining fortune of La Grande Mademoiselle. He
manoeuvred her into paying him 'damages' of 550,600 livres, a
fortune, in compensation, he said, for meddling in his life – without
her intervention he would have prospered under the king's favour.
To do him justice, he spent the money well – he had Le Vau build
him the magnificent Hôtel Lauzun on the Ile St Louis.[6] Possibly
there was a secret marriage between them. They certainly stayed in
one of her castles, occupying adjoining bedrooms. Of course it
didn't last. In the summer of 1683 they literally came to blows. The
parting was final. Even on her death-bed in the Luxembourg, she
refused to see him. He, on the other hand, went from strength to
strength as the king's favourite and was granted a dukedom.

Why bother with this stupid princess and her rapacious para-
mour? Because they illustrate the absolute power of the king Louis
XIV. Even an excessively rich royal princess lived in fear of him;
without the king there was no advancement for a nobly born and
very competent soldier, as Lauzun had started out. The court, like a
black hole, sucked in everybody with the smallest claim to distinction, let alone Molière, Racine, the greatest exponents of French

classical literature. All were swept up. There was no scope for alternative modes of publicly expressed thought. This was *Le Grand Siècle*, the template for French greatness ever since.

In the meantime in Britain, shambolic after the Civil War, the plague, the Great Fire of London and repeated defeats by the Dutch, the king's central power was being whittled down energetically and re-distributed to land-owners and merchants. By the time Louis XIV died in 1715, Britain's king was the German-speaking George I, Parliament was well in the ascendant, and alternative life styles based on religious differences, tolerated. So when a century on, if Jane Austen was minded to take a serious look at her country's history, its 'great period' had been two hundred years earlier, based on the defeat of the Spanish Armada, by weather as much as bravery and skill, and much of the literature of this 'great period' was thought indelicate.

The versions of Shakespeare Jane Austen saw were the adapted ones, and known to be so, the texts re-fashioned at the whim of the actor–director. Authors modelled themselves on whomsoever they chose, for England had no official organisation akin to the Académie Française, to sanctify a body of native literature. While in the eighteenth century France remained emphatically top–down, England at the time of Jane Austen's birth was, if not bottom–up, substantially middle–up.

After the death of Louis XIV, the fame of the Luxembourg palace and its gardens spread, even to Russia – Peter the Great visited in 1717. The palace was renovated and writers took the air in the gardens; Rousseau reciting Virgil of a morning, Bernadin de St Pierre offering to read his works, Diderot letting the side down in his torn *redingote*. (The word is a corruption of 'riding–coat', and describes a double breasted, cut–away jacket.) In 1750 the palace opened twice a week to all comers, showing pictures from the royal collections. This was extremely popular and by 1774, the year before Jane Austen's birth, the Luxembourg estate brought in money, partly from the gardens where chairs could be hired and drinks and books bought at little wooden stands. Not so different from what obtains now.

Come 1778, king Louis XVI's younger brother, the Comte de Provence, moved in. He reckoned the building needed alterations. These were put in hand[7] to march in step with the redevelopment of the whole area where the new theatre for the Comédie Française was being built. There he stayed until July 1791 when, what with the Revolution getting very uncomfortable for the royal family, he managed to escape – he left in his carriage, calmly driving out of the main courtyard.[8]

The Luxembourg became a prison, *maison nationale de sureté*. Doors were bricked up, iron bars placed on windows and a stout wooden fence erected to separate the space immediately around the building from the gardens and park beyond, still open to the public.[9] By the summer of 1793, with the palace fully used as a prison, it held up to 900 inmates. As usual there were some informers, known as *moutons* [sheep], as well as, in October, thirteen members of the Convention (members of parliament), a job lot of English men and women, including Tom Paine, author of *The Rights of Man* and *de nombreux librares* [numerous booksellers / publishers]. Prisoners' families brought in food and clean clothes, or wandered about in the gardens beyond the fence, in the hope of seeing their loved one at a window or being seen by him.

At this stage the regime inside the building offered some solace – the doors of the rooms on a given floor were unlocked, so the prisoners could circulate, talk, play chess. In the evenings some played *vingt-et-un* at about the time when the jailer used to bring in the daily *liste de loterie* [lottery list] and the evening paper. The first gave the names of prisoners due for immediate removal. Carriages waited for them in Rue de Tournon, took them to the Palais de Justice on the Ile de la Cité for a mock trial[10]; the night was spent next door in the Conciergerie prison, ready for the guillotine in the morning. The evening paper gave a list of those executed that morning, that is, the previous evening's gambling partners.

Some prisoners were removed in the middle of the night. These were noisy episodes unless women were involved – they were brave and graceful to the end, according to one inmate. The rate at which these removals [*enlèvements*] happened varied. On one occasion it took one hour to carry off 150 prisoners. Their escorts returned blind drunk, threatening to defenestrate the remaining inmates.

Danton used his time in the Luxembourg to harangue anyone who happened to be walking in the gardens. He clung to the iron bars and shouted his speeches. His window became his soap box. One of his fellow-prisoners, Desmoulins, had been his secretary at the Ministry of Justice; a short-sighted young man, who asked for a new pair of glasses to be sent in, he wanted the better to see his weeping wife Lucille and their little son Horace, as they paced the gardens all day long. Sometimes Lucille was accompanied by Danton's very new young wife, a lady of greater self-control. Danton and Desmoulins were the most prominent of the *révolutionaires qui avaient déplu à leur parti pour avoir reculé devant le tableau des massacres projetés* [revolutionaries out of favour with their parties for drawing back from the planned massacres]. Their imprisonment lent substance to the rumour that Robespierre, their political arch-rival, was about to re-organise the Palais de Justice so that three hundred accused could be tried simultaneously. He was only dissuaded by *la crainte d'inciter une trop grande indignation* [the fear of rousing too great a degree of indignation].

At the end of July 1794 the prisoners inside the Luxembourg heard a great deal of noise from the city – church bells, tocsin, drums. Robespierre's government had fallen in its turn and he was brought to the Luxembourg, as the most comfortable prison available and therefore appropriate for the former Great Dictator. However the head jailer was not relying on the stability of this newest and more moderate government, hence the refusal, on a technicality, to take Robespierre into custody. Instead he was taken to an ordinary prison, where the inmates were much rougher than the educated men and women inside the Luxembourg. He tried to rouse them against the government, to overcome the guards by weight of numbers, but by then all classes longed for an end to the bloodshed. Nothing came of it and Robespierre lost his head on 28 July.

Within the month one palace–full of Luxembourg prisoners had been freed and replaced by Robespierre's former supporters. They included the painter David, who spent his time drawing, painting, planning two large set pieces. The second, *Les Sabines* [The Sabine Women] illustrates a legendary event – the Romans had carried off the Sabine women (a moment frequently painted) and a year later the Sabine men attacked the Romans to reclaim them. The interval had been long enough for the women to get used to their Roman captors and have their babies. David's painting shows these intrepid ladies, interposing their bodies, in various forms of undress, between the combatants and stopping them in mid–fight. It is a moment of dramatic stillness that takes the viewer to the summer of 1794, when the Terror came to an end.

Needless to say, stories of revolutionary bloodshed circulated in England. Jane Austen is likely to have heard particular ones from her cousin Eliza de Feuillide (née Hancock), whose husband was guillotined in February 1794. Possibly more came from her god-father, the Rev. Samuel Cooke, with whom she stayed. He was vicar of Great Bookham, well within gossip–carrying distance of Juniper Hall, that haven for destitute French royalists, so movingly de-scribed by Fanny Burney.

The Luxembourg palace did not stay as a prison for long. The next form of French government, Le Directoire, held its meetings there; the courtyard was the preferred site for celebrations, notably in December 1797, when Napoleon Bonaparte, victorious in Italy, triumphantly presented the peace treaty he had forced on a humiliated Austria[11] as well as all the flags captured in the campaign. There were speeches, music, singing, ladies fluttering their handkerchiefs from first floor windows, according to Madame Recamier, Madam de Staël's great friend. The museum was reinstated and the architect Chalgrin commissioned to remodel the interior, to accommodate the Senate.[12]

The Senate has occupied it ever since, with a short break during WW2, when the German Luftwaffe used it as its regional HQ.

Le Luxembourg — Notes

1 Richelieu: There are two portraits of him in the National Gallery in London, both by P. de Champaigne, one full length and another a triple one.

2 La Rochelle: A picture of the siege, showing very clearly how the British fleet was unable to come to the rescue of the Huguenot inhabitants, is in Dyrham Park, a National Trust property 8 miles north of Bath.

3 New Palace: The building of Marie de Medici's new Luxembourg palace was entrusted to a Protestant, Solomon de Brosse, but in 1615 religious tolerance, especially for people of talent, was still the order of the day. A few years later Rubens was brought in, to advise on the decorative scheme. After moving in, the Queen Mother (as Marie de Medicis was now known) still kept an apartment in the Louvre, which was visible from the main entrance of the Luxembourg, down the present Rue de Tournon, Rue de Seine and across the river.

4 Hunting boxes: Motorists familiar with the area may remember Ratilly, not only for the fairy-tale rise of grey stone from among the trees but, once inside the gatehouse, the cheerful bustle of the pottery or the summer music festival.

5 East wing: The west wing was occupied by her stepmother, her father's second wife. Relations were not easy.

6 Ile St Louis: Baudelaire lodged on the third floor while writing most of *Les Fleurs du Mal*.

7 Alterations in hand: While the work was in progress he moved, with his mistress, into Le Petit Luxembourg, the original house on the site, now at the west end of the complex.

8 Main courtyard: It was his only means of getting away, since at age 36, he already had great difficulty in walking. In his twenty-one year exile, much of it at Hartwell Manor in Buckinghamshire, his mobility decreased, his girth increased and he became known as *Le gros monsieur*.

9 Open to the public: You can find a picture of it in the Louvre. Louis David, the revolutionary painter of the death of Marat (see Revolutionary Paris), was himself locked up for several months. From his window on an upper floor he shows a few inmates in the prisoners' exercise area and a few

members of the public on the far side of the fence. It is his only known
landscape.

10 Mock trial: One prisoner describes how his trial was attended by a number of gossiping women, who sometimes interrupted proceedings by shout-
ing. At the end, one said to another: *Ma voisine, viens prendre le café avec
moi, nous irons ensuite le voir guillotiné.* [Neighbour, come and have a coffee
with me and then we'll go and watch him guillotined.]

11 Austria: Before its defeat by Napoleon's army, Austria had suffered
another affront at the hands of revolutionary France – Marie-Antoinette,
wife of Louis XVI, who had been guillotined like her husband, was an
Austrian princess. At the time in the kingdoms of Europe this was seen as a
particularly heinous offence. While the French might, at the last extremity,
be excused for killing their own royal house, to visit the same fate on a
princess from another country, was totally beyond the pale.

12 The Senate: During the Bourbon restoration, 1814 to 1848, the Senate
was known as *La Chambre des Pairs,* [the House of Peers] and Delacroix invited to decorate the cupola in the library. A monument to him in the
gardens has draped bodies, sweeping upward, bearing palms and laurels to
crown the tight-lipped figure, his overcoat topped with something very like
a pashmina. Also the literary flavour of the gardens was maintained – for
instance by Baudelaire, who played there as a child; or by Henry Murger,
with Mimi on his arm (he wrote the novel *La Vie de Bohème,* on which
Puccini's opera is based), used to meet Victor Hugo for a chat.

Rue de l'Odéon

When James Joyce, with Nora and two children, arrived in Paris on 8th July 1920, his only regular source of income was £100 pa from the British Civil List, operative since August 1916. It seems amazing that at the height of the battle of the Somme and with the Easter Rising fresh in the memory a quick circuit from Ezra Pound to Lady Cunard, Yeats and George Moore to Eddie Marsh, the Prime Minister's secretary, and Asquith himself, should produce this at-the-time-significant sum, for an Irish writer living in Italy.[1] Of course, for a household as extravagant and dysfunctional as Joyce's the sum was totally inadequate. But he was a sponger of the first order, literary genius notwithstanding, and had many financial supporters, Ezra Pound in the first instance.

Within a week of Joyce's arrival, Pound ensured that he met Adrienne Monier of La Maison des Amis du Livres, a bookshop and lending library, at 7 Rue de l'Odéon, and her American colleague Sylvia Beach, whose shop Shakespeare & Company was at number 12.[2] Before the end of the month tentative arrangements were afoot to print *Ulysses*, still unfinished, in France. The text was considered so grossly indecent that no English printer would chance his arm with it in book form, although a few extracts had appeared in magazines as early as 1919. In 1920 episodes published in the *Little Review* had fared less well – the US Post Office had confiscated and burned four issues of the magazine containing extracts; prosecution for obscenity was likely to follow. It did, in February 1921. So with potential American publishers crying off, it was France or nothing.

And so it turned out that French literati rescued the English-language novel. (At the time English was not yet perceived as the emerging global language, about to supersede French as the international language of the educated.) A revolution in the form of the novel was at stake and the French, as instigators and heirs of revolutionary glory, were going to push it. And was not this one the more immediately attractive because it required no effort other than talking and a bit of writing, no sacrifices, not even the exquisitely accurate translation that Jane Austen's limpid irony demands? Besides Joyce was Irish, and the Irish generally anti–English, their Anglo–phobia historically supported by France and the USA. Emotions and interests combined under the banner of France, as the nation above all others that gives literature the prime position in the identities and arts of all nations.

Adrienne Monier and Sylvia Beach took Joyce under their wing. Crucially, Sylvia introduced him to Valéry Larbaud, a minor poet under the name of A.O. Barnaboth (he wrote an unusual ode about travelling by long–distance train), a man of letters with a liking for English writers. Larbaud had translated Coleridge and Landor, and at the time of the introduction was busy on Samuel Butler.

Joyce and Larbaud liked each other on sight. Larbaud was enthusiastic about such portions of *Ulysses* as had appeared in the *Little Review* and wanted to translate them into French. Adrienne was less enthusiastic since she, as editor of *Cahiers des Amis du Livre*, was interested in Larbaud as an original writer from her stable. Come April 1921, Adrienne put Sylvia in touch with her own printers in Dijon, and in September the first proofs of the Scylla and Charibdis episode got back to Joyce. He 'corrected' them, by grossly enlarging them, a habit abominated by printers, started by Flaubert and continued by Proust, although the latter had the excuse of printing most of *A la Recherche* at his own expense.

Larbaud kept up his proselytising efforts and in December 1921 gave a lecture at Shakespeare & Company. Two hundred and fifty people crammed into the shop (looking at the floor space now the figure seems scarcely credible); the mosaic pattern of the book was explained and Larbaud highlighted the novel technique of *monologue intérieur* – surely a lineal descendant of Jane Austen's free indirect speech, that 'modulation from the factual voice of the narrator into (the character's) thoughts and out again, (that) gives an innovatory foretaste of that flickering and subtle immediacy in representation of consciousness which is one of Jane Austen's great gifts to the English novel'.[3] The lecture evoked much applause and the party moved on to Les Deux Magots to celebrate.

Ulysses in English, printed in France, came out on 2nd February 1922, Joyce's fortieth birthday. A second printing in October was sold out in four days. In spring 1924 Larbaud and Auguste Morrel started translating *Ulysses* into French and Joyce started rowing with Larbaud, Adrienne Monier and Sylvia Beach. However, the ladies persevered – in 1929 Adrienne published the French translation; in 1931 Sylvia Beach the eleventh printing in English. By this time both were in some financial difficulty, what with the depression and their own generosity.

For years they had provided a meeting place for writers – with refreshment included – who had no other literary salon to visit. The latest book, the literary man of the moment, the poem about to be given its first public airing, the newest twist to a theory or critical insight, were discussed as among friends, some with recognised achievements, others just starting out. In recollections, Adrienne Monier has been likened to a bee, going from flower to flower, with an encouragement here, an introduction there, a hint to an editor, congratulations, welcoming with equal warmth the acclaimed writer and the talented beginner. Extracts from books were read, recitals given, new writing sympathetically received, conformity frowned on, all in a cheerfully relaxed atmosphere.

Sylvia Beach had developed into an important bridge between English and American writers and their French counterparts. Starting with a bookshop and lending library, she had become agent for Joyce, and poste restante, with banking facilities for some and housing for others. She had, for instance, for several years housed above her shop the composer George Amtheil, Ezra Pound's 'Bad Boy of Music', who wrote incidental music for Yeats and Fernand Leger.[4] Come the war, things got harder. Sylvia, as an American citizen, was in an ambiguous position at the start of the German occupation. The bookshop was on / off. More to the point, she had friends in the country and with their help, most weeks a rabbit – that is meat for a meal – reached Paris. Then one day a German came to Shakespeare & Company wanting to buy *Finnegan's Wake*. She refused. An altercation followed; she closed the shop 'for the duration', as the saying was.

In August 1944 the end was in sight. Allied armies were at the gates of Paris; in the city the communists organised active fighting against the Germans – it was also a convenient moment to pay off old scores. Eisenhower, the Allied Commander in Chief, gave the French column the go-ahead and, commanded by Leclerc, the Free French vanguard came in, closely followed by American tanks. Just as well, for isolated German troops were fighting on, in Rue de l'Odéon amongst others. A jeep drew up outside number 12, a familiar voice called out. 'It's Hemingway,' Adrienne cried. Sylvia ran down to find him in blood-stained, muddy battle dress. He lifted her off her feet, whirled her round, hugged her, to cheers of the suddenly appearing crowd. The ladies had one favour to ask – could Hemingway get rid of the snipers? He was happy to have his soldiers oblige and, waving goodbye, roared off to liberate the wine-cellar of the Ritz.

Rue de l'Odéon — Notes

1 The 1916 Easter Rising, that is in the middle of World War 1, it was a significant attempt by Irish nationalists to rebel against the British. July 1916 was the start of the battle along the river Somme, intended to ease pressure on French troops severely tested further south around Verdun. For the British, it saw the heaviest casualties ever sustained in a single day – some 20,000 killed and 40,000 wounded. The American poet Ezra Pound (1885–1972), author of the acclaimed *Cantos*, knew Lady Cunard, whose network of friends covered both the arts and politics. W.B. Yeats (1865–1939), dramatist, poet and Nobel Prize winner, and George Moore (1852–1933) the novelist much influenced by Balzac, were both approached by Eddie Marsh for an opinion of Joyce, since both were Irish by birth and schooling, and up to speed on Irish literary feuds. Yeats supported the grant from the British government to Joyce. Moore was lukewarm.

2 Do not confuse with the present Shakespeare and Co, on Square Viviani, see Walk Two.

3 Roger Gard in *Jane Austen's Novels – the Art of Clarity*, Yale UP 1992.

4 This happy instinct to hospitality was transferred to the new Shakespeare and Co on Square Viviani, and described in *Tumbleweed Hotel* by George Whitman's guests.

Reading Novels In Paris – 1815-1830

Searching for a Jane Austen-shaped gap through the distractions of Paris is, of course, a pleasure; wander the streets in more or less of a daydream, glance at the figures that made the city the delight to the senses and imagination that it is, and our heroine, back view only, slides in and out of focus. A call to order seems necessary. So take this to be the three raps that precede curtain-up at the Comédie Française, and think back to the 'heavenly half dozen'.

Between 1811 and 1828 London and Paris each saw nine editions of Jane Austen's novels. As far as can be made out, Jane Austen had no knowledge of the French translations. The first in Paris, of *Sense and Sensibility* [*Raison et Sensibilité*] came out in 1815, about five months after the battle of Waterloo, a time when France, defeated, was hosting a multi-national army of occupation. Normality was returning and fortunately the two successive kings of France, younger brothers of the guillotined Louis XVI, managed to maintain it to 1830.

So Jane Austen's view of life, however veiled by translation, fed into a period of consolidation, of generally peaceful rebalancing of the contending power blocs. There was time and space to look around, think, ask questions, about Britain for one – how had Britain escaped the excesses of a revolution and led, through long years, the eventually victorious opposition to Napoleon's France? Translations of English novels were clues to this puzzle. Walter Scott led the field,[1] Mrs Radcliffe was highly appreciated, Jane Austen was an also-ran in this cohort.

Jane Austen came into France on the coat-tails of the *Bibliothèque britannique*. The Genevan magazine had taken four monthly instalments, starting in July 1813, to serialise *Pride and Prejudice*, and similarly with *Mansfield Park*, starting in April 1815, that is during Napoleon's Hundred Days. Readers in Geneva had immediate access; readers in France a few days later, as soon as the bundles of copies, sent by stage coach at concessionary rates, reached Magimel, since 1797 the Paris agent for the *Bibliothèque britannique*; then he had them delivered by hand in the city, or outside it by the variable postal service.[2]

However, when in 1796 Marc–Auguste Pictet had first looked for a distributor in Paris, he chose three other *libraires* – Dupont, Maradan (who later published the first translation of the complete text of *Pride and Prejudice*) and Buisson. The last had published in 1786, three years before the Revolution, *Caroline de Lichtfield*,[3] the long–term best seller by Madame de Montolieu – translator of both *Sense and Sensibility* [*Raison et Sensibilité*] and *Persuasion* [*La Famille Elliot*]. She was a most diligent writer and a very capable networker. By 1815 she had contributed several times to *Mercure de France*, the most prestigious and best capitalised monthly in Paris, published by Arthus Bertrand, one of the major publishing houses in the capital.[4] In April 1815 Arthus Bertrand had brought out a third edition of *Caroline de Lichtfield*, a month before J.J. Paschoud in Geneva[5] had brought out a three volume set of her short stories and she had recently finished her translation, from German, of *The Swiss Family Robinson*, another long–term money spinner. How could Arthus Bertrand refuse his Swiss authoress her version of a novel *dans un nouveau genre* [of a new kind], even though it dwells *trop dans le cercle de la vie réelle* [too much within the confines of everyday life]. She correctly estimated its novelty for French readers, but she doubted its entertainment value. Therefore she jazzed it up, as she admits in her preface, because she feared that such ordinary, every-day events and feelings, without the least reference to the recent agitations and politics, would appear insipid to a readership weaned on stronger fare. So, limpid *Sense and Sensibility* loses its clear–eyed irony in risible sentiment.

It worked. As did similar treatment of *Persuasion* in September 1821. The comparative success of these two, even before their reprint in 1828, was acknowledged by the English translator, Eloise Perks, in her preface to a pretty faithful but heavy–footed version of *Pride and Prejudice* [*Orgueil et Prévention*] for Maradan at the end of

1821. Significantly, none of the straight translations of the four novels merited a reprint.

Jane Austen's novels were lost in an avalanche of literature,[6] increasingly in demand with the return of peace. Literacy rates had risen, and, with a much wider political franchise, reading was something of a democratic activity. However, very few limited their reading to political topics. Novels were the category in demand. Undoubtedly the majority of novel readers were women:[7] novels were seen as their genre, and their insatiable appetite for something so frivolous led to more being written, often by women, and profitably produced and marketed by male publishers.

The format was that of a modern, small paperback, about 19cm by 12, labelled '12 mo' (duodecimo, the size of a sheet folded to make twelve leaves), which was standard for unimportant, short-lived publications[8] destined for *cabinets de lecture*. These were reading-rooms, catering for the large fraction of the educated population who, during the revolutionary and Napoleonic wars, had lost their money but not their taste for reading. Therefore, a cheap subscription, giving access to reading matter in a specific location, or a slightly higher one, to allow taking out books and newspapers, filled a much felt want.[9]

The prices were graded from the cheapest, to give access to just one newspaper read for one hour on the spot, to the most expensive, to allow borrowing any book, newspaper or periodical. The prices were fine-tuned on several principles. The cheapest, for the sporadic reader, was to pay by the session − 20 centimes for newspapers, 30 centimes for newspapers and books, the sessions of unlimited length during opening hours, which were generally from seven or eight in the morning to ten or eleven at night, every day of the year. This suited students and the poorest readers, especially in the winter, when snacks were brought and the whole day spent in a quiet, companionable fug.[10] The most frequently used method of payment was the monthly subscription. Beyond that, tariffs varied − the price of reading a newspaper, to be kept for one hour only, changed depending on the hour of day it was picked up, the previous day's paper being half price; if pamphlets and books for reading *in situ* were added, the price rose; reading exclusively novels was cheaper than reading novels and other literature; taking books out to read at home was half as expensive as reading both at home and in the reading room. Annual subscriptions averaged about 30 francs. The cost of borrowing was increased by a compulsory 5 franc deposit, library fines were 5 centimes a day. It was also possible to subscribe for the number of volumes to be taken out; again novels were 50% cheaper than general literature. An *abonnement pour la campagne* [country membership], for an average of 30 francs, allowed about 30 to 80 volumes at a time. Remember, a standard novel was a three volume publication, and compare with The London Library in St James's Square, that, in 2002, allowed its country members fifteen books at a time.

The establishments also varied in what they offered – some had just a space to read; more offered both a reading space and a section from which to borrow books. Some bookshops had a reading room, many more had a lending library, more still had both. At the top end of the trade were the *salons littéraires*.

A grand one opened in 1826, just east of the Palais Royal, at numbers 44 and 46 Passage Choiseul, a glass-roofed street of small shops still worth wandering down. It consisted of a library on the first floor and a reading-room, devoted entirely to newspapers and journals, including, of course, the *Mercure de France*, on the ground floor. It advertised, amongst its 1120 listed titles ready for borrowing, books on science, natural history, medicine, literature, theatre, memoirs, translations of the classics and the most interesting works in foreign languages, travel books and novels. The catalogue has a subsection, listing the fourteen best-known authors. First, with thirty-four titles, is Madame de Genlis, whose *Adèle et Théodore* Emma refers to with seeming approval but whose *Alphonsine* Jane Austen started and then rejected on the ground of 'indelicacies which disgrace a pen hitherto so pure.'[11] Next comes Walter Scott with twenty-eight titles. Number three is the Abbé Prévost, whose *Manon Lescaut*, a novel within a novel, remains very much read to this day; in his day he was highly regarded for his translations from English, especially Richardson.[12] He weighs in with eighteen titles, closely followed by Madame de Montolieu, author of the best-seller *Caroline de Lichtfield* whose translations of *Sense and Sensibility* [*Raison et Sensibilité*] and *Persuasion* [*La Famille Elliot*] might well have figured among the seventeen titles to her name. Fenimore Cooper has only seven and Fanny Burney brings up the rear with three, but then she only ever wrote four novels.[13] The final subsection of the catalogue lists another 544 titles of novels.

At the other end of the scale were the entirely informal *cabinets de lecture* – one person with a pile of newspapers and an umbrella, a few wooden planks resting on low trestles for benches, with readers coming and going all day. Several were to be found along the Louvre walls. One step up was the *échoppe portative* [portable booth] in the Champs Elysées. But the majority of the 463 listed for Paris between 1815 and 1830 were like shops,[14] at street level, and half of them owned and managed by women. This equality of sexes was in part caused by the large number of modestly-monied, respectable and educated widows, who, in the aftermath of the wars, were looking for a socially-acceptable means to income; secondly, a *cabinet de lecture* had to have a police permit and a woman, with no obvious political leanings during the turmoil from 1789 to 1815, would be more likely to obtain one than a man with known earlier affiliations.[15] There were, of course, unlicensed *cabinets de lecture* and others that sometimes stocked what the police judged to be subversive material. One such was started by a supporter of the now deposed Napoleon; this owner was forced to hand it over to a friend, who also fell foul of the authorities, and also had to part with it to yet another friend.[16] This last, a Monsieur Veret, ran the *cabinet de lecture* as a profitable service to students; situated near the schools of law and medicine, it specialised in books needed by students of both, charged 15 francs a term, asked for no deposit on books taken out and offered a *salle d'études* [a study room] that was, understandably, always full.

However, the majority of *cabinets de lecture* were apolitical, bent on providing entertainment, that is novels. A look at the catalogues of the better-found establishments, that were regularly printed in *Bibliographie de France*,[17] shows that many chose to deal in novels only; for instance, a very extensive collection was held by Madame Cardinal in Rue des Canettes, a street going north from Rue St Sulpice. Half the catalogues were divided into Novels and The Rest; some into Novels, History and Belles Lettres, a division Eleanor Tilney would have appreciated. In general, 80% to 100% of titles refer to novels. The *cabinets de lecture* that carried less than 50% fiction tend to have been part of important publishing houses; these preferred lending out books to providing reading-rooms.

By 1828, when *Raison et Sensibilité* and *La Famille Elliot* were reprinted, sustained, silent reading, the standard practice in *cabinets de lecture*, was fed, in the first instance, by some 140 newspapers and magazines,[18] of which sixteen were devoted to literature and the theatre, another half dozen gave some attention to literature in other languages. The weeklies and monthlies between them offered a view on every topic, ancient or modern, that might take the money and hold the attention of the reader. But if readers persisted in demanding novels, the catalogues helped them in two more ways – there was a subsection on *nouveautés* [new books] for which a higher price was charged, and a list of favourite authors. In these, the names of 104 men and 68 women novelists are mentioned. Again Madame de Genlis, a very prolific author, wins by a neck, with twenty-seven mentions and is immediately followed by Walter Scott, with twenty-six. There are twenty-five mentions of Madame de Montolieu, translator, from English, of Jane Austen and, from German, of Auguste Lafontaine. The latter comes in, under his own name, at number eight. Mrs Radcliffe is at number ten, Fenimore Cooper at eleven. Even Balzac, who learnt his trade by writing gothic novels, rates only five mentions altogether for the several pseudonyms he used before 1829. Only then was he at last sufficiently confident of success to acknowledge authorship of *Le Dernier des Chouans*.

Cabinets de lecture were thickest on the ground round the Ecole de Médicine, and in the area from St Sulpice northward to the river. On the Right Bank, the area immediately north of the Tuileries, around the Palais Royal was even better supplied. Both were haunts of the *grande / haute bourgeoisie* and the *aristocracie financière* [the richest families]. The areas immediately adjoining, those of the merely *bonne bourgeoisie* were also well supplied. But further out, for instance the Invalides area (which, since 1889, boasts the Eiffel Tower) or l'Arsenal (around the new opera house Bastille) had fewer than five apiece. These were the residential areas of the *bourgeoisie populaire bésogneuse et sans argent* [necessitous and moneyless] and skilled craftsmen. In short, *cabinets de lecture* were features of the prosperous, middle class residential areas. Even in this context there was the expected sub-division – on the Left Bank scholars, students and readers seeking literary merit were more likely to find publications to their taste than on the Right Bank. This was increasingly focused on visitors, who came to sample the pleasures of the capital city. Both areas were also reasonably safe for single women to work in. In fact in 1816 one of them moved her *cabinet de lecture* from Rue Jacob (Walk Three crosses it) to 203 Galleries de Bois, in the Palais Royal.

Not that the Palais Royal was altogether respectable from 1815 to the next revolution in 1830. The *Galleries de Bois* and their immediate surroundings pullulated with prostitutes, who doubled as pick-pockets. There were in addition, and again according to Balzac, flower sellers, ventriloquists, street theatre of various kinds and a great deal of noise. The flimsiness of the construction meant that any quarrel in any one of the little shops was broadcast to all. A noisy police raid to confiscate a few dozen copies of a publication rejected by the government censor advertised it effectively and proclaimed the convictions of the publisher, who had hidden away the remainder of the print run. So bookshops, normally the scene of quiet conversation, added to the decibel count. A *cabinet de lecture* in this location hardly fostered the silent concentration evidenced at other addresses. On the other hand, the modest booths hiring out newspapers by the hour, were often in open spaces, mostly along the Champs Elysées, as an extra service to people out for a walk in the fresher air. The actual river banks, especially the north with barges loading and unloading, were considered places of ill repute consequently requiring no reading facilities.

Jane Austen's novels were lost in this welter of publication and noise. There was, however, one *cabinet de lecture* where her books in English may have made it to the bookshelves – Gagliani's.

Long-term visitors to Paris may recognise the name as that of a beautiful bookshop opposite the Tuileries gardens, at numbers 224 and 226 Rue de Rivoli. For many years it had the singular benefit of being open on Monday mornings, so that the last hours of a week-end and the last of the traveller's French currency could agreeably be spent, browsing or talking with the highly informed sales staff, before deciding on a purchase. But the shop's history is better still.

Around 1790 a young Italian, Giovanni Antonio Gagliani travelled from Padua to Paris, didn't like what he found and moved on to London. Here he is said to have married into the book trade, a Miss Parsons,[19] and in 1800 felt safe enough to return to Paris, with the intention of opening a shop to specialise in foreign books. He started the *Librairie Française et Étrangère*, in Rue Vivienne, a street leading north from the Palais Royal, along the east side of the old Bibliothèque Nationale. The war drove his father-in-law back to London, but come 1814 and Napoleon's first abdication, Gagliani was settled in Paris, sensibly judging that his peace dividend consisted of a large, English-speaking clientele, partly army of occupation (as in Thackeray's *Vanity Fair*) and partly English travellers (more than 20,000 in 1821) starved of France. In other words, much the same phenomenon as was repeated in 1945.

He cashed in. He started *Gagliani's Messenger*, a publication intended to help members of dispersed families in re-establishing contact with each other. He produced a *Picture of Paris*[20] for foreign visitors. He opened his *salon littéraire* on a generous scale – 20,000 volumes, with the catalogue regularly updated to highlight the novelties imported, a slew of newspapers in French, German, Spanish, Italian, English ones giving both the government and the opposition views. It was open from 8 am to 11pm. The charge was 4 francs for the fortnight, 6 for the month, 30 for six months and 55 for the year. Expensive, but worth it. An additional attraction was a list of all subscribers, with their addresses, to be consulted for a modest fee by anyone visiting the establishment. This consisted of the lending library service in a building at the far end of the court-yard. In the main building, on the street, a reading–room for news-papers was separate from more rooms dedicated to silent reading or writing, or polite conversation, with coffee. The whole was nearer a club, as English visitors understood the term, than a lending library.

If Jane Austen in English was to be found in any public place in Paris, Gagliani's[21] is the likeliest candidate. Theoretically, John Murray could have placed with Gagliani *Emma*, the third edition of *Mansfield Park*, *Northanger Abbey* and *Persuasion*. Alas, the period documents relating to the detail of Gagliani's transactions no longer exist, nor do John Murray's for the equivalent. The bookshop moved to its present address in 1856.

Reading Novels in Paris 1815-1830 — Notes

1 Walter Scott: *Waverley* came out in 1814, and the translation was selling well before 1817.

2 Magimel: as in Benoit Magimel, the film actor in *La Pianiste* [The Piano Teacher], *Les Amants du Siècle* (with Juliette Binoche), *Le Roi Danse*, etc.

3 *Caroline de Lichtfield*: Maria Edgeworth was a great admirer of Madame de Montolieu, or Madame de Crousaz, her first married name, under which she wrote the novel. In the 'Advertisement' for *Belinda*, a society novel published in 1801, Maria Edgeworth says:
'The following work is offered to the public as a Moral Tale – the author not wishing to acknowledge a Novel. Were all novels like those of Madame de Crousaz, Mrs Inchbald, Miss Burney and Dr Moore, she would adopt the name with delight. But so much folly, errour (sic), and vice are disseminated in books classed under this denomination, that it is hoped the wish to assume another title will be attributed to feelings that are laudable, if not fastidious.'

4 Arthus Bertrand: Visitors to Paris, in the area around Place St Germain des Prés, will find in Rue St Benoit (parallel with Rue Bonaparte in Walk Three) a shop labelled Arthus Bertrand. It sells extremely expensive modern jewellery and knick-knacks. If you penetrate inside, you will discover that it also designs and makes medals, for the Légion d'Honneur for one. The owner, Nicholas Arthus Bertrand, is descended from the publisher, but, moated in secretaries and PAs, does not communicate with independent scholars, a pity since he has documents relating to his ancestor. Another, and communicative, descendant is Yann Arthus-Bertrand, the photographer, whose magnificent book *La Terre Vue du Ciel* [The Earth from the Air] was one of the joys of the year 2000 – and remains so.

5 J.J. Paschoud: He was the Geneva publisher who co-operated closely with the owners / editors of the *Bibliothèque britannique*. This magazine dealt in extracts from English language books (See Geneva – *Bibliothèque britannique*). Once the serialisation had been completed Paschoud often brought out a translation of the whole text. This happened to *Pride and Prejudice* in 1822, translator unknown, as *Orgueil et Préjugé*, the same title as the four serialised extracts in 1813.

6 Avalanche of literature: Publishing as a highly successful commercial venture had been greatly enhanced in Paris before the Revolution by the publication of the *Encyclopédie des Sciences, des Arts et des Métiers*, the eighteenth century sum total of Western knowledge. It had been undertaken by a publisher called Panckoucke, working with printers near Lyon, in Neufchatel and Amsterdam, where exiled French Huguenot printers had

set up viable businesses. (See Huguenots etc.) Printing outside French territory had been necessary because the French official censor, alarmed at the contents of the articles, used a royal decree to put a stop to the enterprise. However, the house of Panckoucke weathered all the political storms. At the time Jane Austen's novels were coming out, it was known for highly regarded translations from Latin, a dictionary of medical sciences and *L'Almanach des 25,000 addresses des principaux habitants de Paris pour l'Année*, a kind of telephone directory before its time, published from 1815 onwards. But Panckoucke had sold *Mercure de France* to Arthus Bertrand at the start of the Revolution, so Madame de Montolieu, Jane Austen's translator, was never part of Panckoucke's stable.

7 Women readers of novels: Of course some men read novels, perhaps as light relief, or to humour their women-folk, or they just liked novels as Jane Austen and her family did, according to her letter 14, dated 18 December 1798. Certainly copies of some pre-Revolutionary novels, to be read in the Bibliothèque Nationale Française, come in beautiful bindings, with armorial bookplates, bearing the names and titles of their erstwhile owners. So at least a few aristocrats thought sufficiently well of the genre to include it in their libraries.

8 Short lived publications: It took Balzac, with his ambition of documenting the gradations and habits of society with the precision that Jussieu was bringing to the classification of plants, to insist on the importance of novels and obtain their publication in 8vo [octavo], reserved for books on serious subjects.

9 A much felt want: A *cabinet de lecture*, that of Blosse, is described, amongst other aspects of publishing, advertising and journalism, in *Les Illusions Perdues* by Balzac. It is a very long and ultimately very depressing book, written with much energy. A much jollier view of a *cabinet de lecture* is to be found in *Un homme d'affaires*, a dramatic story that would make a good comic opera, like Donizetti's *Don Pasquale*. It also has the benefit of being twenty pages long, a point of substance with Balzac – you need quite a lot of French, a good dictionary (his vocabulary is huge) and a head for keeping track of a number of intrigues and historical circumstances, to make sense, let alone enjoy, many of his novels. In England, he was sometimes considered a subversive influence, to the extent that in the three paintings by Augustus Egg, *Past and Present* (in the Tate Britain Gallery, on the Embankment) show the adulterous wife to have been corrupted by reading Balzac. These pictures were displayed in the Royal Academy in 1858, that is eight years after Balzac's death. But, if Ruskin is to be believed, it only goes to show how insidious the Continental poison was in undermining God-fearing Britain.

10 A companionable fug: much as Sartre and Beauvoir used the Café Flore during WW2.

11 A pen hitherto so pure: Letter 49, dated 7 January 1807.

12 Richardson: The Abbé Prévost was something of an Anglophile. He started and edited between 1733 and 1740 a magazine *Le Pour et Le Contre* [For and Against], describing life in Britain; in 1755 he directed the *Journal des Etrangers*, that aimed to familiarise French readers with literature in other languages. He translated and shortened Richardson's *Pamela, Clarissa* and *Sir Charles Grandison*, the second being particularly admired in France and deemed to be the only novel, apart from J.J. Rousseau's *La Nouvelle Héloïse*, to be deserving of serious attention. Richardson had started out as a printer, expanded into publishing and maintained a focus group of lady admirers, who advised him on a woman's take on particular events.

13 Fanny Burney : In 1778 she published, anonymously, *Evelina*; 1782 saw *Cecilia*, published by subscription and from it Jane Austen borrowed the phrase 'Pride and Prejudice' for her own revamped early novel; *Camilla* came in 1796 and kept Fanny and her émigré French husband in funds; *The Wanderer* in 1814 flopped, and was mocked by Jane Austen in her *Plan for a Novel*.

14 Shops at street level: In fact many were opened by regular shopkeepers [*commerçants*] – trade being poor, one possibility of generating income was to clear a part of the shop, scrounge a few chairs, place an order for the daily delivery of a few newspapers and, without a capital outlay, a *cabinet de lecture* was created, relying on the shop's regular, if sparse, clientele to form the nucleus of a new cash flow.

15 Earlier affiliations: These possible retrospective strictures were reinforced by a law of August 1814, (limited to the end of the parliamentary session of 1816) to re-impose censorship on all publications with fewer than 20 sheets; in other words, it covered all pamphlets, the then accepted way of conducting public debate. This was reinforced in November 1815 (that is after the adventure of Napoleon's Hundred Days) with a law *sur les discours et les écrits séditieux* [on seditious speech and writing]. The alternative penalties were prison for anything between six months and five years or a fine of up to 20,000 francs. The last was made more difficult by a shortage of cash, either notes or coin and the very debatable arrangements for credit. In 1819 the journalists' lot was mildly eased with the introduction of trial by jury for professional crimes.

16 From friend to friend: In 1817 Cauchon–Lemair had to hand it over to Foulon, who in 1822 had to pass it on to Veret, who hung on till 1830, when the July revolution ended the kingship of the Bourbon line.

17 *Bibliographie de France*: This was a regular, official publication giving a

less than exhaustive list of books, prints, music published in any one week. All Jane Austen's novels were listed in it. (See The Competition.)

18 Daily publications: By a decree of September 1811 Napoleon allowed only four daily papers. But from the Restoration in 1815, their number started increasing. Some newspapers, especially the better funded and more widely distributed, grasped very soon that it was worth subsidising the subscriptions of small shop and café keepers, to ensure control of the distribution network and with it enlarge market share, at the expense of newspapers of different political persuasions. So in 1824 there were six opposition broadsheets, six supporting the government. By the year 1828, the year *Raison et Sensibilité* and *La Famille Elliot* were reprinted, there were certainly as many as 136, possibly as many as 176, journals.

19 Miss Parsons: Between 1780 and 1801 the only Parsons in the book trade known to St. Bride Printing Library, is James Parsons, bookseller and bookbinder, at 21 Paternoster Row.

20 Picture of Paris: '. . . being a complete guide to all the public buildings, places of amusement and curiosities in the metropolis, accompanied by seven descriptive roads from the Coast to Paris, with full directions to strangers on their first arrival in that capital, by M. Gagliani, Paris, October 1st, 1814.'

21 Gagliani's: The 1833 edition of Jane Austen's novels had sponsors in four capital cities – Richard Bentley, London; Cumming, Dublin; Bell + Bradfute, Edinburgh; Gagliani, Paris.

The Competition

Imagine yourself in Paris in the summer of 1815. The war is finally over, Napoleon on the way to St Helena, the Bourbon King Louis XVIII restored, and life is returning to something like peace and predictability. Middle income men[1] are hanging on to political power, with consequential benefits, achieved during the years of turmoil. It is now a question of adding to or remaking fortunes, lost during the repeated bankruptcies of the state. Ladies are busy remodelling themselves, their homes, recreating polite society. What are they reading, apart from daily newspapers, perhaps a few journals, including a couple devoted to fashion?

With luck the family's pre-revolutionary library is not altogether lost, so the entertaining distraction of a few novels is to hand. Prévost's *Manon Lescaut*[2] remains a favourite, preferred, not least for its brevity, to his translation of *Clarissa*, Richardson's eight volume novel of coercion. This had long been admired for the depth of its characterisation and the tragic quality of the unresolved conflict. It was one of only two examples of the novel genre, both epistolary, to merit serious attention. The other was J.J. Rousseau's equally lengthy *Julie, ou La Nouvelle Héloïse*, a hugely successful work. There were something like a hundred editions between its first printing in Holland[3] and 1800. Its continued popularity during the twenty six years of upheaval lay partly in offering an alternative world anchored in a known landscape on the borders of France.

The public events, pretty few, are peaceful, the drama is entirely personalised. Julie, a rich and beautiful heiress, and her tutor, Saint-Preux, fall in love,[4] become lovers, though this is kept from her parents. Her titled father, a soldier of fortune, refuses to sanction marriage to a plain bourgeois because, a few years earlier, he had become friendly with Wolmar, a rich, aristocratic Russian officer, to whom he had promised Julie. Subsequent internal politics had deprived Wolmar of all his fortune and influence; Julie's father, a man of honour, insists on keeping his word. So Saint-Preux is sent away, and the marriage takes place. There is no hint of Wolmar's raising any objection to Julie being other than a virgin; he settles into the role of enlightened estate owner of Julie's inheritance and fathers a few children. A subsidiary complication involves that stock figure of French fiction, *le milord Anglais*, and Julie's cousin Claire, also in love with Saint-Preux.

A few years later, Saint-Preux having been round the world and acquired a fortune *en route*, returns to Clarens – he has been invited by Julie on her husband's insistence. Wolmar's plan is to prove to Julie that her love for Saint-Preux was calf-love, her real, learnt attachment is to himself. To modern readers his ostensible motive may be questionable, but, fairly rapidly for Rousseau (and this novel runs to 1500 closely printed pages, about the same length of Vikram Seth's *A Suitable Boy*) the affection between Julie and Saint-Preux is seen to persist unabated; there is an accident and Julie dies, explaining that she does so to avoid dishonour to herself and all her circle. Her death-bed declaration is unequivocal:

> Mon ame existerait-elle sans toi, sans toi quelle felicité gouterai-je? La vertu qui nous sépare sur terre nous unira dans un séjour éternal. Je meure dans cette douce attente. Trop heureuse d'acheter au prix de ma vie le droit de t'aimer toujours sans crime et de te le dire encore une fois.
>
> [Could my soul live without you? without you what happiness is there for me? The virtue that separates us on earth will unite us in an everlasting home. I die in this gentle belief, only too happy to pay with my life for the right to love you forever without transgression and to tell you so once again.]

Once you are settled into the book's slow pace, it is enough of a page turner for the reader to engage with the characters as real people. Why is Saint-Preux so meek, so lacking in bottle? Wolmar looks like a plain adventurer, with an eye to the main chance and a cruel streak, but he keeps his side of the bargain. Why is Julie in such a rage to be loved by everybody? She is presented as impossibly wonderful, *rayonnant l'amour* to all and sundry and having this love reflected back. All three are presented as behaving admirably. A modern reader's reaction is at least streaked with impatience. With the grumble out of the way, it is a book that tries to re-invent happiness and love, but in fact shows the first to be illusory and the second, even when returned, never satisfied, always unhappy. In this it is like the view of Racine's passion-fuelled lovers, their endless desire moulded into beauty by love, destined for death.

So, not 'too light and bright and sparkling'. It has 'shade' enough and is 'stretched out here and there' with passages[5] on landscape, suicide, conjugal fidelity, the link between virtuous conduct and happiness, between grief and forgetting, the contrast between the duty to accept the given life and the right to refuse it, or between the dash for pleasure and the appeal of innocence and sacrifice – mostly on the girl's part. Death is the entry to the frozen golden moment, therefore must be total happiness. Nowadays the novel reads as if it ought to be quarried for an operatic libretto, a kind of *Lucia di Lammermoor* without the mad scene. In its day it was fiction staking a large claim for itself, something like a dream flowering into daily life and giving it a new dimension, where feeling, sensibility, imagination permeates every moment.

Some way from Jane Austen, who demands moral integrity from her principal characters. Besides, two unresolved niggles remain – *La Nouvelle Héloïse* is an apt title because Rousseau's book glances back at the historic star-crossed lovers, Eloïse and Abelard, who lived in the early twelfth century. On the other hand, the 1816 translation of *Emma* calls her *La Nouvelle Emma*. Who is she an echo of and what is new about her? That she tries to find a husband for Harriet? Girls being married off at the will of a third party is the standard situation in European literature. Because she is an 'imaginist'[6] and believes that her fantasies make things happen in real life, much as Rousseau hoped to affect daily attitudes? That conviction is demolished several times by Mr Knightley, for one. Because, like Beauty in *Beauty and the Beast*, she wants to stay with her father and therefore delay marriage until after his death? She is talked out of that pretty quickly. Emma, after her several excursions into fantasy,[7] makes the most conventional marriage of all the Austen heroines, the boy next door. Is it that she marries Knight–ley / Preux – the French word means 'valiant knight', who lives at Donwell [Done well] and is not Knightley the least flawed, the socially most enlightened and altruistic of Austen heroes? So it looks as if the novelty resides in a heroine with great, if partly misguided, powers of imagination, who pairs off with Knight–ley, a man whose sterling character, like Saint–Preux's, is his main claim on the reader's sympathy; they are in a higher category, above the other inhabitants and visitors to Highbury. These are lumped together in the subtitle – *Caractères Anglais Du Siècle*, worthy of passing attention but not of admiration or envy.[8] Description of a community unthreatened by external events had little to offer readers emerging from years of strain to outwit national and personal disaster. Also without knowledge of village life in England Jane Austen's sensitivity to the finest social gradations was meaningless, even as a form of escapism.

Emma, when talking with Knightley about Mrs Weston's baby, refers to the theories of child–rearing in *Adèle et Théodore*, a 1782 book by Madame de Genlis.[9] It was sub–titled *De l'Education*. And so it is, both in its advice, on agony–aunt lines, to married and about-to-be-married ladies of the pre–revolutionary aristocracy, and in giving programmes for teaching children. What she has to say about, for instance, handwriting, remains entirely sensible. In addition the book has, perhaps as a consequence of twenty years' influence of *La Nouvelle Héloïse*, one noticeable feature – the carefully brought up son of the family is paired off, almost casually, with the daughter of suitable family friends. He is not asked about his feelings and expresses none beyond a generalised willingness to fall in with his parents' wishes. His sister, however, is consulted at every step, allowed to refuse a very eligible offer, and marries a childhood friend, her inferior both socially and financially. So girls are allowed fine discrimination and delicate feelings; the lads either lack them or over-ride them. Presumably the chaps are fortified by the assumption that, if dissatisfied, a mistress could be comfortably maintained as long as the first essential, marrying a good dowry, has been achieved. It takes another twenty-five years and an English setting for Jane Austen's young men to be uniformly as specific in their tastes as the girls, and, because they have to initiate the relationship, the more vehement in their emotions.

Another very different novel came out in 1782 – *Les Liaisons Dangereuses*,[10] familiar also from stage and screen adaptations. It was considered a thoroughly disreputable novel and as such not meant to come into a lady's hands. But many must have heard of it, fewer read it, perhaps with that disturbing prickle of the skin, when the corruption of youthful innocence and goodness is deliberately embarked upon, just for fun, and described in 477 pages of evil intent and useless hand-wringing. It was a highly successful novel, going through many reprints between 1782 and 1788. Did Eliza De Feuillide, Jane Austen's cousin then resident in Paris, bring it with her when she visited Steventon over Christmas 1782, or did she just mention it as the great *succès de scandale* of the first year of her marriage? In a family as fond of novels as the Austens, it would have been an obvious topic of conversation, perhaps also cropping up on one of Eliza's subsequent visits, in '87, '92, '96, by which time the novel had been translated into English.

For the common reader the question persists, because of the striking resemblance between the title character in *Lady Susan*, Jane Austen's one shot at an epistolary novel and Madame de Mertheuil, the instigator of the tragedy in *Les Liaisons Dangereuses*. Both are evil women (in fact Lady Susan is the only truly evil character Jane Austen ever describes), both intent on domination and acknowledgement of their superiority by the families they destroy, both meticulously plan and execute an attack on the society within which they live. *Lady Susan* is the only one of Jane Austen's works that is consistently serious, without the least hint of comedy. Was it written as a literary exercise, much as art students used to copy paintings by the classical masters? Was Jane Austen trying to extend her range beyond the comedy of the Juvenilia? There the last component is dated 1793. *Lady Susan* followed in 1793-4,[11] just two years before the first version of *Sense and Sensibility*. In its extant version that novel is the only one to retain a tragic story line in the relationship of Willoughby and Marianne, with Willoughby remaining the persuasive villain to the end and Marianne's final rescue less than convincing.

A better preparation for Jane Austen would have been Madame Riccoboni,[12] one of whose brisk, short novels was *Histoire d'Ernestine*. The eponymous heroine, the orphan of domestic violence, is allowed to be talented as a painter of miniatures, and so financially, if modestly, independent. She is pretty dim at recognising her sitter's / admirer's passion, perhaps wisely so, since he is about to enter fashionable, loveless wedlock. Various entirely believable events and people keep her miserable but solvent, until a final *peripetia* sends her, quite honourably, haring off to her sick lover and all ends happily. In this book the chief badge of the heroine's independence and fire is her own decision to travel, accompanied by a servant of course, and to pay for her own journey. A far cry from Emma, who barely stirs outside the shrubberies of Hartfield without a 'walking companion.'

More cheerfully, 1786 saw the publication of *Caroline de Lichtfield* by Madame de Montolieu, who later translated Jane Austen. Entirely virtuous and conventional, the book was extremely successful – it neither enlightened nor scared its readers. A year later came *Vathek*, a pseudo-Arabian gallimaufry written in French by that self-indulgent, crazy, mixed-up rich kid, William Beckford. These days it is a curiosity, worth an idle half day – in its day, as a pseudo-gothic novel in exotic livery, it catered for the taste in horror.

With the Revolution, the preoccupations and tastes of the earlier Ancien Régime did not fade overnight. Demand for the exotic, in the guise of *Paul et Virginie*,[13] another much reprinted best seller, persisted. So did the recurring subject of marriage between a very young girl and a much older man. Madame de Souza[14] had published in London *Adèle de Sénanges, ou les lettres de Lord Sydenham.* Unlike Lolita, in this book a gentleman much past his prime takes pity on a friend's daughter – the adolescent is to be immured in a convent because of her mother's unwillingness to provide a dowry.[15] As he is so decrepit and she so childish, as a newly married girl (there are queries about consummation) she is squired about town by her brother, but the suggestion of incest is dropped as soon as an extremely rich *milord Anglais*, the young Lord Sydenham, arrives on the scene. He is smitten by the gorgeous, unspoilt, unreflective teenager. After much to-ing and fro-ing (which includes ideas about remodelling a garden, the story of a nun who runs away from her convent for a miserable and sickly life in England, and an episode, cribbed from *La Princesse de Clèves*, of the hero stealing a miniature of Adèle), the old husband dies, Adèle is left a very rich widow and sent back to the convent, to await marriage with a husband approved by her highly ambitious mother. At this point, Lord Sydenham and Adèle, who have acknowledged their love for each other, literally buy her freedom, by giving all her money to her youngest brother, to enable him to make an advantageous marriage; only then will her mother consent to be barely civil at her daughter's wedding.

Like *La Nouvelle Héloïse*, this novel berates the social conventions of the period. The author, in her preface, denies any straining after novelty. She aims to:

> inspirer encore de l'intérêt en se bornant à tracer ces détails fugitifs qui occupent l'espace entre les événements . . . c'est la suite de ces sentiments journaliers qui forment essentiellement le fond de la vie.
> [to keep the reader's interest while limited to sketching the fleeting details that fill the gaps between events . . . it is the sequence of these daily sensations that truly embodies the essence of life.]

This is nearer to Jane Austen; as with Riccoboni, the details striven for take account of the economic need to marry and the consequent question – how bearable are these needful marriages? Women are acknowledged as passionate, but allowed to be so only within marriage, as a prelude to motherhood and successful domesticity. Nearer still to Jane Austen is Madame de Souza's 1811 novel *Eugénie et Mathilde, roman de l'émigration*. Three sisters, brought up in different circumstances and with very distinct life-styles, find themselves, at the start of the Revolution, constrained in their father's country estate, then in Brussels, amongst a large and clamorous group of émigrés, and finally, when money is short, in a small village on the north German coast, near Cuxhaven. How do they cope? The account rings totally true to life, the characters breathe, their emotions are vivid, the crowd scenes just at the right focus to sharpen up the concerns of the central characters, the interactions between the sisters, their parents and would-be lovers observed with great precision and sympathy. It is the 1811 version of Mary Wesley's *The Camomile Lawn*, one French early nineteenth century novel worthy of Jane Austen's serious attention.

We know she read the second of Madame de Staël's two novels, *Delphine* and *Corinne*. Both were freely available in Paris before the end of the war, but not *De l'Allemagne*. Published in London by John Murray, Jane Austen's second publisher, it was nearer a travel book, cultural rather than geographical. It gives, among much else, summaries of books and plays by recent German-speaking authors. These were intended to acquaint the French with the peculiar genius of their neighbours, but also nearer the middle of the century, turned out unexpectedly useful to Verdi, always on the look out for likely sources of opera plots.

In general, travel writing was highly popular,[16] even about travelling in France. Here two English writers did well – Arthur Young, who travelled in France repeatedly between 1787 and 1790, and so obtained a very good idea of the ills that fuelled the Revolution. The French translation was published in 1793 by Buisson, a house that often looked to foreign authors and had a few years earlier picked out the best seller *Caroline de Lichtfield* by a Swiss author. Then in 1806, as the 'Continental System' (closing Continental ports to British shipping) was put in place, *Voyages en France, en Suisse et en Allemagne* came out. This referred to journeys undertaken by Dr John Moore, an army surgeon and novelist, and was read with pleasure, by another, Stendhal,[17] while on campaign in Austria.

The year saw another curiosity that prefigures current practice – a novel by Sophie Cottin, another successful writer of the Revolutionary period, was adapted for the stage, with additional music and dances – *Elisabeth, ou les Exilés de Siberie*. A Siberian region, governed by Smoloff, is the prison of Springer, the incognito adopted by a Polish prince exiled for two earlier faults – Springer's very loving wife had been coveted by A.N. Other and he, Springer, had worked for and continues to wish for the freedom of Poland (at that period divided between Russia, Prussia, and Austria). Springer's daughter Elisabeth, loved by Smoloff's son, decides to travel to Moscow and St Petersburg, to beg the Tzar for her father's freedom. (Again, the heroine's courage is proclaimed by undertaking an arduous journey accompanied by only one servant, a poltroon who provides comic relief.) After the usual fictional quota of coincidence, confession, repentance and generosity, in three acts punctuated by song and ballet – including a *ballet grotesque* of boatman with their oars – the predictable happy ending is achieved.

So far, so like modern stage and screen adaptations of Jane Austen. But there is a political undertone. In 1806, the year of the adaptation, oppression by the Tzar of Russia of Springer, champion of the freedom of Poland, could also stand for the oppression by any autocratic ruler, not least Napoleon, as seen by groups opposed to his absolute power even inside France. Further the provincial governor Smoloff, directly responsible for Springer's exile, is himself a victim:

> l'homme sensible qu'un devoir cruel contraint à faire souffrir les autres, est-il moins malheureux que les victimes du pouvoir?
> [if a man of feeling is constrained by his duty to make others suffer, is he less wretched than the victims of his power?]

This could be Rousseau-esque sensibility yeasting its way into the body politic. But also it can acknowledge the appalling moral dilemmas that the violent events since 1789 had faced many. Moral complexity sits oddly in a fashionable entertainment. That is what the show was aiming at. The dedication of 'the book' to Madame Gobert by the script writer is quite explicit – the success of the show, with journalists and punters alike, was due to *les décorations magnifiques* [magnificent scenery and costumes], the inventive ballets, the originality of the music by Monsieur Piccinni,[18] the distinguished talents of the actors assembled at the Théâtre de la Porte Saint-Martin.

This was on the Right Bank,[19] some way from the river and shows how the centre of theatrical gravity had moved away from the traditional Left Bank.[20] The dedication goes on to attribute the polish of the actors' excellence to the training they had received by working in the Théâtre Français, home of the Comédie Française, on the edge of the Palais Royal. Indeed to this day, acting with the Comédie Française is seen as post-graduate training of the most exacting kind.

At long last with the battle of Waterloo, the twenty six years of upheaval came to an end. By November 1815, *Raison et Sensibilité* was in the shops, as well as *Les Capucins*. The author was Madame G. de M. de Faverolles, but in view of its subject, ostensibly by her husband, a captain of dragoons. It sets out to demonstrate that depravity is not a recent development, but was as prevalent in the lifetime of the story-teller's grandfather, some fifty years earlier. Is the time-lapse a nod to Water Scott, whose *Waverley* was an immediate and roaring success? He also times many of his stories to the generation of grandparents, to give them the solidity of seemingly personal reminiscence and a weighty historical context. But here, the fifty year gap is a device to distance the reader from the story which is an old-fashioned bawdy tale, Chaucerian in its cheerfulness, with some late repentance, punishment and death to preserve the proprieties. It is barely readable as a giggle, its only interesting detail (apart from catering for the seeming need to laugh after all the years of high seriousness), an early example of the baddie pretending to be a rich American.

A year after Waterloo, when *La Nouvelle Emma* was listed in *Bibliographie de France*, the same number announced *Adolphe, anecdote trouvée dans les papiers d'un inconnu et publiée par M Benjamin de Constant* [anecdote found among the papers of an unknown man and brought to light by M. Benjamin de Constant[21]]. He was Madame de Staël's long-time lover and his short novel, published first in London, charts the course of a sexual obsession and efforts to escape from it. Totally male, totally French, unputdownable, it feels like being caught in a flood, tossed until washed up on an unrecognised shore. Read it, for the sheer relief of finishing it.

In September *Le Parc de Mansfield, ou les trois cousines* was listed in the *Bibliographie de France*. The added sub-title shifts the focus from Fanny to the whole extended family, giving it a wider, social, rather than intimate, personal focus. La Fontaine's *Fables* and a minor work by Voltaire are mentioned in the same number, as well as, in English 'Cato, 'a tragedy in 5 acts' by J. Addison and *The Heiress*, 'comedy in 5 acts' by General Burgoyne,[22] as performed at the Theatre Royal, Drury Lane, Covent Garden. Printed with authority of the managers from the prompt book. With remarks by M.M. Inchbald.' This was Elizabeth Inchbald,[23] who translated Kotzebue's *Lovers' Vows*, that slow-acting dynamite in *Mansfield Park*.

The diligent Madame de Genlis also had a book published in 1816 – *Jeanne de France*, a fictionalised biography of the deformed but saintly daughter of the French king Louis XI.[24] Jeanne is presented as the unwitting tool of her father; her unrequited love for her husband, the future King Louis XII, combines with her altruism for the benefit of the kingdom, while she suffers, like a patient but unrewarded Grizelda. It reads easily enough for a conduct book – a woman can maintain and even enhance her status by submitting to a patriarchal regime. No whiff of rebellion here.

La Famille Elliot in September 1821 had more serious competition – the first volume of the complete works of Madame de Souza (see above) embellished with engravings, *Aventures de Robinson Crusoe imité* (note that weasel-word) *de l'anglais*, the complete works of Cervantes translated from Spanish (no liberties with imitations taken here), a reprint of *Histoire du chevalier Des Grieux et de Manon Lescaut*, that perennially absorbing masterpiece, and *Histoire d'Ernestine* plus another by Madame Riccoboni (see above). To top it all:

> *Langage de Flore ou Nouvelle manière de communiquer ses pensées sans se voir, sans se parler, sans s'écrire.*
>
> [The language of flowers, or a new means of communicating thoughts without seeing, speaking or writing to each other.]

There must have been life in this poetic convention, since it surfaces to great effect in *Le lys dans la vallée*, Balzac's major romantic novel, heavy with fervour and anguish, which refers to this period.

In November of the same year 7.50 francs was the price of *Orgueil et Prévention*, the first translation of the full text of *Pride and Prejudice*.[25] It was published by Maradan, of Rue des Marais FSG, who, in the same week had another novel listed, the 5 francs, 2 volume, *Vertue et Scélératesse ou la Fatalité* [Virtue and Villainy, or The Fatal Destiny] by M.J. Bocous. Was the title modelled on Jane Austen's? If so, it did nothing for the book. A historical romance (Walter Scott has much to answer for!), set in North Africa for exotic interest, it is inept, repetitive, boring, and has so little to offer that beyond its first twenty, the pages of the copy in the *Bibliothèque Nationale Française* remained uncut until the summer of 2001. Did Maradan think so little of *Pride and Prejudice* in Eloïse Perks' translation[26] that he was happy to launch it together with so poor a novel? There was another translation from English listed in the same week, one by Regina Maria Roche *auteur des Enfants de L'Abbaye* (*The Children of the Abbey*, admired by Emma's protégée, Harriet Smith) and one from the German of Auguste Lafontaine.[27] Add to these another four volumes of the French theatre (a series equivalent to Mrs

Inchbald's *British Theatre*, above) of two heavy-weights Racine and Molière, a translation of the complete works of Locke, and the last two volumes of the complete works of Necker, a man who would be vividly remembered by older readers.

Yet another publishing phenomenon of 1821 and the subsequent year absorbed readers – *Le Solitaire* by Le Vicomte d'Arlincourt.[28] It is another historical romance, but the author had learnt enough from Walter Scott to slot his tale into a precise historical setting – the latter half of the fifteenth century, when the Duke of Burgundy, Charles the Bold, was resisting the power of the French king. To French readers this was familiar territory. Beyond one chapter setting out the duplicity of king Louis XI, father of the saintly Jeanne de France, all the twists in the political and military strand in the plot are neatly plaited into the story. Again following Scott, it is set in a precise geographical location on the borders of France and Switzerland; references to the weather are annotated as familiar to all travellers in the region. On to this solid ground the story is bolted; characterisation is non–existent, the love interest daft, the action ultra–melodramatic. But the whole has enough manic energy to carry a quick reader, riding like a catamaran over the crests of the waves, to the story's conclusion. Its nearest modern equivalent is one of those unbelievable movies on American TV shows in the small hours. The book was phenomenally successful, with repeated printings – the first two sold out in six weeks, the publisher of the third cheap edition told his readers proudly. Critics did not share the enthusiasm, least about the use of language, and d'Arlincourt thought it wise to make some changes, while his publisher stoutly defended him:

> Il y a, dans l'ouvrage de Monsieur d'Arlincourt, des expressions si brillantes dans leur hardiesse, si éloquentes dans leur innovation, qu'en dépit de la critique, elles sont approuvées par le gout.
> [There are in this work by M. d'Arlincourt expressions so brilliantly bold, so eloquently original, that in spite of all criticism, they are accepted by readers of taste.]

Can't say I found them.

This embarrassment of bookish riches in 1821 formed one part of the background of Balzac's *Les Illusions Perdues*, set in this same year 1821. No wonder its hero, Lucien de Rubempré, gives up on his historical novel.

L'Abbaye de Northanger, when its turn came in November 1824, had nothing so startling to contend with – five other novels in its week of publication. A short one, *Le Désert dans Paris*, explicitly refers to the year 1817, when a group of friends are so appalled by post–Napoleonic France that they wish they lived on a desert island. Instead they buy a large property on the edge of Paris, build and stock store houses, set up a farm, amalgamate their libraries (6,000 books all told) and move in.

> Plus d'intrigues, plus de querelles, plus d'envie, plus de médisances. Salut séjour de paix et de bonheur.
> [No more intrigues, nor quarrels, nor envy, nor scandal. Welcome to the home of peace and happiness.]

Very soon things start going wrong and within twelve months all bar one couple are outside the walled enclave. The moral is spelt out:

> Il est imprudent et presque toujours dangereux, dans les choses de la vie, de vouloir s'écarter des idées reçues, ainsi que de la conduite tracé par les convenances.
> [In matters of daily living, it is unwise and generally dangerous to seek aloofness from accepted notions and to behave in an unconventional manner.]

A cautionary tale, allowing for a little irony or laughter, it promotes steady–state convention; the romantic dream of the individual carving out his destiny according to his own feelings and ideas is seen as socially destructive. Yet in the same week, books undermining convention, that is the works of Rousseau, are listed, as well as the memoirs of James II of Great Britain, a pamphlet continuing the argument about censorship of newspapers, plus a four volume translation *Conversations entre un père et ses enfants* made up of little instructive and would-be amusing stories by Maria Edgeworth, Charlotte Smith[29] and Priscilla Wakefield.[30] And to crown it all, *Practical Observation concerning sea-bathing* by Dr A.P. Buchan, in French bar the title. He was in favour, so giving some credence to Mary Musgrove, who tried it in Lyme in November,[31] an event to us as unlikely as the apple blossom in July, that Edward Austen-Knight was the first to complain to his sister about.[32] The uncomfortable theory of the period held that the colder the sea-water and the ambient air, the more health-giving the exercise. Consequently Eliza de Feuillide / Austen, Jane's sister-in-law, took her sickly little son to Margate during the coldest months of 1790 into 1791.[33]

December 1827 saw yet more editions of the complete works of Molière, Voltaire and Chateabriand's to date[34] and a pamphlet on J.E. David as a historical painter. There was a reprint of *Raison et Sensibilité* and a new translation of *Kenilworth*. The latter had been so highly regarded by Victor Hugo, then an angry young man, that he turned it into a play titled *Amy Robsart*.[35] Walter Scott was hugely popular for his radical invention – the historical novel about ordinary people in precisely described actual locations, mainly in Scotland. Specific regionalism made Scotland glamorous and exotic, the odd mythic figure, like Meg Merrilies or Jeanie Deans, adding to local colour and reminiscent of earlier story-telling styles.

This larger than life element in English writing had another boost in 1827 – Charles Kemble had taken his company of actors to Paris, to perform Shakespeare in English. It was a thunderous triumph (Berlioz, for one, was profoundly affected), the national and romantic features of the plays being particularly admired. In this enthusiasm for wide-brush effects (what Scott called his 'Big Bow-Wow strain'), so alien to Jane Austen, *Raison et Sensibilité* sank without any public notice, although it is the only one of the six novels with tragic scenes, arguably fit even for opera – the party (in volume 2 chapter 6) where Marianne is rejected, and Willoughby's confession (volume 3 chapter 9).

The following year the reprint of *La Famille Elliot* retained its subtitle – *ou l'Ancienne Inclinaison*; presumably an allusion to the proverb: *Vielles amours et vieux tisons s'allument en chaque saison* [old love and old embers flare up at any time]. The other reprints mentioned in the same number of *Bibliographie de France* are Ovid's *Art d'Aimer*, *La Princesse de Clèves*, an enduring masterwork of psychological insight and poetic images,[36] and *Zélie dans le Desert*, by Madame Daubenton. This had originally been published in London in 1787, but also sold at three addresses in Paris. A re-print forty years after first publication suggests that the conventional novel of pre-revolutionary France was still in demand. It is the usual story of girls, their lovers and proposed arranged marriages. To avoid these, they embark on a ship bound for Batavia (modern Jakarta), are shipwrecked en route, the girls separated from the men, have then to cope on their own, starting, as in *Robinson Crusoe*, in a cave – they meet *Le bon solitaire*, a Frenchman of course, who on Sumatra has a farm with sheep and goats and makes his own cheese. A couple of deaths and a few years of solitary living later, Zélie meets up with her lover, who has managed to save enough from the shipwreck to recreate a French-style interior. More months of agonising whether to sleep with him without benefit of clergy, end in happiness and a couple of children. Eventually all the characters are re-united, the necessary official marriages, to ensure social respectability, take place, and on return to France they build themselves a desert in a wood.

Scholars and readers with quirky tastes read these novels now. The vast majority of them, by women writers, share weakness in the use of language through their over-numerous pages. Some are better organised (*Adèle et Théodore*, for instance), some have arresting ideas (*Corinne*), or added value as historical documents (*Eugénie et Mathilde*), but you would not re-read them to savour the sentences. Theoretically therefore, foreign literature should not have suffered just by translation. However the French had late in the eighteenth century strong ideas about what a translation should do – French taste was absolute good taste, therefore the French turn of mind was in total unison with the human spirit.

Consequently translation involved, if at all possible, perfecting the original, embellishing it, making it over to give it a national (French) appearance, in short naturalising a foreign plant. When it came to works in English, this was difficult because they displayed exaggerated individualism, a love of freedom (from literary conventions at least) and a bent for independence that bordered on indiscipline. This had to be accepted in a book that sets out to instruct the reader; then the translator 'owes his public the author such as he is' thought Charles Pictet de Rochemont. But not in novels. Prévost, who was very practised at translating, complains – *Monsieur Richardson perd de vue la mesure de son sujet et s'oublie dans les details.* [Mr Richardson loses the thread of his narrative and meanders off into details.] Add to this the demands of fashion / what will sell, you get Madame de Montolieu's free translations, *les belles infidèles.* Madame de Staël entered the fray by daring to assert that beauty is not absolute, nor the French taste the only acceptable one, although – she added in swift support of chauvinism – probably the purest.

Without going into arguments about purity of taste, the main use of translations was that they should be acceptable to French taste and cover their costs, if no more. Familiarisation with foreign literature was secondary to the book being for French readers 'a good read'.

One of the best was *Melmoth the Wanderer*, by C.R. Maturin. It sold so well that Balzac could not use the name for one of his projected works[37] until after the death of the author in 1824. It was one of the most successful gothic novels both in France and England, centred on a character who blends features of The Flying Dutchman, Count Dracula and Faust, with episodes relating to separate historic periods and locations. With these it satisfied the newly aroused demand for a genuine historical context supported by local colour of comparable accuracy, first awakened by Scott in France through his trusty translator, Madame Defauconpret. Sweeping the board during the period 1815–1830 (the period covered by Balzac's string of contemporary novels *La Comédie Humaine*) Scott was the second most popular writer whose books are listed by lending libraries (*cabinets de lecture*).[38] In English neither Maturin nor Scott are seen as inventing the language of the modern novel, Jane Austen's particular contribution to English literature. They invite admiration for their large scale effects, the variety of their invention in both plot and description. Besides, Scott's sense of history as a continuum weighing upon and shaping each generation, appealed to a generation that had just lived through a historical turning–point. French readers were not alone in feeling that in 1789 history had changed into a higher gear and produced in record time a completely new mega–memory of characters, themes, images, to feed the collective imagination and give a lode to be quarried for unprecedented creativity.

Where does Jane Austen fit into this? Her novels are neither gothic nor historical, nor an archival record of trials in the immediate, turbulent past. They are everyday tales of everyday people. The everyday theme of marriage is unburdened by sexual worries, the insistence on good behaviour comes from Protestant self–orientation to moral integrity, the tribal memory of arbitrary coercion is very far in the past and unsanctified by the peaks of literary achievement. Her villains are not beyond redemption, her heroes and heroines are imperfect, but manage to fight their corner courteously and successfully. With the *Bildungsroman* barely in its stride, Marianne, Emma, Elizabeth and Darcy are obvious examples of characters growing into better people and the last two are nearest to revolutionary. In Paris, *Pride and Prejudice* comes most insistently to mind – Elizabeth's transgressive behaviour, disregard for rank, insistence on equality. Darcy the thoughtful – and generous – realist, who feels his way out of rank and into happiness by way of 'the utmost force of passion'. This is traditionally the preserve of the French literary genius – the heroes of Racine, for one, experience love as an involuntary affliction. But here the hero questions behaviour as prescribed in literature and, with the heroine, also in life; between them they undermine the social system and its concomitant power base. All this passed totally unremarked as the two translations of the full text of *Pride and Prejudice* sank without a ripple. As does, to this day, the clear–eyed, steady gaze, through a lens of irony without cynicism and humour without malice.

Northanger Abbey was disregarded, partly because it parodies gothic novels that were going out of fashion by the date of its publication, partly because it sailed under the colours of Pigoreau, the money–grabbing publisher who provided trashy novels for lending libraries. *Mansfield Park* did not fit the perceived view of a girl governed by religion – instead of going into a convent, the heroine measured herself by the standards of her clergyman lover and through deft manoeuvring, obtained the three highest gifts of secular life – *l'amour, la fortune et la gloire*. *Sense and Sensibility* and *Persuasion* make it to a re–print only on the reputation of the translator and the distortions she imposed to make the originals more attractive to French readers; *Emma* came out with an *Avertissement* that presented the book as a cultural travelogue, the picture of manners and morals in a half–recognised habitat:

> French travellers to England will recognise the customs, habits, manners of small towns, or what used to be called the provinces. Those who have never visited the country, will get to know our neighbours without stirring. Readers are warned that these pages contain no amazing adventures, no enchanted castles, no slain giants; everything is natural. After reading *Emma* readers may be convinced that the author pictured the characters from life and that the events described took place in the neighbourhood.

This just would not do for readers used to appalling hardships imposed from above by 'them' and barely recovering from the consequent, ground–level miseries suffered by 'us'. The contrast with a group of 'us', who are successfully active in their own interest, without interference, who are predominantly cheerful, constrained by their private desires and emotions, not by major public ills, that picture was just too foreign. Interest can not be held by such a personalised, undisturbed view of life. These novels could not be worth serious attention.

The view was put succinctly by Philarète Chasle[39] nearer the middle of the century – Jane Austen, as well as Fanny Burney, was a grand-daughter of Richardson, distinguished by the harmony of delicate perception. But she is heavily implicated in the crime of the modern (that is early nineteenth century) English novel:

'c'est de ne plus reconnaitre de principe élevé, de ne pas tomber d'une source haute et importante, de ne pas exprimer un sentiment vaste et puissant'.
[It no longer acknowledges any over-riding principle, neither stems from an exalted and vital origin, nor expresses any vast and mighty feeling.]

In one word *vulgaire*, as Madame de Staël labelled *Pride and Prejudice* as early as 1813.

More surprisingly, in 1882, a gentleman who had taught French in London[40] pronounced:

Elle ne fait jamais l'appel à l'émotion, ni au rire, encore moins à l'humour pour produire l'effet voulu!
[She never makes use of feeling, nor laughter and even less frequently of humour to obtain the desired effect.]

How good was his English?

It took more years and a former ambassador[41] to the USA to get the point:

C'est elle qui eut le plus d'influence, ouvrit la voie la plus large, et qui garde aujourd'hui encore le plus de lecteurs.
[She had the most influence, opened up the widest course and to this day, retains the most readers.]

Clearly a man whose grasp of English was at the needful level. He concludes:

On la devine à la lire telle qu'elle fut, bonne, spirituelle et jolie.
[From reading her books you guess her to be such as she was, kindly, witty and attractive.]

Maybe. Just as, maybe, the French have steadily underestimated

Jane Austen because she proclaims the possibility of happiness – to
be sure rational happiness, backed by a sufficiency of money, but
genuine and sustained none the less. For her heroes and heroines,
personal integrity, self–fulfilment, marital harmony and social use-
fulness are compatible, to be realised by all men and women of
goodwill and good sense. This optimism in a great writer is rare. In
the English core Great Tradition only George Eliot shares it
(granted Henry James is American and Joseph Conrad Polish). But
cast your mind back over the French titles that have cropped up
repeatedly throughout this book – *La Princesse de Clèves*, *Phèdre*,
Manon Lescaut, *La Nouvelle Héloïse*, all summits of French literature,
all tragedies. Scroll forward to *La Chartreuse de Parme*,[42] *Madame
Bovary*,[43] *Le Grand Maulnes*,[44] *Le Diable au Corps*,[45] *A la recherche du
temps perdu*,[46] all eminently readable, all most beautifully written, all
punctuated by disasters, ending in a final one, all signally short of
laughter, although Stendhal allows himself a quota of smiles and
Proust a much thicker dusting of irony. The tragic view, pessimism,
is the most glaring distinction between serious literature and novels
by women, for women, before about 1830.

If women writers met the seeming need for happy endings with
gusto, what did they know that men did not? That women of the
period, living at home, quiet and confined, like Anne Elliot,[47] have
their feelings prey on them, and lives of quiet desperation are in-
compatible with successful child rearing. So theoretically happy
ending stories are the cultural expression of biological imprinting,
the need for them catered for within the gender.

So Jane Austen loses out again. She was only a woman and just too
damn' English.

The Competition — Notes

1 Middle income men: Electors had to have an income of 300 fr pa and candidates 1000 fr pa.

2 Prévost *Manon Lescaut*, a novel within the much longer novel, *Memoires d'un homme de qualité*, 1731.

3 Printing in Holland: The full text had been objected to by the French censor, but pirated editions, the first by Robin, were soon on sale.

4 Fall in love: This is the same situation as in Kotzebue's *Das Kind der Liebe*, first performed by amateurs in private in 1790, that is 29 years after *La Nouvelle Héloïse*. In 1798 Kotzebue's play was translated and adapted by Elizabeth Inchbald, as *Lovers' Vows*. It was highly successful on the London stage and figures largely in *Mansfield Park*, Jane Austen's fourth novel, written some fifteen years later. The scene in the play in which Amelia (the echo of Julie) declares her love for her tutor Anhalt (the echo of Saint Preux) is the one that Mary Crawford and Edmund, highly attracted to each other, rehearse with Fanny's help, both unaware that Fanny herself is in love with Edmund. The rehearsal happens in the East Room, normally Fanny's private refuge. So not only is her territory invaded but, as prompter, she has to help them declare their mutual attraction by means of the play's text. This highly charged scene seems amplified by its double literary reference and raises the possibility that Jane Austen at least knew of Rousseau's *La Nouvelle* Héloïse, (a reasonable assumption in a family known to enjoy novels), much as these days novel readers would know of a novel by Solzhenitsyn.

5 Passages: Jane Austen's letter 80 of 04.02.1813, in Deirdre Le Faye's editions, 1995, OUP, on receiving her copy of *Pride and Prejudice*.

6 An imaginist: Emma calls herself this in vol. 3 ch. 3.

7 Excursions into fantasy: In that she resembles the heroine of *The Female Quixote*, 1752, by Charlotte Lennox, enjoyed by Jane Austen, letter 49 of 07 & 08.01.07, in Deirdre Le Faye's edition, 1995, OUP.

8 Admiration or envy: English critics and adapters of the novel, notably Andrew Davies, see Highbury and its secondary inhabitants as the essence of the novel. To the French translator, writing the *Avertissement* that precedes the text of the 1816 edition (see above), it and they are more like a familiar zoo.

9 Madame de Genlis: A feisty lady, governess to the children of the Duc d'Orléans, Philippe Egalité, cousin to King Louis XVI (see Revolutionary Paris). This particular book was published in 1782. She was a prolific and highly popular novelist, and left copious and entertaining memoirs. She visited England, crops up in Fanny Burney's diary for 1785, and was a

friend of Thomas Holcroft, the actor, dramatist, Jacobin novelist, who translated both her books and Madame de Montolieu's best-seller *Caroline de Lichtfield*. See Geneva, The Translator.

10 *Les Liaisons Dangereuses*, 1782: If the novelist Stendhal, a native of Grenoble, is to be believed, the plot is based on events in that city, witnessed and discussed by Choderlos de Laclos, when the author, an artillery officer, was stationed in the city. Even Stendhal, writing in 1837, avers that he met and spoke with an old man who had personally known the evil Madame de Mertheuil. A staunch republican in his youth, Stendhal became acquainted with English novels through *Bibliothèque britannique*, (see Geneva, *La Bibliothèque britannique*).
He visited England in October–November 1821 and came away with an impression at odds with Jane Austen: 'Women don't exist in English society, as if they were abolished . . . it is not husbands or eunuchs who keep them out of society, but their own wish and their idea of what is fit and proper, and its opposite.' He goes on to explain that they don't sleep around. A faint English echo of *Les Liaisons Dangereuses* is *The Delicate Distress*, by Elizabeth Griffith, 1769.

11 There is an alternative theory put forward by Professor Marilyn Butler that Lady Susan was written as late as 1809.

12 Madame Riccoboni, 1714–1792: an actress who specialised in the plays by Marivaux, she wrote a number of epistolary novels and adapted Fielding's *Amelia*.

13 *Paul and Virginie*: by Bernardin de Saint-Pierre was first published as part of *Etudes de la Nature*, a more poetic text than its name would suggest. The novel, something between Enlightenment, romanticism and pastoral, based on a true incident, is still worth reading.

14 Madame de Souza: Another very feisty lady, she was an émigrée in England and later, in very straitened circumstances, in Hamburg. Fortunately her second husband was the Portuguese ambassador to Paris, and she lived successfully and prolifically ever after.

15 Provide a dowry: The same financial shortcoming in Manon Lescaut's family led to her being taken to a convent, when a stop *en route* enables Des Grieux to meet her, and set in motion the roller-coaster ride to perdition.

16 Travel writing popular: *Bibliothèque britannique* responded to this demand – in 1811, 54% of the pages of its *Littérature* section was devoted to travel, by 1813 the proportion had dropped to 40%. Overall fully one third of its pages were given to descriptions of places outside Great Britain.

17 Dr John Moore: He also wrote novels, one about a good man and another about a bad one. Perhaps his main claim to fame is that he was father to Sir John Moore, the commander killed during the 1809 retreat to

Corunna, and commemorated in elegy, formerly learnt by heart by school children:

Not a drum was heard, not a funeral note
As his corse to the ramparts we hurried . . .

18 Monsieur Piccinni: This was Antonio Piccinni, grandson of the Piccinni whose *Iphigénie en Tauride* competed with Gluck's. See Walk One. The original novel had been translated into English in 1807.

19 Right Bank: The metro station is the St Denis exit of Strasbourg-St Denis. The gateway is still standing at the crossroads of Boulevards Sébastopol and St Martin, on the direct line, by taxi, between Gare du Nord and Ile de la Cité.

20 Traditional Left Bank: See Palais Royal and the Comédie Française.

21 Benjamin Constant: See Geneva, Madame de Staël. Constant's attempt to disclaim ownership of his narrative took in very few readers of his time. Was he after the limited protection of a convention used by Henry Mackenzie some forty years earlier? He had used similar feints to distance himself from his narratives in *A Man of Feeling* (1771) and *Julia de Roubigné* (1777). For both men writing novels was a secondary occupation – Constant was a politician, Mackenzie Comptroller of Taxes for Scotland. Even after Mackenzie's younger friend, Walter Scott, showed that writing serious novels could be both respectable and lucrative, the practice was, arguably, suspect in men aspiring to a rôle in public life.

22 General Burgoyne: He is better known for losing the battle of Saratoga and thereby unburdening Britain of her American colonies.

23 Elisabeth Inchbald: She was primarily an actress and edited *The British Theatre*, a large collection of plays in repertory over many years, but more memorably wrote *A Simple Story*, 1791, still worth reading.

24 Louis XI: 1423–1483. He was known as 'The Universal Spider'. Wisely avoiding Paris, his palace was at Plessis les Tours, from which he managed his unruly subjects and neighbouring states quite ruthlessly and eventually, with much success.

25 *Orgueil et Prévention*: The publisher chose this title because he knew that a rival publisher (Paschoud) based in Geneva, was also about to produce a translation with the commonly accepted title of *Orgueil et Préjugé*. This had been given in 1813 to the extracts published by *Bibliothèque britannique*.

26 Eloïse Perks' translation: It was not the first time Maradan had tried a translation from English. In 1798 he had published a translation of *The Adventures of Hugh Trevor*, by Thomas Holcroft, a novel that manages to combine the picaresque with the political-didactic. Holcroft himself had earlier translated both Madame de Genlis' *Veillées au Chateau* and Madame de Montolieu's best-seller *Caroline de Lichtfield*.

27 Auguste Lafontaine: Not by Madame de Montolieu, although she used this German writer as the richest quarry for her talents.

28 Le vicomte d'Arlincourt: If an author had a title of nobility, this is always spelt out in full on the title page of these novels.

29 Charlotte Smith, 1748–1806: *The Old Manor House* (1793) and *The Young Philosopher* (1798) are two of her novels which feature the newly emancipated USA as an actual place, with characteristics very distinct from Europe, not used just as a narrative convention, a means of getting a character off-stage for a considerable length of time, with attendant difficulties of communication by letter.

30 Priscilla Wakefield: She rates a footnote in Jacqueline Pearson's *Women Reading in Britain 1750–1835*, CUP 1999, as the author of *Domestic Recreation*; 'or Dialogues Illustrative of Natural and Scientific Subjects', 1805.

31 Swimming in November: *Persuasion* vol. 1 ch. 11 and vol. 2 ch. 2.

32 Apple blossom in July: *Emma*, vol. 3 ch. 6. Edward's comment in W.H. Pollock *Jane Austen, her contemporaries and herself* (London, 1899) quoted in *Jane Austen: a family record* by W. and R.A. Austen-Leigh, and Deirdre Le Faye, the British Library, 1989.

33 Sea bathing : See *Jane Austen – A Family Record* by W & RA Austen-Leigh and Deirdre Le Faye, The British Library 1989.

34 Chateaubriand's works to date: His *Voyage en Amérique*, referring to a journey of 1791, had been published earlier in the year and was now added to the lengthening canon.

35 *Kenilworth*: Walter Scott's novel came out in English in 1821. In 1829 the play was turned into an opera by Donizetti, titled *Elisabeta, o il Castello di Kenilworth*.

36 Madame de la Fayette's novel was rapidly recognised for the masterpiece it is and translated into English in 1679, that is within a year of its first publication. Did Jane Austen know it? For Henry Tilney's exposition of the woman's rôle in dancing, prefiguring that of her rôle in marriage (*Northanger Abbey* vol. 1 ch. 10) effectively deconstructs the moving scene when Madame de Clèves dances with the Duc de Nemours, without knowing who he is; up to that point they have never met but are irremediably drawn to each other.

37 Balzac learnt his trade with a handful of gothic novels, written under several pseudonyms; he finally acknowledged only *Histoire de Jane la Pale* in his collected works.

38 Listed by lending libraries: the most popular was Madame de Genlis (see above) and the third most popular was Madame de Montolieu. Madame Guénard de Méré, author of the bawdy *Les Capucins*, comes in at number four, and Madame de Souza (see above) at five.

39 Philarète Chasle, 1798–1873: He taught modern languages at the Collège de France, the very attractive building on the south side of Rue des Ecoles. It is a major centre of research and learning, founded in the sixteenth century by a king anxious to counterbalance the intolerance of the university. He also wrote *L'Oeuil sans Paupière*, a fantastic tale published in 1832, as part of a collection titled *Contes Bruns*. An English translation featured in *Fantastic Tales* (Penguin 2001) edited with an introduction by Italo Calvino.

40 A gentleman who taught French in London: H. Testard, officier de l'Académie, professeur de Français à Londres in *Histoire de la litterature anglaise depuis ses origins jusqu'à nos jours*, 1882.

41 A former ambassador : J.J. Jusserand, *Le Roman Anglais*, 1886.

42 *La Chartreuse de Parme*, Stendhal, 1839.

43 *Madame Bovary*, G. Flaubert, 1857.

44 *Le Grand Maulnes*, Alain–Fournier, 1913.

45 *Le Diable au Corps*, R. Radiguet, 1923.

46 *A la recherche du temps perdu*, M. Proust, 1913–1927.

47 Anne Elliot, *Persuasion*, vol. 2 ch. 11.

And Finally . . .

Alas, Jane Austen in French is not going to win any prizes now, any more than she did 180 years ago – the translations obscure her greatness, based as it is on her language. She created the seamless language of English fiction:

> Her art succeeds in moving in and out of the minds of her people, and in and out of the crowds and communities. The combination of such social notation with such analysis of the consciousness transforms our sense of what the novel can do.[1]

English-speaking readers of the twenty-first century are scarcely aware of this, because her model has become the standard one, from which later idioms, of James Joyce for instance, developed.

She doesn't fit in France. There, to this day, her ostensible concerns look marginal, mean-spirited, at best quaint. At the time when her books were first rendered in French, they must have been almost freakish; they fitted into no category, being so unsensational, so lacking in invention or tragic episodes. This was too distant from the tastes of the first readers of Jane Austen in French. Her books, especially the unadorned translations, were like offering chamber music to listeners with a life-long habit of heavy metal. French national consciousness had been moulded by that sacred monster, Napoleon, and before him by the triumphs and horrors of the Revolution, the weight of earlier French history and the consequent literature. Jane Austen, essential to the mainstream of English consciousness, operates in a moral universe close to the Genevan, much further from the traumatised French of 1815 to 1830. The French were, and overwhelmingly remain, immune to her language and irony, 'so seductive, so intoxicating' that 'insidiously sucks' the reader in, as Colin Firth, a self-confessed admirer of 'European tormented novels' discovered,[2] her language more spell-binding in the original than filleted in however faithful a film script. How easy to relax, to slide into her self-sufficient imaginary world, so immediately recognisable in its events, characters and their inner lives, 'the most probable fiction', as Byron's future wife declared.[3] And so inviting to all readers, to re-interpret in their own image, to illuminate their own moral universe.

After living with the project of this book for a few years, the strongest lasting impression is of enormous suffering, on a continent-wide scale. It is not just the primitive blood-lust, however unbelievable it is that the French, the world's most enlightened country in the eighteenth century, gave way to it, even sanctified it with revolutionary theory. How could they bring themselves to do it, this descent into savagery unseen in Europe for more than a century? The same question was asked by my parents' generation, when evidence for the Holocaust started coming out of Germany and equally, they could not believe it.

In the case of France, the misery lasted from 1789 to 1815, a lifetime of twenty six years. Worse still, between the episodes of slaughter, there was hunger, repeated bankruptcies, foreign wars, privations of every kind, total disorder of daily life of a pervasiveness we can hardly imagine. Paris had the worst of it, much like London during the shorter second World War. Geneva was an oasis of comparative stability. From Geneva came the sanity of scientists keeping in touch across national boundaries and the practical concern for the needy on its streets. From Geneva came also the one unequivocal goodie to emerge from the crowd of characters mentioned in this guide book – Charles Pictet de Rochemont, editor of the Littérature section of the *Bibliothèque britannique* who introduced Jane Austen to the Continent. He was also sufficiently down-to-earth to pioneer, demonstrate and publicise improved methods of agriculture and husbandry; he was sufficiently public-spirited and skilful to negotiate unity and independence for the Swiss cantons, to create a country of inviolable territorial integrity and perpetual neutrality. Drink to his memory; there aren't many like him.

More prosaically and personally writing this book was a journey, starting, very properly in the old kitchen of Jane Austen's cottage in Chawton, Hampshire, where the curator was the first to listen and encourage. The route went no further than Chur, in Graubünden (Coire, Grisons), and the most exotic mode of transport was the Glacier Express. *'Ce n'est pas Christophe Colomb'*, said a French friend. Quite right, but the discoveries en route, apart from the research ones, gave it the air of a quest. There was an enchanted castle, the enormous Bibliothèque Nationale Française, with impregnable doors, metallic walls, passages more like space-ships than human habitations, guardians who oscillate unpredictably between barely suppressed hostility and cheerful support. There was the wonderful tribe of librarians in libraries across three countries, patient, interested, informed, supportive, strict about enforcing the 'pencils only' rule. The kindness of strangers came spectacularly from three Swiss scholars – Marie-Claire Loup, at the Bibliothèque Publique et Universitaire in Geneva, J-D Candaux, the historian of Geneva, and Valerie Cossy of the University of Lausanne. There was the extended family of friends and Austenites, who listened, asked questions and sprang into action – books were given, lent, located in out-of- the-way libraries; a certificate of serious intent – essential for French libraries – came from one, a reference for another library from a second, a third searched through his family archives; others walked the streets of Paris, took photographs, read, discussed, disagreed, suggested. Time, attention, food and drink were provided – several were already familiar with the variety of highly drinkable Swiss wines, one shared my delight in the excellence of the Royal Society's library steps, none had experienced the reliability and comfort of the dedicated metro line from Madeleine to Bibliothèque Nationale Française.

Conversation about books proliferated, heads nodded over books crying out for authors – why is there nothing geared to the common reader and readily available on the shelves of the local library about, for instance, translations from French and German, theoretically available to Jane Austen? Of the translators Charlotte Smith has a £47 book to herself, Elizabeth Inchbald a book in English and a sympathetic account from the University of Lille, Thomas Holcroft better known as a Jacobin. What is wanted on the topic is something patterned on the excellent *Dr Johnson's Women* by Norma Clarke.[4] Another book crying out for an author is about the Swiss diaspora in London of this period. And what about the Swiss in Canada?[5] While we are about it, why is there nothing about British colonists who left the infant United States? In all the busy cheering of the newly enfranchised Americans this episode of political cleansing is forgotten.[6] If nothing else, the exodus lends itself to 'Gone with the Wind' treatment, as the odd remembered family anecdote testifies.

'Get a bee in your bonnet about Jane Austen and see where it gets you,' was the toast proposed by a friend.

Where indeed? First, the hope that young, clever, bilingual scholars, with reputations to make, will tackle this area, for a start spell out the difference between French and English novels by women of this period; is it more apparent than real, and if so, why? Then to urge you all who happen upon this book, go to Paris and enjoy the city, perhaps with a little bookishness along the way. (Or even Geneva perhaps.)

And finally, go back to re-reading Jane Austen's novels. You don't realize how good they are until you have read others, many others by her contemporaries and successors. Without a smidgeon of doubt, hers are the best.

Bon voyage!

And Finally . . . Notes

1 What the novel can do: B. Hardy. *A Reading of Jane Austen*, The Athlone Press, 1979.

2 Colin Firth: Quoted in Birtwistle and Conklin *The Making of Pride and Prejudice*, Penguin and BBC Books, 1995.

3 Byron's future wife: Quoted in Park Honan, *Jane Austen – Her Life*, Phoenix Giant Paperback, 1997.

4 *Dr Johnson's Women* by Norma Clarke, Hambledon and London, 2000.

5 Swiss in Canada: A throw away line about members of the Prévost family (Prévost himself having been an important collaborator on the *Bibliothèque britannique*) settling in Canada appears on page 264 of D.M. Bickerton's *Marc–Auguste and Charles Pictet: The Bibliothèque britannique and the dissemination of British Literature and Science on the Continent*, Slatkine Reprints, Geneva 1986. There is also the inconclusive evidence of the youngest Pictet brother, traced to Montreal in 1790. (See Geneva: The Pictet Brothers.)

6 Political cleansing: Even the *Cambridge Modern History* gives it only a short paragraph, mainly concerned with the sale of abandoned land holdings.

Time Line

1572 Massacre of Protestants on St Bartholomew's Day in Paris.

1588 Defeat of Spanish Armada by England under Elizabeth I.

1598 *Henry V* by Shakespeare
Edict of Nantes under King Henri IV to allow Protestantism by law.
End of religious wars in France.

1603 Queen Elizabeth 1 of England dies;
James VI of Scotland becomes James I of Great Britain.
Troilus and Cressida by Shakespeare.

1610 *Cymbeline* by Shakespeare.
Louis XIII new boy-king of France.

1611 Authorised Version of the Bible (the King James Bible) published.

1616 Shakespeare dies. Cervantes dies in Spain.

1643 Louis XIII dies, his son Louis XIV is another boy-king.

1648 Civil War (*La Fronde*) starts in France.

1649 Charles I of England beheaded = end of English Civil War and start of
Cromwell's Commonwealth.

1652 Civil War (*La Fronde*) ends in France.

1660 Peaceful restoration of Stuart Monarchy in England, Charles II is the
new king.
Le Bourgeois Gentilhomme by Molière well received in Paris.

1662 The text of the *Book of Common Prayer* is finally settled and becomes
standard in the Church of England.
Protestant churches throughout France closed.
Ecole des Femmes by Molière well received in Paris.

1664-5 Great Plague in London and throughout England.
Le Tartuffe by Molière seen as highly controversial.

1666 Great Fire of London.
Le Misanthrope by Molière a great success in Paris.

1667 *Andromaque*, Racine's first great success.

1672 *Bajazet* by Racine, successful tragedy.
L'Avare and *Les Femmes Savantes* successful comedies by Molière

1673 *Le Malade Imaginaire* by Molière. He dies.

1674 *Iphigénie en Aulide* by Racine is a huge success.

1677 *Phèdre* is the last of Racine's tragedies.

1678 *La Princesse de Clèves* by Madame de LaFayette, the first psychological
novel.

1685 Edict of Nantes repealed. Protestantism is outlawed in France.

1688 James II of Great Britain, who had converted to Catholicism, is deposed.

1689 William of Orange and his wife, Mary Stuart, become joint sovereigns of Great Britain.

The Bill of Rights limits the king's power and confirms the Protestant religion for Great Britain.

1697 Perrault's *Contes de ma mère d'Oye*.

1699 Racine dies.

1714 George I of Hanover becomes King of Great Britain. He speaks no English, to the benefit of the power of Parliament and government by prime minister.

1719 *Robinson Crusoe* by Daniel Defoe.

1726 *Gulliver's Travels* by Jonathan Swift.

1740 *Pamela* by Samuel Richardson.

1745 Prince Charles–Edward Stuart lands in Scotland, tries to reclaim the throne of Great Britain and is defeated. This series of events is the subject of Walter Scott's *Waverley*.

1748 *Clarissa* by Samuel Richardson.

1749 *Tom Jones* by Henry Fielding.

1751–1772 35 volumes (11 of plates) of *Encyclopédie ou Dictionnaire raisonné des sciences, des arts et des métiers* published.

1755 Dr Johnson's *Dictionary* published.

1761 *La Nouvelle Héloïse* by J.J. Rousseau published.

1775 Start of American War of Independence.

Jane Austen born, J.M.W. Turner born.

1778 *Evelina* by Fanny Burney published.

1783 End of American War of Independence.

1786 *Caroline de Lichtfield* by Madame de Montolieu published.

1787 *Decline and Fall of the Roman Empire* by Edward Gibbon published.

1789 Start of the French Revolution with crowd storming the Bastille.

1791 King Louis XVI of France accepts constitution.

Mozart's *Così Fan Tutte*. Lavoisier's Table of 31 Chemical Elements. King Louis XVI and family try to leave France, are caught and returned to Paris.

1792 France declares war on Prussia, Austria and Sardinia.

France declared a republic. September Massacres.

1793 England at War with France. King Louis XVI executed.

Reign of Terror. Marat murdered by Charlotte Corday.

Roman Catholicism banned in France.

Queen Marie–Antoinette executed, Philippe Egalité executed.

French troops driven out of Germany. Louvre becomes an art gallery.

1794 *Songs of Experience* by William Blake.
Danton and Desmoulins executed, mass executions, Robespierre and
St Just executed.
Slavery abolished in French colonies. Ecole Normale and Ecole
Polytechnique open in Paris.
1795 Metric system introduced. Bread riots and more terror in Paris.
Napoleon appointed Commander in Chief in Italy. Austria signs
armistice with France.
Directoire government in France to 1799. In Geneva *Bibliothèque
britannique* starts.
1797 *Camilla* by Fanny Burney. Napoleon defeats Austrian army in Italy.
1798 *Lyrical Ballads* by Wordsworth and Coleridge. Nelson destroys
French fleet in Aboukir Bay.
French capture Rome, Pope leaves as prisoner; French occupy Malta
and invade Egypt successfully, overrun Kingdom of Naples.
Republic of Geneva annexed into France.
1799 Napoleon enters Syria, returns to France, becomes First Consul,
appoints Talleyrand as his foreign minister.
Louis David exhibits *The Sabine Women*.
1800 British recapture Malta. *Castle Rackrent* by Maria Edgeworth.
Napoleon again defeats Austrian armies in Italy and Austria .
A. Volta produces electricity from a battery of zinc and copper plates.
De la littérature dans ses rapports avec les institutions sociales by Madame
de Staël.
1801 Act of Union of Great Britain and Ireland. Nelson defeats Danes off
Copenhagen.
Jane Austen leaves Steventon for Bath. French troops leave Egypt.
J.J. Lalande's *Catalogue of Stars* published in Paris. Goya *The Two
Majas*.
1802 Peace of Amiens. *Delphine* by Madame de Staël.
1803 War with France re-starts.
1804 Napoleon proclaimed emperor of France.
1805 Nelson defeats Franco–Spanish fleet at Trafalgar and removes threat
of invasion of England.
The Lay of the Last Minstrel by Walter Scott.
Napoleon defeats Austro–Russian armies at Austerlitz.
1806 French armies defeat Prussian, enter Berlin and Warsaw.
Building of Arc de Triomphe starts in Paris.
Continental System, closing all ports to British shipping and vice versa,
starts.

1807 *Hours of Idleness* by Byron. *Corinne* by Madame de Staël.
   Travels in Latin America by A von Humboldt published in Paris.
1808 France invades Spain, Napoleon's brother takes over as King of Spain.
   The Inquisition in Spain abolished.
1809 Wellington starts slow but successful campaign against French in
   Spain.
   Jane Austen moves to Chawton.
   Napoleon defeats Austrian armies again, annexes the Papal States.
1810 *Lady of the Lake* by Walter Scott. Napoleon's apogee.
1811 **Sense and Sensibility.**
   Luddites destroy industrial machinery (see *Shirley* by Charlotte
   Brontë).
1812 *Childe Harold's Pilgrimage* (Cantos 1 & 2) by Byron.
   Napoleon invades Russia, has to retreat through the winter, with huge
   losses.
1813 Wellington defeats French in Spain and enters France.
   Pride and Prejudice. Adapted in four instalments as *Orgueil et Préjugé*,
   published in *Bibliothèque britannique* in Geneva.
   Napoleon defeated in Leipzig, French expelled from Holland.
   De l'Allemagne by Madame de Staël published in French in London.
1814 **Mansfield Park.** *Waverley* by Walter Scott.
   French defeated again, Napoleon abdicates and is banished to Elba.
   Congress of Vienna opens, to define peace terms.
1815 *Guy Mannering* by Walter Scott. Humphry Davy invents miner's
   safety lamp.
   Raison et Sensibilite published in Paris.
   Mansfield Park adapted in four instalments and published in
   Bibliothèque britannique in Geneva.
   100 Days = Napoleon's attempt to re-claim throne is defeated at
   Waterloo.
   Restoration of French Bourbon monarchy under Louis XVIII.
   Second Peace of Paris. Treaty of Vienna.
   Swiss Federal Pact ratified: Confederation of 22 contiguous cantons,
   with permanent neutrality and inviolable territory.
1816 **Emma** and *Childe Harolde's Pilgrimage* (Canto 3) by Byron published by
   Murray in London.
   Le Parc de Mansfield and *La Nouvelle Emma* published in Paris.
1817 **Jane Austen** dies.
1818 **Persuasion** and **Northanger Abbey** published in London.
   Endymion by Keats, *Frankenstein* Mary Shelley.
   Allied troops leave France.

1819 P.B. Shelley *The Cenci*. T Géricault *Le Radeau de la Méduse*.

1820 George III of Great Britain dies, the Prince Regent takes over as George IV.
   Ode to the Nightingale by J Keats. *Ivanhoe* by Walter Scott. *Prometheus Unbound* by PB Shelley.
   Méditations Poétiques by A de Lamartine.

1821 *The Hay-wain* by John Constable. *La Famille Elliot* (a.k.a. *Persuasion*) published in Paris.

1822 *Orgueil et Prévention* published in Paris.
   Orgueil et Préjugé published in Geneva and sold there and in Paris.
   De l'Amour by Stendhal. *Symphony No 8* (The Unfinished) by F Schubert.

1823 Robert Smirke designs the British Museum. George IV presents the library of George III to the British Museum. It now forms the golden core of the British Library.

1824 *Leaping Horse* by John Constable.
   French law compensates aristocrats for losses during the Revolution.

1826 *The Last of the Mohicans* by J Fenimore Cooper.
   Cinq-Mars by A de Vigny.

1827 Battle of Navarino, victory for combined fleets of Great Britain, France and Russia leads to Greek independence.

1828 Reprints of *Raison et Sensibilité* and *La Famille Elliot* in Paris.
   Les Trois Mousquetaires by A Dumas.

1830 July Revolution in France, King Charles X deposed.

1832 **Bentley Edition of Jane Austen's novels.**

1834 *Tour of Connemara* and *Helen* by Maria Edgeworth.

1835 *Le lys dans la vallée* by H Balzac.

1837 Dickens' *Pickwick Papers* in one volume. First instalments of *Oliver Twist*.
   First part of *Les Illusions Perdues* by H Balzac.

1838 Last instalments of *Oliver Twist*. First instalments of *Nicholas Nickleby*.

1840 *The Old Curiosity Shop*.

1841 *Barnaby Rudge*.

1842 Dickens first tour of America.
   Balzac's Preface to first collected edition of *La Comédie Humaine*.

1843 *A Christmas Carol*.
   Les Illusions Perdues completed.

1847 First part of *Dombey & Son*.
   Jane Eyre by Charlotte Brontë.
   Vanity Fair by W M Thackeray.

More Books

Informal and conversational this book may be, it still involved long, pleasurable hours sitting over books and documents at home and in libraries. These were:

In Geneva: Bibliothèque Publique et Universitaire, and the city archive library; in Chur / Coire also the city and archive library.

In Paris: Bibliothèque Historique de la Ville de Paris, Bibliothèque Nationale Française site François Mitterand, Bibliothèque de la Sorbonne, Institut Mémoire de l'Edition Contemporaine.

In Great Britain: the Bodleian Library, the British Library, Guildhall Library, National Army Museum Library, National Maritime Museum Library, the Royal Society Library, St Bride Printing Library, University of Glasgow Library, Westminster City Archives, Westminster Victoria Library.

More books were purchased through Jane Austen Books, Chicago and John Sandoe Books, London.

The most useful books were not necessarily high on entertainment value. So, on pleasure bent, here is a dozen of the most diverting or riveting:

Mémoires d'Outre-Tombe: F de Chateaubriand, Pléiade 1950

Lire à Paris au temps de Balzac: Françoise Parent-Lardeur, Ecole des Hautes Etudes en Sciences Sociales 1999

La Chute des Aristocrates: Jacques de Saint-Victor, Perrin 1992

Eugénie et Mathilde: Madame de Souza on microfiche in BNF, 1811

Voltaire's Coconuts: Ian Buruma, Weidenfeld & Nicholson 1999

On the Eve: Vincent Cronin, Collins 1989

The Forbidden Best-sellers of Pre-Revolutionary France: Robert Darnton, W.W. Norton & Co Ltd 1995

James Joyce: Richard Ellman, OUP 1982

Women Alone: *Spinsters in England 1660 to 1850*: Bridget Hill, Yale UP 2001

Paul's Letters to his Kinsfolk: Walter Scott, Constable 1815

Secret Service: *British Agents in France 1792-1815*: E. Sparrow, Boydell Press 1999

The Beast and the Blonde: Marina Warner, Chatto & Windus 1994

See also:

A Bibliography of Jane Austen: St. Paul's Biographies, Winchester and Oak Knoll Press, Newcastle, Delaware, 1997.

Index

The Author

Vera Quin went to nine schools in five countries and then to Girton College, Cambridge, where she read English. The bulk of her working life was spent at the Learning Disabilities Clinic at St Thomas' Hospital and in schools trying to teach learning–disabled children. She wrote, with Dr Alan Macauslan, *Reading and Spelling Difficulties* 'A Medical Approach' and *Dyslexia* 'What Parents ought to know'. She lives in London.

Cappella Archive provides a mastering service
for the written word. The typeset book
file is stored in a digital archive
and copies are individually
printed to order.